THE
SECRETS OF YOUR
RISING
SIGN

THE SECRETS OF YOUR
RISING SIGN

*The Astrological Key
to Getting What You Want*

WILLIAM LAMB
WITH **WEBB HARRIS JR.**

FAIR WINDS
PRESS
GLOUCESTER, MASSACHUSETTS

Text © 2004 by William Lamb

First published in the USA in 2004 by
Fair Winds Press
33 Commercial Street
Gloucester, MA 01930

Library of Congress Cataloging-in-Publication Data available

ISBN 1-59233-038-X

10 9 8 7 6 5 4 3 2 1

Cover design by Laura Shaw Design
Book design by Laura Herrmann Design

Printed and bound in Canada

Dedicated to my many faithful listeners and treasured clients.

TABLE OF CONTENTS

INTRODUCTION

Awakening to Self-Awareness: Seeing Myself as Others See Me

Y ou hear me say it on the radio time and again: "There are no problems that cannot be solved with a more clear, more accurate awareness." And the most helpful awareness that any of us can possess is an awareness of ourselves.

My view from high atop the stellar staircase on the Mars mezzanine in the Milky Way Mansion here at the William Lamb World Center has shown me that much of the dissatisfaction we experience in life, from minor annoyances and petty displeasures to general unhappiness and painful regret, is the result of a lack of awareness of ourselves and our circumstances. We fail to acknowledge our true strengths and weaknesses, to understand the relationship between our inner desires and our outward projections, and to appreciate the connection between our daily behavior and the immutable truths of the planet we live on.

My own life has been a case in point. As a younger man, I was unaware that the positioning of the moon, planets, sun, and stars in relationship to the time and place of my birth determined the elements and aspects of my human nature. I didn't know that the intensity with which I faced the world was a result of the influence of the moon. I never suspected that my impetuosity and my temper were determined by the Sun, or that the likability which so often manifested itself in my relationships with others originated in my rising sign and, if exercised wisely, could prove itself an uncannily useful tool in acquiring the things I really wanted.

So I blundered through life as many of us do, with quite tragic consequences on one occasion. I lashed out in anger when defied, I rushed into courses of action without forethought, I didn't see the merit in other people's opinions, and I brooded and pouted when things didn't go my way. But what sometimes makes the past so hard to swallow is that, all the while, I carried within myself the very traits and skills that could have created a much more successful and happy outcome.

Over the years, my study of and devotion to astrology has identified those innate traits and skills and has taught me how overwhelmingly important it is for William Lamb, the Horoscope Man, to use them to everyone's advantage. Among other things, I learned the following remarkable and invaluable lessons: My natural stubbornness could be forged into focused determination; my natural likability could serve as the foundation for polite diplomacy; and my natural insightfulness could be concentrated like a laser on the words and conduct of others, allowing me to better understand their wants and needs. In short, I could truly be myself yet still project a more flattering, endearing, and cooperative William to friends, acquaintances, and colleagues.

Now I follow this path to the best of my ability. And, in turn, I've been rewarded with a lot more personal and professional success, a larger circle of friends, and a more joyous existence.

Believe me when I say that my life's mission is to help others do the same. And this book is one more way to accomplish that. Not so much through lecturing or dispensing heavy-handed advice, but by helping others to be more aware of themselves through astrological insight. By becoming more mindful of the astrologically determined positive and negative traits at their disposal, they can realize their goals and objectives. Or, as I often phrase it on the air, "to actualize their ego."

There are no problems that cannot be solved with a more clear, more accurate awareness. And the most helpful awareness that any of us can possess is an awareness of ourselves.

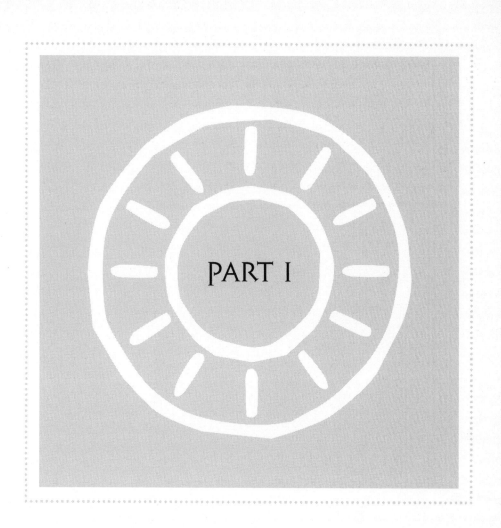

PART I

REALIZING

CHAPTER 1

PERSONALITY POWER
ACTUALIZING THE EGO FOR FUN AND PROFIT

When someone asks, "What's your sign?" and you respond, "I'm a Leo," you're defining your identity by the part of the sky the sun was in on the month and day of the year you were born. For instance, a woman whose birthday falls on August 1 was born during the thirty days between the end of July and the bulk of August when, from an earthly perspective, the sun passes through the constellation Leo. So Leo is her "sun sign," and when asked, she answers instinctively, "I'm a Leo." But there's much more to this Lordly Leo lady's makeup than the simple position of the sun on the August day of her birth. At the moment of her first breath, the moon, the earth's galactically connected planets, and the stars were all positioned somewhere in the heavens in relation to her geographical birthplace, and all of them, from their particular positions, exert important influences on her. It's important to understand that these positions would be very different if she'd been born even three or four hours earlier or later in the twenty-four hour cycle. So knowing the precise time of her birth is critical in determining all of the astrological influences upon her nature.

Over the years, a de-emphasis of this simple, yet crucial, fact has resulted in a striking loss of awareness and has misled many people. And this frustrates me. As a professional astrologer and a front-row observer of astrology's amazing truths, I cringe when I hear astrologers attempt to describe or to counsel a person after ascertaining nothing more than the person's birthdate, because, unfortunately, both the description and the counsel are at best incomplete. The time of day we're born is easily the most important piece of information on anyone's complete and accurate birth chart.

Of course, your sun sign is very significant: It provides insight into how your ego works. (To many people, the term "ego" carries a negative connotation and is often mistakenly equated with self-centeredness. I'll be employing a much different usage. I use "ego" to represent the exertion of our "will" into the world around us. Simply put, we can think in terms of inner desires.)

Imagine a man driven by a craving for money, devoting almost all of his time and energy to pursuing financial gain. He loves to sit in his customized counting room at the end of the day, fingering his stacks of currency. His self-worth is directly connected to the acquisition of dollars and cents. He knows what he wants, and at some point in his life he mapped out his strategies for getting it. We're talking now about the elements of his will.

But here's an important question: How does this man behave in his pursuit of financial gain? What exactly does he project to the people around him in his attempt to accomplish his purpose? Do they see him as a greedy old Scrooge? A driven entrepreneur? Or a financial genius? Perhaps they see a budding philanthropist. How does he "package" his efforts? What does he look like? How does he sound? Is he an open book to his peers, or is he a conundrum? Does he possess successful people skills? Or is he overly forceful? These questions relate less to his ego expression and more to his personality and physical type, which are the immediately obvious things about him. And these specific, obvious qualities are determined almost solely by the time of day he's born, not by the time of year. They're determined by his rising sign; the sign precisely on the Eastern horizon, from the perspective of his birthplace, at the moment of his birth, as the earth turns in its twenty-four hour cycle.

This is true for each of us: Our rising sign determines our most obvious qualities. And ultimately we should ask ourselves these crucial questions: How well do these qualities complement our ego expression? And how effective are we at using them to get what we want?

For almost thirty years I've practiced astrology as my sole source of income, and amazed radio and television audiences with my specific insights into their personalities and circumstances. And I've done this primarily on the basis of the time of day they're born. When people call into my radio shows, I often ask them not to reveal the month, day, and year of their birth. I ask simply, "What's your time of birth?" This allows me to demonstrate how much specific information can be gleaned from birth time alone. I talk to them on the level of their day-to-day behavior, give advice based on their natural tendencies, help them emphasize the positive traits and minimize the less productive ones. This allows them to get what they want in life with more ease and frequency. They're always astounded by my insights and surprised to find that, even without a knowledge of their sun sign, these characteristics are so apparent to me. It makes for great radio. In these instances, I'm dealing with what they project to others most immediately and obviously. I deal with personality and physical type, what they project into the world in their attempt to satisfy, or actualize, their will.

Now let's return to that Leo woman. It's very likely that, from time to time, she flips through astrology books, turning to the Leo pages to read a little about herself. After all, it's human nature to be curious about ourselves. What's this book have to say about me? she wonders. And, generally, she'll read something like this: "Leo is regal. Leo is proud. Leo demands respect. Leos are often artistic. Leos desire recognition."

Maybe some of this rings true to her. But maybe some of it doesn't. As a matter of fact, unless she was born at dawn, her rising sign, the personality factor, wouldn't be Leo at all. If she was born, instead, shortly after dawn, her rising sign would be Virgo, the sign of modesty. We would say she's a Leo with Virgo rising, and this would give her a much more modest demeanor. Not a lordly, regal personality at all! Let's call her Cynthia, and let's imagine one possible scenario that might depict her life as Leo with Virgo rising.

Cynthia is an oil painter who prefers to make a big impression, reflecting that artistic Leo ego expression. She spends much of her free time painting beautiful and dazzling landscapes. Verdant, green meadows, with majestic mountains in the background. Azure skies above and, here and there, puffy white clouds casting shadows on the fields below. She gives great attention to detail because her Virgo personality is both productive and unusually aware of details. But Cynthia is so detail-oriented that her wonderful landscapes are never quite finished. She's after perfection. And in her own estimation, she has yet to paint the perfect landscape. The green is never quite green enough. The azure is never quite azure enough. And the clouds' shadows are never exactly proportional. Consequently, her perfectionism never allows her landscapes to make it to a spot on her living room wall. She'd like to display her works and be appreciated by others as an artist, getting the attention most Leos crave. She wants to be recognized as a painter. But do you see what's happening? Cynthia's Virgo perfectionism is getting in the way of her Lordly Leo ego expression.

But let's create another scenario and suppose that, instead of shortly after dawn, Cynthia was born at noontime. Her sun sign remains Leo because her August 1 birthday hasn't changed. But the time of day she was born now gives her a different rising sign. Cynthia becomes Leo with Scorpio rising. She's handy, sexy, full of gusto, immensely discriminating and determined. And both Leo and Scorpio, being fixed and determined, are very prone to dismiss what they don't agree with and to reject what they don't prefer. She might still be a painter of landscapes, but now she's not likely to be such a perfectionist. She's already convinced her work is superb. Her problem isn't that her paintings are never finished: In addition to the four landscapes hanging on the walls of her den, she has fourteen more propped against the wall in the spare bedroom. But Cynthia has a different problem now. With Scorpio's usual aversion to feeling vulnerable and reluctance to risk rejection, she's willing to show her work only to those people she's reasonably certain will applaud her efforts. So only a select few are ever invited into the inner sanctum mysterious Scorpio uses to protect herself from possible rejection. "Most people don't appreciate good art anyway!" she insists, avoiding rejection but leaving her self-confidence intact. Yet by carefully hand-selecting as her audience only those people whose opinions are sure to flatter her Leo ego, she's denying herself the greater acceptance she desires. The end-result is the same as it was before.

If only Cynthia could be longer on courage and accept her feelings of vulnerability for the very human feelings they are. Not fetters and chains of inhibited confinement. Just a natural part of who she is. With a strong dose of self-awareness, she's better equipped to overcome her inhibitions and to opt for the bigger piece of cake: universal recognition.

Now let's talk about Joe. He's a Likable Libra with Lordly Leo rising. His Libra sun sign creates a desire to want to share his time and space, to get along with people, to be liked by them, to have fun with his friends. But whenever he calls his buddies, they're always busy. At least they say they are. Sometimes, however, after a particular buddy tells Joe he can't go to the football game because he's got to help his daughter with her chemistry homework, Joe, on his lonely drive to the stadium, sees that same buddy rushing into the neighborhood sports bar. Why does this keep happening? After all, Joe is extremely fond of his friends, always trying to be considerate. With his generous Leo personality and his Likable Libra willingness to share, he often offers to pay their way if they're a little short on cash.

What Joe doesn't realize is that others don't see his obliging Libra ego as quickly as they see his "all full of myself" Lordly Leo personality. He has allowed his fierce Leo pride to overshadow some of the best characteristics of his Likable Libra ego. Unwittingly, he appears much more self-absorbed than he means to. Joe thinks he's being friendly by inviting others to the ball game—yet it never occurs to him that he rarely asks them what they would like to do! Maybe Joe's friend would rather watch the game on the sports bar television than go to the stadium. Maybe Joe's friend has many other pals who hang out at that sports bar. Maybe Joe's friend doesn't like the lines or the food at the stadium. But with Joe, it's always Joe's way! He never thinks to ask his buddy, "Would you rather just watch it on the sports bar big screen?" If he would just be a little more aware of how people are reacting to him, a little more sensitive to others' preferences, a little more Libra, Joe would find himself spending less time alone.

In each of these instances, we find people undermining their will with their personalities. They see themselves in a certain way, but they're not very aware of how others view them. They know what they want in life, but they're not projecting themselves in a way that helps them get it.

In this book, I hope to show you how to integrate your ego with your personality in such a way that your ego is healthily satiated, complemented by your personality, allowing for more success and less disappointment in life. I'm hoping to show you how to get what you want naturally with your own unique set of characteristics. It's a matter of seeing yourself more completely and discovering better ways to react to your experiences.

Look at it this way. Any characteristic can be a strength or a weakness. Consider caution. An old proverb says, "Look before you leap." Don't rush into decisions without weighing the consequences. But another old proverb says, "He who hesitates is lost." Don't spend so much time analyzing potential consequences that you end up missing opportunities. Well? Should we always wait at least three days before signing on the dotted line, or should we just take a deep breath and sign the damned papers before someone else beats us to the punch?

Better that we ask which response suits us, and under what circumstances. Sometimes, exercising great caution serves us well. At other times we just miss the bus. Is our caution prudent, or does it cause us to see-saw? Do others perceive us as level-headed? Or do they see us as dawdlers? It really does make a difference!

My clients tell me that the astrological insights I've shared with them have increased their happiness and success in life. I hope to do the same for you. There really are no problems that can't be solved with an increased awareness. I love it when I'm stopped on the street or in some other public place by people who want me to know I've helped them change their lives for the better. Among other things, astrological self-awareness gives us a more discerning sense of timing, and it allows us to improve our reactions to the consistent experiences our lives on earth present to us. Just as grass is green, sky is blue, and blood is red, arrogance repels people and positive, winning ways create an ideal situation where everyone benefits.

CHAPTER 2

FROM GUESSTIMATION TO REALIZATION

THE TIME AND PLACE OF YOUR BIRTH

From the preceding chapter, you can see just how crucial it is to identify your rising sign in order to understand exactly what and how your personality projects to the outer world. While your core ego, the realm of your inner desires, is the domain of your sun sign, the outward "you" that family, friends, and colleagues encounter every day, including even your physical appearance, is mostly the domain of the rising sign. Many years of passionate study, experience, and reflection have convinced me that, though the interaction of the sun sign and the rising sign is by no means the only important combination of astrological elements in a person's birth chart, an awareness of that interaction, and of the extremely important influence of each upon the other, is the key to comprehending precisely how others see us. And, in turn, this information becomes our guide to getting what we want in life. Often, other people fail to understand our wants and needs because we simply aren't projecting the things we think we are.

In Part III, the largest section of this book, you'll be able to find specific personal descriptions tailored to your own sun sign/rising sign combination. But for that information to be as accurate and useful as possible, it's imperative that you be certain of your true rising sign. Because the earth is a continuously rotating sphere, completing a full turn approximately every twenty-four hours, the constellation on the eastern horizon from any specific geographical vantage point isn't fixed for long. So you must know two things about yourself to accurately determine your rising sign: (1) your place of birth and (2) your time of birth.

While most people know the place and date of their birth, many people don't know the exact time of day they were born. Some people don't even know if they were born in the a.m. or the p.m. If you do know the precise time, and you were born between 40 degrees north latitude and 40 degrees south latitude (that is, north of Tamuca, Chile; Mar del Plata, Argentina; and the island of Tasmania; but south of Provo, Utah; New York City; Madrid, Spain; and Beijing, China), then you might be ready to turn to the next chapter. But if you don't know the exact time of your birth, or if you were born outside these geographical parameters, you absolutely have to do your best to access this data.

Here's my advice:

Consult your birth certificate. If you're thirty-five or younger, you'll probably find the exact time of your birth indicated there. If you don't have a handy copy of your birth certificate or if the time isn't indicated, sometimes all you have to do is ask relatives. Chances are someone will remember fairly well the time of your birth, and they might even know who would have a copy of the certificate stowed away in their attic.

But if this common-sense strategy fails, there are other options. Often, the medical records department of the hospital in which you were born, or the city or town hall of your birthplace, can be of help. These institutions can sometimes provide your specific birth time—even when this information is absent from your birth certificate!

Also, the Internet is a Godsend for locating and securing such records, especially with the increased worldwide interest in family genealogies, as well as searches for birth parents and birth siblings. At the time of this writing, typing "find birth certificate" into any good Internet search engine turned up dozens of businesses able to quickly find birth certificates for a reasonable fee, as well as sites like the official home page of the Centers for Disease Control and Prevention, on which visitors can find their respective state governmental agencies responsible for maintaining these documents. A person born in Florida, for instance, can procure a copy of their birth certificate from the Office of Vital Statistics at the Department of Health and Rehabilitative Services for less than ten dollars.

Now concerning the geography of your birth and its sometimes profound effect on your rising sign, the best course of action anyone can follow to insure the accuracy of the identification of their rising sign is to have a professional astrologer prepare a genuine astrological birth chart. This will remove all of the guesswork. Various encyclopedias and websites are available to help laymen manufacture a chart, but I encourage you to utilize my contact information to benefit from my specialized and personal assistance in this most important step, especially if you were born north or south of the aforementioned cities.

In the toughest cases, I'm also able to perform what we astrologers call an astrological rectification of your birth chart, which is "working backwards" from what we do know about you to construct what we at first do not know, i.e., the concrete elements of your birth chart. In the hands of a competent astrologer, an astrological rectification is quite trustworthy and very useful.

CHAPTER 3

ASTROLOGICAL INGREDIENTS
THE WHOLE COSMIC KIT AND CABOODLE

I began Chapter 1 with a brief discussion of how a modern overemphasis of the sun sign, sometimes to the exclusion of other astrological elements, often results in incomplete or even misleading information. If my knowledge of a client's astrological makeup were limited to the sun sign, I would possess a solid understanding of the inner will, the ego, the core desires. But what about the personality? What about the emotional nature? Moods? Personal aesthetics? Thinking skills? Communication skills? And what about the character? How are responsibilities approached and rewards received? True, I could learn about some of these things through simple observation and interaction, but it's a poor astrologer who has to follow a client around all day to document behavior.

In leading you into a more complete awareness of your rising sign personality and its relationship to your sun sign ego, I want to be careful to avoid this same mistake. Because the rising sign determines how we project ourselves to others, becoming, in essence, the tool we use to get what we want, knowing all we can about this sign and how it complements or impedes our inner will is crucial to ensuring our happiness and fulfillment. This truth is the heart and soul of this book. But there's certainly more to a birth chart than just these two factors; in fact, the rising sign itself can be influenced by other elements of the chart.

Consider the positions of the planets at the time of your birth and how they affect the total person. The planets can exert such a strong influence on the operation of the signs that I refer to them as "the engines of the signs." Consider Mercury. Among other things, Mercury influences the relationship between the mind and mouth, how we think and communicate. When I look at a birth chart and see Mercury sitting in a "fixed" rising sign (Taurus, Leo, Scorpio, and Aquarius), this tells me that my client is very strong and steady-minded, finding it easy to concentrate when she needs to. Mercury in an "active" sign (Aries, Cancer, Libra, and Capricorn) creates a restless mind, enamored of physical activity, and creating the potential for "busy dizzy" activity for activity's sake. And Mercury in a "flexible" sign (Gemini, Virgo, Sagittarius, and Pisces) denotes a quick-minded, curious person but sometimes with less of an ability to focus.

Venus influences love and money, how we show affection and handle our finances. Mars influences our energy level and our passions in general. The child who's boisterous at the dinner table, aggressively interrupting adult conversation, often has impatient Mars configured with talkative Mercury on the eastern horizon.

Jupiter and Saturn are character planets. Jupiter affects the philosophy of life, the level of benevolence and forgiveness. Saturn affects the willingness to give oneself to personal discipline and responsibility, and also affects loyalty and respect. It can also create tendencies toward jealousy, fearfulness, and materialism.

Even the "New Age" planets—those that, because of their distance from the earth, escaped man's attention until modern times—are very important. Uranus, discovered in 1781, gives strong attitudes; it can create argumentativeness, and humor and magnetism, too, but possibly a stressful, disagreeable nature. Neptune, discovered through mathematics in the nineteenth century, is the planet of imagery and gives a good eye for proportional beauty, a photogenic physical nature, a vivid imagination, and, too often, deceptiveness. And Pluto, undiscovered until the early twentieth century, is the planet of intensity, investigation, psychology, and psychoanalysis, able to bestow a gift for ferreting out the hidden and perceiving what's generally concealed to others. I personally have Pluto to thank for my insights as an astrologer; he sat directly overhead when I was born, as if presiding over my life's destiny.

Our Moon, too, being the closest celestial body to the earth by far, is an intrinsic part of the astrological equation, dramatically influencing our emotional nature. The Moon on the eastern horizon at the moment of birth generates extreme sensitivity in women and a gentlemanly quality in men. When she inhabits those fixed rising signs, she gives a steadier and deeply emotional nature and sometimes makes us overly subjective and serious. In the active rising signs, she dispenses a restless emotional nature. And in the flexible rising signs, she creates a lighter, more flexible, and widely fluctuating emotional nature, a useful ability to get over things quickly and avoid unproductive sulking and pouting.

This illustrates the usefulness of a competent astrologer who's almost always able to delve beneath the superficiality of the typical astrology handbooks, with their all-encompassing platitudes and wide generalizations, to scrutinize the nuances of character, personality, and demeanor.

But what's important to note about all of this is that without access to a comprehensive birth chart, we can't pinpoint the exact positions of these elements: True astrological self-knowledge remains, at best, incomplete. Remember our painter friend, Cynthia, from Chapter 1? In the scenario in which she was Leo with Virgo rising, Cynthia was fiercely devoted to fine details in the landscapes she painted. She was after perfection in her art, but she always disappointed herself in her pursuit of just the right green and just the right azure. Unwilling to hang these "less than perfect" paintings on her living room wall, she kept them hidden from view, which left her unfulfilled. She deeply yearned with her fixed and determined Leo ego to be acknowledged for her artistry by friends and family.

We were able to see this much about her knowing only her sun sign and rising sign. But how much more complete is the picture when we know that her Moon is in Aries! This makes her a bit impatient and impulsive, qualities that don't serve her perfectionism well. Maybe Cynthia's perception that her azure isn't quite azure enough is more than illusion; maybe her impulsiveness prods her to move on to a new landscape before the current landscape is sufficiently polished.

And if we know that her Mercury is in Cancer, we can rest assured that her manual dexterity ensures that her fingers are in tune with her emotions.

Knowing that both her Mars and her Pluto are close together in Virgo would explain her untold reserves of energy and would also suggest an extreme level of intensity. All that energy and impulsiveness! No wonder she moves from painting to painting!

Her Venus in Gemini reveals a studious sharp-mindedness, an eye for details. Her Jupiter in Aquarius serves her well in any quest to find and fit in with associated artists' organizations to promote her work.

But all of this, as wonderful as it is, lies beyond the scope of this book. Astrology in its fullness is too large a science to be effectively condensed. And we astrologers do a disservice to ourselves, our public, and the field itself, when we pretend that one or two signs tell all.

Beyond the sun sign/rising sign combination to which we'll confine ourselves in the following pages, there's really only one other astrological element that we can speak about with certainty in the absence of a birth chart: the sun. Here, organized according to the birth time classifications you'll find in Part III, is a nutshell description of the sun's influence. You can confidently add this information to what I have to say later about your specific situation—but bear in mind that the sun is just one ingredient in the whole cosmic kit and caboodle.

The Influence of the Sun

✴ If you were **born around dawn**, a sunny disposition becomes even sunnier, while a naturally less-than-sunny disposition benefits from the glow of the sunrise illuminating the darkness. Willfulness and a robust physical nature are likely.

✴ If you were **born shortly after dawn**, you probably require some isolation to regenerate your energies. You're likely a natural at working behind the scenes in a position of service to others.

✴ If you were **born at mid-morning**, you'll show some magnetism and friendliness. The sun tends to make you a good team-player. And you live today with tomorrow in mind.

✴ If you were **born around noontime**, you've a willingness to take charge and oversee things. You're a good manager. You're sensitive to disrespect, and generally won't abide it.

✴ If you were **born in the early afternoon**, you're more carefree and hopeful, with a better-than-average faith in life. You tend to behave in winning ways, with a happy-go-lucky disposition. You're usually ready to forgive and to look at the bright side.

✴ If you were **born in the mid-afternoon**, I'd expect an intriguing and mysterious quality about you. You might be aware of things that aren't so obvious to others. Your life's pattern would manifest an unusual protectiveness involving the necessities of life: food, shelter, clothing, career, and cash flow.

✴ If you were **born around sundown**, you would be an attentive partner. With a tendency to enjoy the company of others, you exhibit a natural ability to share your time and space in sociable ways.

✴ If you were **born early evening**, helpful and productive behavior fulfills you, and an obvious modesty is likely. You tend to be analytical in your approach to life, and you've a keen awareness of details.

✴ If you were **born mid-evening**, there's a bit of "Good Time Charlie" about you. You're fond of children and sometimes exhibit childlike qualities yourself. You're much better than average at earning positive attention, possibly with a flair for the dramatic.

✴ If you were **born 'round midnight**, sensitivity and caution usually manifest themselves. You take a custodial approach to responsibilities, and your life circumstances are often unusually involved with home, family, and real estate.

* If you were **born in the wee hours**, you love to move around. You're chatty, quick-minded, intellectual, and given to an academic approach to life, but possibly a bit scattered.

* If you were **born pre-dawn**, you've a good eye for quality. You exhibit a lot of focus, determination, and confidence but a good deal of stubbornness, too. You're generous on the one hand, but inflexible on the other.

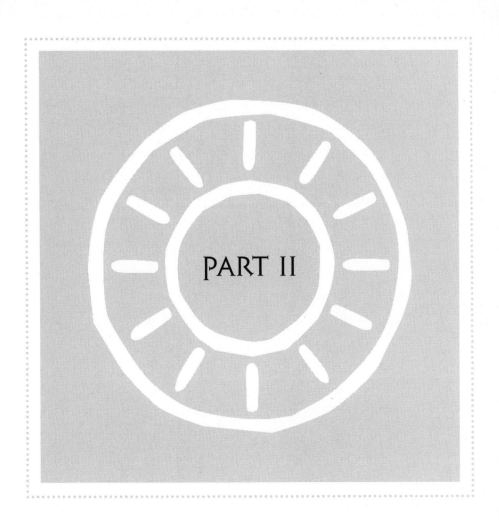

PART II

DISCOVERING

CHAPTER 4

WHICH IS YOU?
RECOGNIZING YOUR RISING SIGN

Here are some general descriptions of the rising sign personalities. But remember: The sun sign and other astrological influences will usually impact the degree to which these qualities manifest themselves.

 From childhood, Action **Aries** is charming. With an adorable smile, rambunctious behavior, and a crazy, restless zip zip spirit, kids with Aries rising become the grown-up early birds who catch the worm. People with Aries rising are at the door before the party starts, prompt to the meeting table while the business papers are still being shuffled. To say the least, they're short on patience.

They exhibit a childlike honesty throughout life and expect an honest, direct approach from others: They're easily annoyed by people who are less than candid.

These folks are up-and-at-'em, bright-eyed, bushy-tailed, shoot from the hip, "Ask me, I'll tell ya," honest injuns.

Physical type: a physical resemblance to parents or grandparents; good muscle tone; an attractive forehead
Favored color: bright red

Taurus, the Banker, the Beast of Burden, is steady-as-he-goes. People with Taurus rising are deliberate, focused, and don't like to be rushed. As children, they're generally slower about things, absolutely stubborn, grouchy when hungry, and not easily roused from sleep. Into maturity these characteristics remain. These people are bothered by impracticality, and are sometimes vain and a little grumpy. They need their animal comforts. They're "Keep it simple, stupid!" types, potential pouty faces, and sticks in the mud, but they're usually generous and always steady with their efforts.

They often say, "Don't crowd me! Get outta my way! I know what I'm doin'!"

Physical type: broad shoulders; low voice; a broad smile with a lot of teeth; possibly a plodding gait, with a bit of clumsiness in the feet

Favored colors: pastels

 Chatty-faced, "Hi! How ya doin'? Where ya from? I been there! See ya later!" Jitterbug **Gemini** is the icing on the cake of the zodiac. People with Gemini rising are sincere and unassuming, adept at making other people feel comfortable in their presence—just genuinely nice folks.

From their early years, they're incredibly curious, annoying adults with endless questions, "What's this? What's that? Why? Why? Why?" Their inquisitive nature usually leads them to an interest in books and learning that follows them into adulthood.

These people are inherently agile, and capable of juggling two or three tasks at once. They're quick-minded, and fond of displaying intelligence.

Physical type: a youthful appearance

Favored colors: pale yellow, light gray

He's the willing worker! Thin-skinned and sensitive, with a gentle demeanor, Cautious **Cancer** is always politic and often found working long hours in public places, taking advantage of an ability to avoid giving offense. People with Cancer rising get the job done in a utilitarian, worker-bee fashion.

As children, they love to earn and stash money and, even in youth, they've a penchant for saving rather than spending. Cancer children are usually industrious, sensitive, cautious about almost everything, and quite loving toward their mothers.

Sentimentality towards the past helps these folks learn from their experience but sometimes leaves them emotionally inhibited, hesitant to embrace today's opportunities. In these cases, they live in the past rather than learn from it. They make themselves scarce if faced with rejection but are cagey when threatened and skilled at avoiding intensity. They can be very noncommittal: "Don't fence me in! Don't back me into a corner!"

Physical type: short shuffle in the walk; sometimes poor eyesight

Favored colors: olive green, forest green, smoky gray, silver

Lordly **Leo** exhibits a generous and sunny disposition. People with Leo rising are bold and assertive, and possibly unruly as children; they resent being told what to do. But their willful independence breeds confidence and competence in adulthood, creating consummate showmen, effective attention-getters, and masters of the big impression.

With lion-hearted fearlessness and a good dose of romantic appeal, these people stand out from the crowd. They believe in doing it right the first time. "Stand aside. I'll generously show you how to do this, and you can do it the next time." They're often fond of jewelry and might come off as a bit too full of themselves.

Physical type: healthy robustness; able to get by with relatively little sleep; noticeable crown to the head

Favored colors: gold, orange, forest green

 Almost too aware of the little things, people with **Virgo** rising fidgeted with their clothing in their grammar-school days, toyed with the zippers and buttons, and grew up analytical, nit-picky, and skeptical. Virgo, the Worry Wart, counts heavily on intellect and is extremely productive. These people love to be helpful, but on a bad day they display an "I just can't handle it! I've been sick!" attitude.

These folks are blessed with a strong eye for detail, and a natural intelligence equips them to ferret out problems, work out the kinks, and fix what's broken. And they like to think they're smarter than others: They love trickery! It feeds their ego. They'll sometimes use a flippant comment just to extract and analyze a response.

Physical type: youthfulness; sometimes a fading chin

Favored colors: navy blue, forest green

 Always obliging, with superb people skills, Likable **Libra's** ingrained childhood politeness blossoms ultimately into an adept social skillfulness. People with Libra rising are masters of diplomacy! "What can I do for you?" They enjoy the company of others and don't like to be alone. They often nose in, and are sometimes better off minding their own business.

"Eenie-meenie-minie-moe, left or right, I don't know... Oh, hell, wait and see." If their options aren't inspiring, these folks are indecisive.

And they usually have a good eye for style and color.

Physical type: sometimes sharp facial features; usually well-proportioned, with long, attractive, shapely legs

Favored color: greenish blue

Suspicious and intense, with an intimidating depth in the eyes, Mysterious **Scorpio's** aversion to feeling vulnerable can be traced to childhood: people with Scorpio rising were wary of strangers and not often eager to say much. Scorpio women, especially, find it very difficult to disclose themselves to others, even to their closest friends.

These folks are amazingly insightful. I see what you're doing, they say to themselves. They have a red meat approach to life, are full of gusto, and given to energetic activity. Their "Grab the handle, we're outta here! Do it now, think about it later!" attitude sometimes creates an overachiever.

There's often a mechanically skillful and/or artistically inclined quality to Scorpio rising, even from the earliest years.

Physical type: deep eyes; sometimes a noticeable muscularity; in women, shapely and voluptuous, or a tendency toward problems with weight

Favored colors: maroon, dark red, black

 Sweet and optimistic, Happy-Go-Lucky **Sagittarius** is the winner of the zodiac. People with Sagittarius are hopeful dreamers, with a forgiving "It's okay! We'll do better next time!" character.

In youth, they're spontaneous and speak up like Dennis-the-Menace, saying the wrong things at the wrong time, but with such candor their parents usually find them more amusing than embarrassing. (Sagittarius is the sign of "foot in mouth," or speaking without thinking, an activity that can sometimes be offensive.) Sagi-magi-ragi-ttarius children sometimes enjoy too much adoration from their elders, ending up spoiled in childhood and arrogant as adults. They think themselves above things and ignore negativity as if it doesn't pertain to them, but their ultimately winning ways, forgiving nature, and hop-skip-and-jump, eight-cylinder, full-throttle, "saddle up, we're outta here" behavior, easily earns them love and adoration.

Physical type: good posture; agility; a spring to the step

Favored colors: purple, royal blue, deep pink

Capricorn, the Wise Old Goat, is always in charge. With a business-is-business attitude, people with Capricorn rising strive to earn recognition for their accomplishments. They usually exude a respectfulness that puts them in good stead with their superiors. But they're so calm, cool, and collected that they sometimes wear a face of stone, even exhibiting insensitivity. They believe in "take it on the chin" and "the buck stops here."

Capricorn children are often cooperative and easy to raise; they value the approval of authority figures, handle responsibility well, act older than their years, and sometimes delight in "bossing" people around. They're prone to jealousy. They grow up accomplished, authoritative, and bossy. "Do what I say! And don't raise your voice to me!"

Physical type: well-defined jawline; sometimes a bony face

Favored colors: brown, medium grays; businesslike tones reflecting the Capricorn regard for moderation

 Electric, magnetic, and friendly on a good day, sour and disagreeable on a bad one, **Aquarius,** the Electric Light Bulb, is the Mr. Big Attitude of the zodiac. People with Aquarius rising are funny-boned, good fellows well met, with a "best foot forward" approach. They can be stiff-spined and argumentative. Today this, but tomorrow that. They do what they want to do and think what they want to think. They say, "No," but explain, "Yes." How frustrating! Their words don't always match their message, but their attitude is always showing. They sometimes carry a chip on their shoulder.

These folks are wound tightly and are given to laughter to release stress, and their laughter is contagious in a positive setting and nervous if in disfavor with the people around them. Aquarius children can get on laughing jags, even when they're in trouble, and for Mom and Dad it's sometimes hard to learn that this is simply the Aquarius way of relieving tension.

Physical type: whether unusually tall, or unusually short, Aquarius' appearance is always unique

Favored colors: shocking blue, bright yellow, something electric and vibrant

Gentle, kind-hearted, tranquil and serene, Peaceful **Pisces** dislikes intensity and contention. People with Pisces rising are very uncomfortable with confrontation. "Don't ask me," they say. "You might disapprove, and I can't endure your disfavor; it weighs too heavily on my psyche." As youngsters, these folks are always cooperative and easy to handle. After all, they don't want friction. Even into adulthood, they can be scaredy-cats when it comes to others' disapproval.

These folks are good listeners. They absorb on an emotional level exactly what's being said. Their mouths are shut, but their ears and feelings are open. They're Christ-like cosmic travelers, sometimes feeling a little earthbound but longing to soar like an angel. They enjoy their solitude, peace and quiet, and the shadows of nighttime.

Physical type: delicate appearance; sometimes pale-skinned

Favored colors: emerald green, sea green, midnight blue

PART III

INTEGRATING

my loyal radio audiences and personal clients are extremely familiar with one of my favorite dictates: "We get what we want by behaving according to the positive traits of our sun sign." I'm emphasizing the word "behavior" here because, in this book, we're focusing particularly on the domain of our rising sign, the sign that determines our personality and physical type, the characteristics most obvious to the people around us. Remember: our personality is the tool we use to get what we want, to satiate our will or ego expression. So in order to get what we want in life, it's important to ask ourselves these questions: How do others really see us? What do they assume about us based on the behavior we exhibit? In what ways does our rising sign personality complement our sun sign ego? In what ways does our rising sign enhance our most positive sun sign traits? Does it possibly over-intensify them? Does it possibly obscure them? This kind of self-awareness allows us to modify our behavior in ways that boost others' confidence in us and our abilities, and encourage their willing cooperation.

In this chapter, you'll find a brief, precise description of each unique sun sign/rising sign combination. And this information will be most useful to you if you keep in mind the principles discussed in the preceding chapters and, especially, the fundamentals of your rising sign description in "Which Is You?"

It's also helpful to remember that the signs can be categorized by their modality and their representative element. When considering both your sun sign and your rising sign, it's useful to keep in mind each sign's modality and element. They give you a "nutshell" encapsulation of chief characteristics, motivations, and challenges.

THE MODALITIES

1. FLEXIBLE: Gemini, Virgo, Sagittarius, and Pisces

Also known as the "mutable" signs, the flexible signs are Gemini, Virgo, Sagittarius, and Pisces. All four of these signs exhibit more of an ability to lighten up and go with the flow than the other eight signs of the zodiac. They're typically more light and lively, and more apt to entertain new ideas, even if they sometimes lack the concentration needed to always get to the bottom line. These flexible signs share the challenge to be more deliberate and focused, to be willing to slow down enough to avoid confusion or miss the point.

2. ACTIVE: Aries, Cancer, Libra, and Capricorn

Also known as the "cardinal" signs, the active signs are Aries, Cancer, Libra, and Capricorn. These four signs exhibit more restlessness than the other eight signs. There's a sense of "I've gotta do something" and a tendency to be enamored by activity for activity's sake. These active signs share the challenge of identifying the source of their behavior: Are they motivated by true inspiration? Or are they rushing around because they feel like the crap's going to hit the fan? Or maybe trying to avoid feeling lazy and unproductive?

3. DETERMINED: Taurus, Leo, Scorpio, and Aquarius

Also known as the "fixed" signs, the determined signs are Taurus, Leo, Scorpio, and Aquarius. These four signs are better able to focus and concentrate than the other eight signs. They share a deliberateness and a powerful ability to focus and endure, but they also share the challenge of avoiding stubbornness and closed-minded rigidity.

THE ELEMENTS

The four elements are fire, earth, air, and water.

* The fire signs are Aries, Leo, and Sagittarius. These signs are motivated by inspiration, and their inspiration often rubs off on others.

* The earth signs are Taurus, Virgo, and Capricorn. These signs require a practical earthly reward to motivate them.

* The air signs are Gemini, Libra, and Aquarius. They are motivated by concepts and ideas.

* The water signs are Cancer, Scorpio, and Pisces. They're motivated by their emotions, exceptionally prone to subjectivity, and apt to erroneously feel responsible for things they can't control.

CHAPTER 5

THE ARIES SUN SIGN
AND ITS RISING SIGN PERSONALITIES

THE ARIES SUN SIGN
March 21–April 19

These are the bright-eyed, bushy-tailed, childlike smiley faces among us. They're straightforward and sometimes painfully honest, but they're always expedient and trying to get on with it. As one of the four "active" signs, Action Aries is characterized by restlessness and impulsiveness. Arians have an innate need to be doing something. Things often seem to them as if they aren't moving fast enough: The money they need for a new car takes too long to accumulate; the meeting to discuss a desired promotion is scheduled too late in the week. They show up early for everything. Their expedient impatience can be a useful tool, but it can also be a liability, depending on what sign is rising. Arians' early arrival usually implies that they'll do more than their fair share, contributing sizably to the productivity of the team; with an eager beaver demeanor, they always do more than expected, without complaining. They might be extremely "busy dizzy," spiraling into too much of a rush, and shouldering others' responsibilities as well as their own. When their attitude is positive and optimistic, their efficient contributions always meet with approval. But if they're mired in pessimism, succumbing to a nagging feeling that "the crap's gonna hit the fan," they run around like a chicken with its head cut off, pushing and aggravating the people around them. They sometimes tackle tasks less from inspiration and more from obligation. But the energy expended doesn't faze them because their anxiety dictates, "Well, I've gotta do something, even if it's wrong!" This restlessness often robs them of a healthy serenity. Without an adequate level of self-awareness, Arians are just too mindlessly pushy and impatient, spinning their wheels and wasting their time.

Aries is a bit more egotistical than the other active signs, but with their childlike charm and honesty Arians win favor and enjoy a great amount of trust from others because they're courageous enough to put their cards on the table, removing all suspicion. You never have to wonder what they're up to; they're obvious to even the most casual observer. And because of their springtime "summer's coming" attitude, they usually expect improvement in time—so inspiring others is a simple matter. With a positive attitude and a bit of focus, their puppy dog ways are a joy to behold.

Aries Born Around Dawn:
Aries with Aries Rising

Buckle up and hold onto your hat if you've a mind to keep up with these people. And if you can't keep up at the gym, don't hang around them! These hard-body peacocks are obviously pleased with the impressive physique they work so energetically to maintain. And even if they're not well-proportioned and physically fit, they still enjoy the physical realm much more than the rest of us. They're full-blown, springtime puppy dogs! They enjoy competition and physical release, so sports and the out-of-doors are usually high on their list of favorite things. Activity is their forte. Though dawn births often have a sunny disposition, these Arians might come off as overly confident. But Arians born around dawn are usually so childlike-honest, they get away with their egotism almost every time. Unlike Lordly Leo, for instance, they don't leave the impression that they think they're better than others. When they storm in eager and insistent, they're seldom opposed and often welcomed.

Arians with Aries rising are Action Aries personified and therefore easy to read. They earn trust and cooperation through their willingness to reveal themselves. Their motive is seldom obscure, so no one needs to wonder what they're up to. Aries is a ram, and these prototype Rocky Mountain bighorns are as straightforward and ram-like as it gets: They're expert climbers, fit and trim, and blessed with seemingly endless reserves of energy. You've seen these animals fight on television nature shows. They lower their heads and charge directly forward—there's no deviousness or guile. They strike their target, back up, and bolt forward again. Arians born at dawn are Energizer Bunnies with rams' horns. They're born initiators. With an innate cleverness, they carry out their agenda expediently. They do best if they have the reins because they're not likely to stand by and watch others take the lead. But once they've established their ground and set things in motion, they'll willingly hand the wheel over to others to avoid boredom—they're ready to move on to the next challenge. They're extremely restless, with an adventurous spirit. They're drawn to vocations that allow them a great measure of independence. They're so hands-on they need a boss like a hole in the head!

But these Arians do need to steer clear of that God-awful impatience that breeds mishaps and irritability. Their restless, anxious, and pushy behavior can be very bothersome and a real pain to others. They might rush their peers, interrupt a speech before the point's been fully made, or steal the best seat when they show up early for a board meeting. If they can see themselves objectively and avoid that kind of behavior, they'll charm the pants off of everyone in the room.

Aries Born Shortly After Dawn:
Aries with Taurus Rising

Aries the ram teams up with Taurus the patient beast of burden! These people have all the directness of Aries born around dawn, but they're much more intense, deliberate, focused, and determined. They're much more willing to sit in the boss's chair and stay there; they actively earn their way and patiently wait for him to leave. The ram and the bull are pretty good complements, though Arians with other birth times will be better at "lighten up and move along." This combination does need to avoid heavy-handed overkill. But the patience of Taurus, the Banker, can actually mitigate these people's Action Aries restlessness. These folks are better equipped to accept sedentary roles, and they're usually more patient and determined. But hopefully that doesn't mean they're listless or immobile. Their Taurus personalities do a lot of serious deliberation, yet they usually get things done effectively and efficiently. They might paint the entire house unnoticed, leaving others to wonder, "How the heck did they do that!?" The answer is their blend of Aries expedience and Taurus "cut the bull." They don't waste time with non-essentials as much as other Aries types. They're sometimes drawn to banking, accounting, and other fields where they can keep their eye on the bottom line; they find satisfaction in keeping track of things, particularly material things. And with Taurus rising, they sometimes prefer a mouthy microphone, where they can use their articulate voice to display and popularize their charming Aries ego. The fearless bull overcomes stage fright pretty quickly.

At their best, Arians with Taurus rising can be extremely generous, showing their affection with material gifts: money, a meal, or a tasteful keepsake. They have an unusually warm touch.

Both the ram and the bull are horned animals, but the ram's horns are designed to bruise, while the bull's horns gore and draw blood. So Aries is generally less intense than Taurus. For instance, Aries's childlike innocence is almost never mean-spirited. These particularly "bullish" Arians need to draw on their springtime "summer's coming" attitude and lighten up. They may need to moderate their speech a bit, and be less stern towards and demanding of others. They need to avoid aloofness and accept disappointment with less gravity. If they accentuate their generosity, exercise their willingness to do whatever's necessary to get the job done, and take their pleasure in the self-satisfaction of a conscientious effort, these Arians will not only find success—they'll be able to slow down and enjoy it!

Aries Born Mid-Morning: Aries with Gemini Rising

Watch out! It's a ram on wheels, with sports car steering! If you can't keep up, stand aside. Or be ready to change directions at any moment. Talk about multi-tasking! Arians with Gemini rising are brimming with bright ideas and arrive with their sleeves rolled up, asking all the necessary questions to get the job done quick as a whistle. And they're flexible with everyone involved. Because they're adept at communicating and making "connections," they're often found giving instruction in front of a class or working in shipping—making deliveries, piloting a plane, or even driving a bus. They also make splendid writers. They can keep two or three, or even four things going at the same time. Communicating and connecting gives them lots of acquaintances, so they can recommend a good roofer or an honest mechanic off the top of their head.

These Arians love to talk, so they stay in touch. However, they're not usually good at slowing down and keeping things focused and orderly. Off-topic ramblings aren't uncommon, and their friends have to be willing to go with the flow. They get bored quickly, and it's easy for them to become scattered, to plan too much to do and leave themselves spread too thin to do the job punctually and properly. They plan insufficient intervals between their many appointments, so when they're forced to wait for everybody to show up, they end up running behind for the remainder of the day. They need to better budget their time. Arriving too early and anxious—or harried and late—undermines their natural Aries charm and always makes everything more difficult.

Jitterbug Gemini's chatty curiosity, in tandem with Aries' "early bird catches the worm," creates a person who wants to know everything right now and isn't afraid to ask, indicating a sincere interest in other people. At their best, these Arians are charming and conversant, with an inoffensive light touch. They're the original Mr. Nice Guys, the "icing on the cake" of the zodiac. But they might tend to ramble on well after their point has been made, allowing conversation to drift toward gossip or some other superficial or irrelevant nonsense, and possibly divulging privileged information. They need to know when they've said enough, and learn to be patient and quiet enough to let people consider their position—because their position is very likely to be unselfish.

Aries Born Around Noontime:
Aries with Cancer Rising

Now here's a switch: a cautious ram with a practical purpose, avoiding rejection as a matter of course, less direct and more cagey, but still "busy dizzy" much of the time.

Until they're inspired by their Aries fire, these people use caution in all their dealings. But once they're sure of the situation, they bound off and take the lead with their high-stepping Aries enthusiasm. With Cancer's sense of utility adorning Aries' energy, you get a willing worker with a buzz saw mentality, always willing to do what's expected, no matter what. But their Arian efficiency comes with a cautiously sensitive and human touch. Their Cautious Cancer personality is wonderfully plugged in to others' emotions. They're so keenly sensitive that they can deal with people in an unobtrusive, yet useful and effective way. Even when their Aries egotism flares and their impatient honesty speaks bluntly, these Arians usually avoid giving offense due to the couth provided by their Cancer sensitivity. Vocationally, they're well-suited for work in most public places, particularly retail establishments or restaurants, but they also succeed as apartment managers or realtors. They're superb overseers, but their employees better wear some comfortable shoes—there's a workaholic mentality here that's never afraid to tackle big jobs, work long hours, and accept schedules that others might find intolerable.

Because Aries and Cancer are both active signs, the Cancer personality complements the Aries ego quite well, but certain Cancer elements, especially that reticent emotional nature, have to be acknowledged and contained to keep these people from succumbing to a pretentious, busybody attitude. Deception never benefited honest Aries, but it's always an easy insincerity for willowy, womanly Cancer. Remember, Cancer is naturally cagey. If Arians with Cancer rising allow themselves to become resentful, they'll instinctively move into a behind-the-scenes "attack mode." Because they feel their own emotional pain too deeply, they suffer their wounds forever, fostering emotional scars that inhibit their ability to jump at opportunities and enjoy their success. This sort of behavior can seriously undermine their natural Aries honesty and charm.

It's always in these folks' best interests to put their cards on the table, speak the truth with discretion, and trust that others will respond favorably when their sensitive and considerate personality lets their bright-eyed, bushy-tailed ego shine through.

Aries Born Early Afternoon:
Aries with Leo Rising

Nobody else in the zodiac makes a bigger "early bird catches the worm" splash than Aries, and here it's wrapped up in a warm, sunny, robust, big impression, Lordly Leo personality. Upbeat, springtime Aries' positive, honest, and expedient character sets the stage beautifully for Leo's "Stand aside, I'll show you how to do this" attitude. These Arians leave a striking impression. They're good at inspiring others and taking the lead on things. However, they're not the best followers; they don't like being told what to do. They're naturally independent, and when it's necessary to spend time in the underling's chair, they'd better have a very long leash to satiate their restlessness. Arians with Leo rising are great promoters and fabulous entertainers. In fact, they're usually entertaining, no matter their particular career. But their life's work might lead them to promotional positions. They're usually good salespeople, as long as they're left alone to do things their way. Working out of town or on the road might well be their cup of tea—that is, if they can pull themselves away from their adoring family. Leo rising usually makes for an invested parent. They're ideally equipped for starting a small business, although their Aries impatience might require them to hire someone else to do routine and tedious managerial tasks or lengthy inventories.

Leo's magnanimous generosity is one of these people's more endearing traits. They give freely of their time, consideration, and means. Leo's fondness for children coupled with Aries' competitiveness might lead them into coaching youth sports, although, ultimately, they're a bit hard-driving and not so long-suffering, given their "do it right the first time" attitude.

Leo is, above all, the consummate showman, so when Leo rises the impression left with people is paramount. Because Arians are already given to a healthy opinion of themselves, Arians born early afternoon need to steer clear of coming off as self-absorbed and self-serving. So as not to compromise their Aries childlike honesty and charm, they need to be aware of how they're being received and adjust their reactions accordingly. The best showmen are always aware of how their audience is receiving them. These Arians can expect screaming success if they remember to always manifest a clear and genuine interest in the people around them.

Aries Born Mid-Afternoon:
Aries with Virgo Rising

When helpful, productive, intelligent Virgo teams up with take-the-initiative Aries, a great troubleshooter emerges. These quick-minded, clever "Johnny-on-the-spot" types track down problems and put out fires, with little to no spirit of self-importance—unless you question their intelligence! They're extremely competent if anything needs to be counted, sorted, or stored in an expedient and orderly fashion.

Virgo is keenly aware of detail. Vocationally, these Arians are splendid merchandisers, wizards at inventory control, and fabulous accountants. They take naturally to the department store and might also gravitate towards medical professions or precision carpentry. But whatever the field, it's the proclivity toward analyzing, diagnosing, and making corrections that drives them. They're genuine Mr. Fix Its!

However, these Arians do need to keep a close eye on their insecure Virgo, the Worry Wart. Virgo's analytical nature can degenerate into pickiness. So they focus too tightly on inconsequential matters, fussing over semantics, criticizing the insignificant, or announcing some blinding skepticism subconsciously designed to allow them to believe whatever they prefer, never mind reality. They feel this allows them to hide under a cloak of confusion, disclaiming responsibility for anything and everything. And, man, oh man, can they be annoying with their shrewd flippancy, saying things that they know aren't true just to get an energy-draining reaction from the people around them. So, ultimately, Arians with Virgo rising might leave a negative impression without ever realizing it. Is that outsmarting themselves, or what? Yes, their Virgo helpfulness and productivity work wonderfully well in tandem with their Aries eagerness, enhancing their natural charm, but propelled by Virgo's more negative traits, these Arians can unwittingly do themselves a grave injustice. Objectivity is the cornerstone to truly productive accomplishment and recognition.

Aries Born Around Sundown:
Aries with Libra Rising

When Aries' innate charm is accompanied by Likable Libra's polite, considerate nature, we get a person with superb people skills, much beloved by others. For Arians with Libra rising, the social aspects of life should provide warm rewards and pose few problems. They interact superbly with their peers and colleagues, giving meaningful attention to what others have to say. So they flourish in part-nerships of any kind. They're natural deal-makers. They're highly effective politi-cians and successful lawyers. Whatever they put their hand to, they possess the skills to make it work. But the hallmarks of these people's success are "one hand washes the other" relationships and smooth networking. It's not always *what* they know, but *who* they know, that brings them their next inspiring opportunity. They might even experience "chance" meetings that provoke a first-impression affinity or even a feeling of instantaneous recognition. It's not uncommon for people born around sundown to feel as though they know another person upon first meeting.

However, that's not to say that Arians born around sundown are without weaknesses. Certain Libran tendencies can undermine some of the best Aries qualities. Their Libra personality can lean towards a paralyzing indecisiveness that's much at odds with Aries' need to get on with it. For instance, they might find themselves facing a deadline but lacking confidence in their associates, leading them to uncertainty and vacillation; and in the end, their Aries need for action will eventually cause them to succumb to the "do it yourself" syndrome. This can actually limit their effectiveness by increasing the risk of overload. So whom they align themselves with in their life is unusually important and influential to their destiny.

Another area of possible concern here is that Libra's propensity to meddle in other people's affairs, without invitation, can be intensified by their Aries impulsiveness. And with their desire to keep everyone happy, these Arians can seem a bit hypocritical, telling everyone exactly what they want to hear. They might agree with two or three contradictory statements from different friends or colleagues, intending only to keep everyone happy, but ending up appearing two-faced and ultimately detracting from the honesty that normally serves Aries so well. But, all in all, these are darling people with fair and considerate ways. You'll have a hard time finding more loyal friends and honest partners.

Aries Born Early Evening:
Aries with Scorpio Rising

Buckle up if you intend to ride along with these people, because they're always on the move! Aries' impulsiveness is accentuated by "full of gusto," "do it now and think about it later," "grab the handle and break it" Scorpio. These are the two most active, energetic signs in the zodiac, and the only two signs ruled by red hot, horny, handy Mars! But Scorpio does a much better job at "look before you leap" than Aries does. Mysterious Scorpio always looks for what's not obvi-ous to others, so these Arians are usually more deliberate and strategic in their purpose. Adept at reading other people's motives, and not so given to letting the cat out of the bag, Arians with Scorpio rising are ready enough with information that others truly need to get the job done—but they work on a "need to know" basis. They're not likely to say more than is necessary, and they certainly won't divulge any secrets.

As extremely energetic as Scorpio tends to be, the Aries susceptibility to a "busy dizzy" lifestyle is increased in this combination. To ensure direction and moderation instead of purely helter-skelter physical behavior, Arians born early evening need to remind themselves that spring always follows winter, and that all things in due time is, simply put, the way of the world. Some earthly wisdom can ease their load, bolster their optimism, and certainly improve their effectiveness. Much of their frenetic behavior is the result of anxieties about idleness rather than positive inspiration. They're too enamored by behavior; they believe being sedentary is downright sinful. So maybe they should take a lesson from nature: Even a twitchy squirrel finds a moment to sit still in the sunshine once he's gathered food and procreated.

With less intensity and more patience, these Arians are gifted managers. They're independent and handy, so they might make a good foreman at a construction site. They enjoy this kind of busy work—and their childlike, active Aries might just make it look like play! They're good at reading between the lines, deciphering clues, and perceiving hidden meanings, so they usually know where others are coming from. They also make formidable detectives, skilled psychologists, and even highly competent engineers, forensic scientists, and physicians. But in any role, professional or personal, they usually earn their rewards from the get-go, getting things done even before they're asked, leaving themselves very well-equipped to succeed and receive the benefits they're so hell-bent to have.

Aries Born Mid-Evening:
Aries with Sagittarius Rising

When Happy-Go-Lucky Sagittarius, the Wild Thing, embellishes the adventurous Aries ego with inspiration and winning ways, the result is a live wire with an encouraging word, who's a lot of fun to be around. Arians with Sagittarius rising are diversified. They'll start a business and make a success of it, but will soon feel the urge to bound downrange to see what's new and interesting. They're sometimes military personnel whose Aries breeds a warrior and whose Sagittarius carries them to foreign lands. They're the civil servants who climb the political ladder, or the attorneys who rise to judgeship. They're the troubleshooters who quickly put things in order, then hurriedly move along to the next pressing problem. Give these people an office with no windows, and you'll drive them stir crazy. They enjoy the outdoors, and since Aries the Ram and Sagittarius the equestrian Archer are both hoofed animals, they're comfortable in the role of the rancher. They love their wide open spaces!

Without moderation, however, these Arians can perpetuate a lot of superfluous and even reckless behavior. Their Aries egotism assures their off-the-wall Wild Thing that they look marvelous in outrageous clothing, and their Aries impulsiveness can't wait to saddle up and move along. So exotic, or gaudy, or even clownish—they're off and running, and making quite a spectacle of themselves. And they're so full of Pied Piper promise and inspiration that everyone wants to follow.

Exaggeration and broken promises are their nemesis, along with mindless comments and thoughtless behavior. They just get anxious! It's difficult for them to slow down and think things through, even as well-intended as they are. Always wrestling with their impetuosity, they desperately need to learn how to hold their horses and see the effect they're having on the people around them. They absolutely need to be true to their word and fulfill their promises. As long as their associates find them refreshing, sporting, and maybe even roguish, they'll retain their good graces; but when they cross that line into frenzied and reckless behavior, people back off, knowing that a mishap—not to mention danger—is just around the corner. And—oh, brother—do these people love their danger! Testing the waters and taking it to the limit are their favorite pastimes.

Aries Born Around Midnight:
Aries with Capricorn Rising

Arians with Capricorn rising are ship-shape, by-the-book, and disciplined, the trusted "keeper of the keys." They're never the mouse at play while the cat's away; they won't leave early when the boss is out of town. They're competitive hard-bodies not only in their attitude, but sometimes physically, as well. And it's a bit difficult to know how much sensitivity exists here. They're awfully ambitious and accomplishment-oriented, and their hands-on management style equips them to run businesses of any type. Long hours usually don't faze them, and they love to be on the move. They're active in the home and with family, too, but hopefully they don't take their parenting so seriously that they run their household like an Army barracks. They're just so thorough and in charge! Yes, these folks are good moms and dads, and wonderful organizers, but they're born slave drivers for any "business is business" purpose.

Arians born around midnight need to use a little finesse and "put some icing on it." If they'll give an encouraging word, they'll make things work a little easier. They're too serious and sober, and potentially sour in their authority. For them, human interaction can become mindless competition. And the fact that they always win doesn't help: it fuels their "get ahead of everyone" mentality. They simply need to allow their charming Aries to show through. Enough demanding hard ass already! It makes everything more difficult than it needs to be. Here's an interesting prospect: Stop treating everyone like a competitor and get more cooperation.

Some of the best qualities of both Aries and Capricorn can, in tandem, actually cause difficulties. The Wise Old Goat is quite capable of accomplishing great things, but these people need to avoid letting their strengths become their weaknesses. Building on their loyal, diligent, and respectful behavior serves them wonderfully through life; it reveals them as incomparably dependable and earns them the seat of authority. Their instinct is to be visibly fair and equitable with the responsibility of leadership. Both the Aries Rocky Mountain bighorn and the Capricorn mountain goat are ambitious high climbers and know how to watch their step so as not to stumble and fall. They wisely calculate their moves and pick and choose their path to success and recognition. If they'll compete only with themselves rather than others, they'll earn the support they need to get what they want and do the best job imaginable in one fell swoop.

Aries Born in the Wee Hours:
Aries with Aquarius Rising

With an "all for one and one for all" attitude, Arians with Aquarius rising are "on deck, at attention" team players, genuinely well liked and often quite popular among their peers. Their friendly magnetism keeps them completely connected and in good favor. They're often on the city council or wearing a uniform of some kind, in service to the community with their friendly demeanor coupled with a natural straightforwardness. They're inclined toward big projects requiring technical aptitude, and their Big Attitude Aquarius might put them directly in the fire-truck driver's seat, the airplane cockpit, or at the ship's helm. They've always read the manual from cover to cover. And they're alert and prepared for any emergency—they know each team member's proper position and the location of the necessary tools to get the job done. When the crap hits the fan, they're Johnny-on-the-spot, a cool head in the face of danger. No one shouts "This is no drill!" as formidably as these people do.

However, Aries' ego and impulsiveness can stoke the snarly, stressed-out, chip on the shoulder, argumentative downside of Aquarius, the Electric Light Bulb. Yes, their fearless nature and soldier's spirit serve them well when the platoon is under fire, and they're indispensable when the smoke is billowing from a neighbor's house, or when the barbarians storm the city gates; it's their inner tension that equips them to take the ball and run with it, narrowly averting whatever tragedy is at hand. But inevitably they carry their stressful demeanor into less trying situations. Aquarius' uptight anxiety remains alive and well. They're frayed and uptight on a Monday evening, coiled on the couch like a cobra. Rather than bite the hand that feeds them, they might do well to go outside and blow off steam by jogging around the block or playing basketball with their chums. Anything to help them relax. If these Arians can control their inner ferocity, they'll earn not only cooperation, but adoration, from others, with a delightful blend of Aquarius magnetism and Aries innocence.

Aries Born Pre-Dawn:
Aries with Pisces Rising

Always fascinating, and sometimes glamorous! When the Aries ego is complemented by a whimsical, somewhat delicate, Pisces personality, the result is a tantalizing blend of charisma and artistry. Arians with Pisces rising have a wonderful eye for beauty, and they're superb at imaging. As the sign of illusion, Pisces often gives them a photogenic quality. They take naturally to the manufacture of images and the production of motion pictures; in fact, the creation of all forms of illusion is in their bailiwick. Cameras and photography are a significant part of Pisces' domain. However, these Arians are rarely driven solely by prospects of financial reward; they thrive instead on achieving personal satisfaction and the creation of beauty, and if they can find in life what truly inspires them, they attain ultimate happiness as well. Active research with an open mind, exposing themselves to all the world has to offer, ensures that discovery. They shouldn't sit idly, with crossed fingers, wishing and waiting for their destiny to fall into their lap. Often they gravitate towards people-helping institutions like schools and hospitals, or to vocations and lifestyles that take them to the sea. The nuts and bolts of everyday living on the cold-as-stone planet earth can overwhelm these bright-eyed and bushy-tailed, but wistful, Arians. They truly need something that stimulates their spirit, something they can create, transform, or perfect. Delicate Pisces and agile Aries often combine to form a skilled ballet dancer or a charming actress. Hours spent alone honing their craft, even into the quiet and lonely wee hours, will never seem burdensome, but always inspiring, if they've found their artistic niche.

However, this combination of charm and artistry creates a shrewd inoffensiveness that often allows these Arians to get away with untold mischief. They should avoid becoming too delighted with their own intriguing cleverness; they might end up indulging it to their detriment.

The Pisces need for peace moderates the vigor of Aries, producing a sensitivity unwilling to rock the boat; these folks often keep their mouths shut, preferring their motives to be unseen. But their polite civility tempered with timidity can arouse suspicion. If others begin to wonder what they're up to, or why they refuse to put their cards on the table, ulterior motives will be suspected and people will be less prone to extend the cooperation that makes life so much easier. Arians born pre-dawn simply need to have the courage to show their Aries honesty and build trust by revealing themselves. There's nothing to lose! When they're willing to stick their neck out, they'll find that, more often than not, their contributions will be enthusiastically welcomed.

CHAPTER 6

THE TAURUS SUN SIGN
AND ITS RISING SIGN PERSONALITIES

THE TAURUS SUN SIGN
April 20–May 20

Taureans are patient, persistent, and practical, with an eye for quality in people and things; their attention is always on the bottom line. Knowing precisely what they want and exactly what the price should be, these people are focused and determined and have little tolerance for nonsense. They want visible results from their investments. Like your banker, they'll give you more time, as long as the goal is in sight, the strategy is mapped out, and it all makes practical sense. Taurus, the Banker, the beast of burden, is level-headed and sure-footed.

These folks are serious and patient, allowing themselves to effectively fill their role and obtain their objectives. But depending on their rising sign, the level of seriousness and intensity might actually exceed what's really necessary; overkill can cause difficulties with friends, peers, and colleagues who find them too rigid and intolerant. In these cases, they need to lighten up and not take life so seriously. While it's important that the beast of burden keep his eye on the ground to maintain his footing, Taureans need to be careful not to lose perspective, becoming so obsessed with the here and now that they forget to look up and envision the future. They're so wrapped up in their own agenda that they forget to accommodate their surroundings. It's understandable that they're so focused and steady; they put all their weight into their decisions and rarely hedge their bets, making it difficult to recover from any error in judgment.

So moderation and a forward-looking, light and lively, open mind can be difficult for these bulls to maintain. However, other rising signs might mitigate the natural focus that serves Taureans so well, weakening the bottom-line mentality they require to realize their ambitions.

Taureans are innately generous and quite willing to share their comforts and material wealth. They love to indulge their senses. Taurus *is* the sign of sensuality. They're tasteful and discrete, with an eye for value, but sometimes not so easy to approach. They respond well to dignified treatment. While an undignified infraction almost always elicits their aloof intolerance, leaving them distant and unavailable, a more respectful approach will move them to trail along peacefully with a ring in their nose and a flowery wreath around their sturdy necks. These, too, are positive traits that some rising signs will enhance while others will obscure. Self-awareness is always the key.

Taurus Born Around Dawn:
Taurus with Taurus Rising

Double Taurus, double intensity, double focus and determination. Taureans with Taurus rising are Taurus, the Banker, personified. Even physically, a broad smile with lots of teeth, broad shoulders, and narrow pelvic bones are not uncommon. Will these Taureans harness and channel their formidable strengths? Or will they end up demanding, intolerant, overly serious and unpleasantly intense, burning bridges and engaging in overkill? Moderating their anger and developing a softer touch is the key here. When they remember, "Father, forgive them, they know not what they do," all is well. Of course, it's true that ire and indignation can be powerful motivators, but when anger becomes mindless rage it never brings back a desired response. So if the bull declines to snort fury and fire when he sees red, he'll avoid being the matador's victim. Keeping his cool has its rewards!

Taureans born around dawn have no problem identifying and focusing on the bottom line. After all, that's Taurus' forte. But their focus can become so obsessive that they lose sight of everything else. Sometimes they just don't see the larger picture; their single-minded purpose disallows them to see the light at the end of the tunnel. They feel their disappointments too intensely. But if they give themselves time to chew on things, they dig out the simple facts every time. It's all a part of getting to the bottom line, of being certain that the terms suit them and the rewards are realistic and desirable. It's their nature to stick with a project until hell freezes over, and if a particular deal takes an unexpected dive, these Taureans are liable to drive it straight into the ground. They don't always know when to quit. When they succeed, they really succeed. But when they mess up, the ceiling falls in. The problem is gluttony—even at the dinner table! Ask them how much food they ate, and they'll tell you they ate it all! But there's a lot of tastefulness here. Yes, double Taurus' appetite is sometimes over-developed, but if you need someone to help you find a good value, these are the folks to call. They expect their fabrics to be expertly woven and their food to be deliciously seasoned. There's a lot of vanity here as well, so they usually opt for tailored clothing rather than loose-fitting and flowing things. They love to show off their physical form.

They're great salespeople, giving simple explanations and refusing to take "No" for an answer. As businesspeople, whatever they build, they build to last. "Shoddy" is not in their vocabulary. If they'll keep their eyes open, exercise their deep loyalties, and give others the benefit of the doubt—if they'll react to adversity with tolerance and flexibility, and let their broad, sexy smile break through the seriousness, they'll acquire all the comforts and enjoyment of life they envision.

Taurus Born Shortly After Dawn:
Taurus with Gemini Rising

Gemini, "the nice guy," usually does a good job of lightening up Taurus the Banker; Gemini's "icing on the cake" sincerity adds a lot of tolerance and flexibility. So the nimble, spry, chatty-faced Jitterbug Gemini personality can be a real blessing here. Gemini rising provides the beast of burden an open mind, and while Taureans usually do profit from lightening up, they need to remember that "loose lips sink ships." They need to avoid spilling the beans. Much depends on how well they've done their homework, allowing themselves to truly grasp the situation. Gemini loves to talk, so spewing opinions is a joy. But if enlightenment is missing, those opinions might be a bit heavy-handed and better left unspoken. Taureans run the risk of taking a position not based in reality, so "Don't confuse me with the facts" sets in. Taurus is the master of "I just talk, I don't listen" bull-headedness, so he needs to avoid just rambling on. Taureans with Gemini rising are quite capable of self-undoing, so they have to remember that once the police officer has pulled them over and whipped out his pen, the time for running off at the mouth is past. Some silent respect works better. And being by themselves is rejuvenating; it helps them to see themselves in context, assimilating who and what they are, and what they think. This is how they regenerate their energy: Solitude is a useful tool. The bull is innately a down-home creature, not always prone to wander away from the pasture. These people like their home turf; their home neighborhood is their comfort zone. And they often enjoy reading. There's an intelligent curiosity in Gemini that likes to be satiated.

Taureans born shortly after dawn make great teachers. They impart information articulately and understandably. In any event, they like to be involved with things that have a practical purpose, things that satisfy the Banker's no-nonsense mentality. And since Gemini is the domain of vehicles and transportation, these Taureans might make splendid truck drivers: Their Taurus can sit, while their Gemini travels and chats with other truckers on the CB. But, please, none of that raw language over the airwaves!

Taurus Born Mid-Morning:
Taurus with Cancer Rising

"Still waters run deep." These people are usually cautious and contemplative, and not very willing to risk rejection. But Cancer is a world-class thrifty nickel and practical Taurus loves a bargain, so Taurus with Cancer rising is very effective at accruing material things. Real estate being one of Cancer's preferred domains, we might find these Taureans exercising their diligence in renovating properties or selling houses. In any case, Cancer's cautiously clever industriousness is a fitting complement to Taurus' determined, do-the-deal mentality. Their mid-morning birth inclines them to lift their head and envision the future. These Taureans will sacrifice today's reward for tomorrow's promise in a heartbeat. And there's too much Cancer sensitivity here to burn many bridges. Rather than self-destruct if their offer is rejected, they'll simply wait patiently until the buyer reconsiders and returns next week. There's a magnetism in this combination. Cautious Cancer's reticence curbs a lot of Taurus' bullishness, making these Taureans very industrious colleagues and competent supervisors, especially if they keep that forward-focus, letting bygones be bygones in the course of life's inevitable misunderstandings. Though neither the crab nor the beast of burden is known for networking skills, the mid-morning birth makes for well-connected people who know their way around the community.

Cancer is usually family-oriented, so these folks love to provide for their own. Their material generosity with loved ones is quite admirable, but they also need to be generous in their judgments and emotional reactions, willing to give counsel with no strings attached. For instance, they're extremely fond of their children but often have very concrete and inflexible ideas about what directions their kids should take in life. Taurus' "my way or the highway" mentality merges with Cancer's clinging possessiveness. There's sometimes a fierce tenacity in this regard. They'll willingly shell out the money for college tuition but will then attempt to control the course of study, disapproving if their children choose the wrong field. And when this happens, they've gotten themselves smack dab in the middle of someone else's space, preventing that person from making her own choices. Of course, this proves to be overly controlling, bad management. If these Taureans will back off just a bit, if they'll give people room to breathe and allow them their right to pursue their own path, they'll find themselves greatly appreciated and endeared to the people they care most about.

Taurus Born Around Noontime:
Taurus with Leo Rising

Now these people take the bull by the horns and pursue their goals with a "stand aside, I'll show you how to do this" attitude. They're super determined, masterfully competent, and striking in their delivery. Lordly Leo's pride, fearlessness, and "do it right the first time" mentality is a good complement to Taurus' practicality and focus. Leo is characterized by confidence and competence, always putting on a hell of a show and leaving a big impression. If Taureans with Leo rising do their homework and learn their material before taking a position, they'll successfully sway people in their direction. When they know what they're talking about, these Taureans can sell ice to an Eskimo.

Taureans with Leo rising tend to put themselves out in front of the pack. Bullishly headstrong and prideful, they don't respond well to a lot of supervision. They insist on their independence and work best on a long leash. In the boss's office, they might be difficult to work for. They can be very demanding. They deeply disapprove of lackadaisical behavior and can be highly intolerant of what they perceive as a lack of initiative. But if they become too "my way or the highway," they run the risk of breeding resentment and might be left alone to do everything themselves. They need to remember that most people aren't as intense about everything as they are.

Leo's showiness blended with Taurus' vanity can result in a big, fat, gold watch on a man's wrist and expensive bracelets, necklaces, and earrings on a woman, leaving the impression that these Taureans are well-heeled. Just as they're generous with others, especially their children, they like to be generous with themselves. And this obvious generosity can actually be one of their most effective tools. Far from bribing others, their gifts are meant to show affection and appreciation, two of the most important things to them. They want to be recognized for a job well done and they expect a little gratitude for their most competent efforts. They don't react well to being slighted, and they'll come down heavily on those who seek to take advantage. If they remember to extend to others the same respect they expect for themselves, Taureans born around noontime will find people engaging and cooperative every step of the way.

Taurus Born Early Afternoon:
Taurus with Virgo Rising

These are unassuming, cooperative people with a youthful appearance and a good eye for style and quality in people and things. And they're masters at efficiency and precision. Their Taurus "cut the bull" teams up with Virgo's keen eye for functionality, equipping them to get things done lickety-split. Both Taurus and Virgo are "earth" signs, motivated by practicality, so these Taureans actively seek out what's most productive. This is always their best strategy. Virgo possesses a busy mind that enhances the Banker's ability to cut to the chase, so these people do the job with precision, leaving time to spare. As long as they don't get bogged down making mountains out of molehills and losing the forest for the trees! Virgo, the Worry Wart, is easily side-tracked by analytical pickiness. But the best antidote for Virgo's fussiness is Taurus' "keep it simple, stupid." The beast of burden is strong and durable, so Virgo's insecurities should be minimal in this combination. The key here is embodied in Johnny Mercer's popular song: "Accentuate the positive; eliminate the negative."

Taureans with Virgo rising are often found in vocations that require licensing. They believe in monitoring, but they themselves usually don't need much supervision. Virgo is always the willing worker, and Virgo mitigates Taurus' bull-headedness with a more flexible and intelligent mind; these folks like to exhibit a helpfulness where other Taureans might stomp, stamp, and snort. Virgo's penchant for keeping busy can turn these analytical Bankers into humming buzz saws. Taureans born early afternoon are inclined toward medicine, nutrition, fashion, and all things personal. You might find them selling furniture or pharmaceuticals. With Virgo's head for analysis and Taurus' money sense, they might be teaching economics. With Virgo's love of finery and Taurus' eye for quality, they might be interior decorators, Park Avenue haberdashers, or merchandisers of exquisite jewelry. They love what's stylish, tasteful, and attractive. They might even be virtuoso violinists. There are a great many possibilities, but, in any event, these Taureans are infinitely more delicate and precise in their behavior than many other "bull in the china shop" Taureans.

Taurus Born Mid-Afternoon:
Taurus with Libra Rising

These people are polite but determined, and if they exercise good judgment, doors of opportunity open pretty easily. Libra's catch-phrase for success is, "It was who I knew, not what I knew, that put me in the seat of opportunity." Word of mouth and "one hand washes the other" partnerships are Taurus with Libra rising's bread and butter. Yes, Taurus can be bull-headed and obtuse, but with obliging Libra rising Taureans are keenly aware of how they're being received. So adjusting their behavior to fit the occasion is an easy matter. They know how to benefit from enhancing other people's resources, setting up win/win situations that produce a snowball effect: They give two and get four, they give eight and get sixteen. So a Likable Libra personality improves Taurus' (the Banker's), ability to fill his coffers. Not a bad deal, don't you think? They learn quickly to put some icing on the cake, to be diplomatic, fair, and equitable. Deal-making is their forte; they can succeed in any vocation really, but litigation, investment banking, or stockbrokerage are a snap for them.

A Taurean born mid-afternoon is a people-person. Venus's rulership of both Taurus and Libra creates an energy of attraction; pretty Venus, the night star, is always the planet of love and money. There's an element of beauty here that attracts people, things, and opportunity. These are people-pleasing people-watchers, never bored at the train station, airport, or food court.

If these Taureans create problems for themselves, it might be with their willingness to oblige. At the moment, they might agree to something too hastily, realizing only later, in a time of reflection, just what they've gotten themselves into. They suddenly comprehend that they've agreed to something that doesn't seem fair to their "give and take" Libra. Now they're faced with changing the terms of the agreement after the fact, leaving themselves open to appearing less than true to their word. This is rarely a good strategy for someone who relies a great deal on business and personal relationships. Focusing on the bottom line, keeping the machinery of their relationships well-oiled and in good working condition, these are Taureans' keys to success.

Taurus Born Around Sundown:
Taurus with Scorpio Rising

These are some serious go-getters with pretty good people skills, considering how hell-bent they are to get what they want. Taurus determination and Scorpio gusto add up to voracity! There's almost too much energy in this combination, a passionate, hot sexuality, a sensual touch, a tendency to bite off a great big chunk; they drink life in gulps rather than dainty sips. This is no lackadaisical bull, frittering away the afternoon in a quiet meadow. These Taureans are get-up-and-go gluttons. With a Taurus ego and a Scorpio personality, the patient, plodding determination of Taurus translates into an intense focus on the seemingly unattainable. These Taureans always aim high, taking on projects that others find daunting. But resourceful Scorpio and persistent Taurus can handle just about anything. There's a "do it now and think about it later" attitude here that's demanding and dauntless. These people recoup their investments and then some. And they rarely falter. Their grandiose objectives are no mere pipe dreams. They're realistic and workable.

The investigative qualities of Mysterious Scorpio can help the Banker ferret out the bottom line no matter where it's hidden. Some Taureans see only the obvious, but not these. Taureans with Scorpio rising are formidable sleuths. They're the sorts of detectives who always have more questions and never take "No" for an answer. They don't wait for an invitation. They're already sitting in the suspect's bedroom when he returns home and turns on the lights. They're the scorpions underneath the bedsheets, and every bit as dangerous when riled. They're superb auditors, undertakers, and investment bankers.

Their dinner time birth keeps them keenly aware that one hand washes the other. They're wisely accommodating, getting the cooperation they need to realize their ambitions. And if they remain vigilant to avoid stubbornness, oafishness, and vanity, they work toward their goals with reasonable amenability, earning approval from their peers, and walking off with exactly what they came for.

Taurus Born Early Evening:
Taurus with Sagittarius Rising

"Sagittarius" derives from the Latin "bull-slayer," which might make it seem like a Sagittarius rising sign is a poor complement to a Taurus ego, but not so: Sagittarius gives the bull a smiley face and winning ways! Sagi-magi-ragi-ttarius, Mr. Happy-Go-Lucky, slays most of Taurus' less-buoyant traits, such as bull-faced frowns and closed-minded stubbornness. If these Taureans retain their determination and bottom-line sensibility, they're upbeat, inspiring, and quickly able to endear themselves. They're often gifted politicians with a "big kid" demeanor. They've a bit of "Jolly Old King Cole," and they know what they're doing. Even when some Taurus bullishness prevails, Sagittarius' onward and upward attitude is usually able to clean up the mess and move along. When the bull throws all his weight into what turns out to be a poor decision, creating a fiasco of colossal blunders, the leaps-and-bounds of Sagittarius the traveler puts him way down-range and out of sight when the crap hits the fan. Sagittarians are lucky people!

Because they are outdoorsy and sports-oriented, Sagittarians are sometimes inclined to outdoor vocations. With the bull as their sun sign, they might be rodeo-riders or A-1 ranchers. Normally, Taurus leans toward the sedentary, but in tandem with Sagittarius, the Wild Thing, they might get antsy sitting down or staying indoors too long.

Problems, however, can arise if Sagittarius arrogance couples with Taurus' stubbornness. They become rather self-centered and pompous. This is especially true if in formative years the grown-ups were too permissive. As adults they can become "holier-than-thou" given their "spare the rod, and spoil the child" background. Another area of concern is Sagittarius' agility and nimbleness leading them to opinionated judgments and a "pie in the sky" outlook. But if their Sagittarius optimism remembers to promise only what Taurus can realistically deliver on time and in good order, all is well. If they avoid these potential mistakes, they end up in the winner's circle every time.

Taurus Born Mid-Evening:
Taurus with Capricorn Rising

Combine common sense with a business-is-business personality, and you get a powerfully practical person who can make things happen. Taureans with Capricorn rising are the businesspeople who have the goods their competitors only wish they had, and they drive a hard bargain in selling them. They're the people in charge: serious honchos who know that what goes around, comes around. In this combination, Capricorn, the Wise Old Goat, presents a well-thought-out business concept to Taurus, the Banker, who contemplates it, chews on it, and gets to the bottom of it; then—and only then—does he agree to fund the project. Both signs are earth signs, motivated by practicality; their eyes light up when rewards are tangible and plans feasible. Taureans born mid-evening, more than any others, are apt to end up in charge, with most of the profit still in their pockets. But they need interests outside their career that will help to broaden their perspective and give them a well-rounded experience. It's their nature to be all work and no play, leaving them to feel like they're always on the time clock, but all work and no play really does make Jack a dull boy.

There's an eye for quality and sensible approach to life that ensures financial stability here, as well as the security and satisfaction that financial stability provides, but true happiness won't follow the dollars and cents unless these Taureans look beyond the material. If they don't, they're apt to be left alone in their ivory towers. They simply need to lighten up, keep a sense of humor, and not take it all so seriously. Capricorn's sour disposition and bossy ways are partially responsible for their impressive achievements, so these traits shouldn't be curbed entirely—but they need to be vigilant on bad days, when it seems everyone's full of error. Storming around like know-it-alls, and threatening to fire their best workers, is a prescription for disaster. They need to slow down, take a deep breath, recover their "calm, cool, and collected" demeanor, and conjure a Wise Old Goat smile. One of their most useful tools is their Taurus generosity.

Usually, that generosity shows up in how they reward their employees monetarily. But they need to broaden the scope of their generosity to create enduring friendship and warm relations. In this way, others won't bypass them altogether.

Taurus Born Around Midnight:
Taurus with Aquarius Rising

Aquarius is all about attitudes—BIG attitudes! So these people need to know exactly what they're projecting. Are they magnetic jokesters, or are they sourpusses? Does the Aquarius personality add electric magnetism to the focus and patience of Taurus? Does it create the most contagious funny bone you've ever met? Does it lead the plodding, big mouth bull to a book or two, creating a well-read, fully enlightened, self-aware dreamer and doer with the gumption, the wings, and the technological know-how to become an airline pilot? Or does it instead provoke Taurus' bull-headedness and closed-mindedness, resulting in an argumentative quality that amounts to a sour chip on the shoulder, creating an obnoxiously opinionated pain in the neck who might well be the worst bigot on the block? Aquarius does have an innate will-to-disagree, and in tandem with Taurus' stubborn streak it can be a source of bad attitudes. But if Taureans with Aquarius rising live their lives with an open mind and a thirst for more humor and camaraderie, they become the determined community-minded social workers who are motivated by a marvelous spirit of brotherhood; they understand that we're all in this together and "what I do to you, I do to me." If these Taureans cultivate tolerance for ignorance and error, they become the determined, enlightened teachers who always illuminate and never give up on even their most challenging students; they're always ready to assist them in understanding that their efforts will be rewarded with accomplishment and recognition. If they refrain from offense or insult, they'll find that the sky's the limit. Flexibility and tolerance are the keys here. Their magnetism will draw people to them, and their "good fellow well met" team player will reveal itself. They're witty and sharp-minded public servants, but also possess an eye for the simple truth that, in concert, provide the grist for a hilarious experience

The Banker doesn't care much for surprises in life, but Aquarius, the Electric Light Bulb, loves sudden happenings. If there's an emergency, Taureans born around midnight rise to the occasion with mechanized precision; when friends and acquaintances deliver pleasant surprises, they revel in the collegiality. So if these somewhat inflexible Taureans will lighten up and inculcate the buoyancy of the Aquarius-determined air sign into their nature, they'll be at the groundbreaking of the latest community project and voted the new hands-on city councilperson who leads the community to astronomical improvements. They'll even discover special delight in the world where otherwise they'd never have found it.

Taurus Born in the Wee Hours:
Taurus with Pisces Rising

A whimsical Pisces personality works rather well with the patient, long-suffering Bull. It gives a lighter touch. These people listen as well as speak, and they're better at peaceful solutions than other Taureans. A more gentle approach augments Taurus' ability to make things easy, yet fruitful. With an open mind, Pisces absorbs what's being heard, and delivers her newfound understanding to Taurus' sharply focused Beast of Burden brain, where it is practically applied. Pisces becomes more stabilized and Taurus more amenable. These people are formidable researchers—Pisces loves to snoop!—and when they know their material, they're very effective teachers: Taurus knows how to "keep it simple, stupid!" With Taurus' nose for money and Pisces' affection for the nighttime, they're comfortable behind the cash register at the 24-hour convenience store, though their imaginative Pisces might give them a penchant for creative writing. These are the soft-spoken people who pick up that obscure sound or little bit of missing information; their busy minds hum with shrewdness; and they're masters at painting the picture that conveys their message and creates the circumstances they prefer. There's versatility here; but most of all there's that Pisces eye for beauty and illusion. When they're at their best, they do a hell of a job, without much fanfare. And they might be found on either end of the camera: On one hand, they don't always prefer attention, but on the other, Pisces is photogenic.

But Pisces is also the wimpy scaredy-cat of the zodiac. So these bulls might inflict their bullish ways—then run away and hide! They might say things of great magnitude in a very soft, almost inaudible, tone, because they really prefer to be silent.

When Pisces rises, Taurus' materialism is sometimes satiated in the most fascinating ways, but Pisces often gets disillusioned with earth's bounty. Pisces' watery emotions prefer living things. Financial security and earthly comforts have their merit, but maybe not quite as much for these imaginative Bankers. An ideal position might be building homes with a charitable organization akin to Habitat for Humanity, or some other worthy cause.

Taurus Born Pre-Dawn:
Taurus with Aries Rising

No one needs to sit and wonder where these people are coming from! They're direct as can be, and they're apt to be very impatient with coyness or any other form of insincerity. Both Aries the ram and Taurus the bull are horned animals, implying a straightforward approach to life. With their Aries childlike innocence and charm, they earn a lot of trust and are usually well-served by putting their cards on the table, but their impatience, coupled with Taurus' heavy-handed intensity, can easily lead to overkill. The key here is to be respectful of everyone's space. If these people are oblivious to how they're being received, they're likely to be too forceful. Being the first at the board meeting in typical Aries early-bird fashion often leaves the good impression that they're eager-beaver willing workers, but unwittingly stealing the boss's seat and seeming to usurp his authority with bullish bluntness seldom pays off. These Taureans know how to be punctual and are always ready to do their fair share, and even take the lead if necessary, but with their Banker's single-mindedness and good dose of vanity, they often need to tone it down a bit. Slowing down just enough to make others feel accommodated earns them a lot of trust and cooperation. And if they'll use a little tact, they might even hit the jackpot; but staying aware of how people are reacting to them is essential.

These Taureans need jobs that require lots of activity. Aries rising loves to be physical. They're great initiators with a sterling ability to follow up and complete the task. There's an abundance of self-motivation and a dogged persistence. As outside salespeople they're pounding the pavement early and knocking on doors until they find a buyer. Especially when they're promoting something like building materials, or financial products such as insurance or stocks, they're extremely effective. They're also competent behind a microphone, articulate and succinct, able to handle attention, and even reveling in it with little to no stage fright. Having been adored as youngsters, and still carrying a childlike charm, they're sometimes charismatic radio personalities. And after work, you might find narcissistic Taurus with hard body Aries rising in the weight room. They love to look good, and they probably need to blow off steam.

With a good sense of self-worth, a keen eye for quality in people and things, a generosity that earns them friends, and a dignified candor that breeds respect, Taureans with Aries rising have the potential to achieve great things. But they'll need to be fair and use some tact.

CHAPTER 7

THE GEMINI SUN SIGN
AND ITS RISING SIGN PERSONALITIES

THE GEMINI SUN SIGN
May 21–June 21

Geminians are the most curious creatures on the planet! At their best, they're chatty, informed, congenial, sincere, and especially flexible people; they're the "icing on the cake" of the zodiac. They're alert and open-minded enough to consider any and all options in their quest for fun and profit. These folks are pleasingly pleasant Mr. Nice Guys, the friendly strangers on the elevator; they're courteous and conversant, and, better yet, they're always willing to share at least a tidbit of information that will inform and amuse. Their ability to obtain interesting data and cordially disseminate it is powered by three major Gemini characteristics: a love of intelligence, a silver tongue, and a delightfully breezy, "Hi! How are you?" Jitterbug Gemini demeanor. They love to talk and communicate in every way: between cities on highways and byways; in discussion; or while illustrating points and selling products in their glib and congenial manner. On the computer, they're naturals in the chat room.

But as is the case with all sun sign egos, the rising sign personality has a profound effect on these characteristics, enhancing, obscuring, or undermining them. Gemini's biggest weakness is a lack of focus. When these folks are dependable and ship-shape, they're held in high esteem; but when they spread themselves too thin, showing up late or not at all and offering up little more than some rambling nonsense or mindless chatter as excuses, they come off as flaky nitwits. Focus, concentration, and determination are the keys here. Rising signs that decrease Gemini's ability to follow through with focus and determination need to be acknowledged and consciously tempered. Gemini's insatiable curiosity and penchant for gathering information can create a very well-informed person, but Geminians are often so eager to display their trove of trivia that they jump to conclusions before they've gotten the point. The complexities and nuances of the deeper meaning might totally elude them. When this happens, they cheat themselves of intellectual depth, their knowledge remaining shallow, incomplete, and superficial. The Geminian's challenge is to take time to focus, and do so without dampening their light and lively enthusiasm.

Gemini Born Around Dawn:
Gemini with Gemini Rising

These people are busy-minded chatterboxes! They're full of questions, and they give new meaning to multi-tasking. No one juggles two, three, or four things at one time as efficiently as these quick-minded, quick-moving flit-arounds. They might be unsettled, but they're incomparably pleasant!

Geminians with Gemini rising are Jitterbug Gemini through and through. They never get bored. They'll always find something that interests them. Though many other astrological factors can influence the physical type, the usual Gemini youthful appearance and slightly built body are typical here. They love to be in motion, walking, jogging, or bicycling through the neighborhood, waving to neighbors or stopping briefly to chat. Ping-pong and tennis usually appeal to them; anything that flits back and forth or changes directions quickly is their bailiwick. The exercise of to-and-fro is even at work in Gemini's love of reading: These folks are often fast readers, adept at scanning words. But slowing down to absorb the meaning and retain the information is very important. Their curiosity is boundless; they're often drawn to magazines and newspapers that offer up information in neat, little packages. But it's easy for them to miss the point. (Be ready to repeat yourself when talking to them!) Their rush to finish the first article and move quickly to the second, so they can share what they've learned, can leave them totally oblivious to the heart of the matter. They'll miss the exit while eyeballing the road map, dooming themselves to thirty wasted minutes on a godforsaken side road, unwilling to ask directions for fear they'll appear stupid.

And these Geminians do love to drive. They'll be willing to give you a ride to the ends of the earth, and you'll definitely enjoy the trip. They love gadgetry, too, whether it's at their fingertips on the dashboard or sitting in the entertainment center. Information-giving gadgetry—like global positioning systems, calculators, and computers—are especially their cup of tea. Eager to share what they know and naturally pleasant, Geminians born around dawn are especially equipped to gather information and answer questions in positions such as telephone directory assistance or classroom instruction. But a deliberate pursuit of mental focus is recommended if they're to be truly knowledgeable as opposed to scatterbrained.

Gemini Born Shortly After Dawn: Gemini with Cancer Rising

These people have all the congeniality of Gemini, but they're considerably more emotionally cautious and sensitive. This makes them more aware of how they're being received and gives them a willingness to adjust themselves to fit the occasion. They love to be accepted! Cautious Cancer avoids rejection like the plague, so they're very sensitized to their environment. In tandem with the Gemini ego, the inoffensiveness and unassuming demeanor of a Cancer personality creates a gentle and well-intended person. Cancer is the Mother Goose of the zodiac, so these Geminians take pleasure in catering to the needs of family and friends. But they do need to be on guard against letting Cancer's workaholic nature and Gemini's lack of focus merge in such a way that they get lost in their surroundings, doing for others without noticing how they're being affected themselves. Geminians with Cancer rising get so busy taking care of what they perceive to be their responsibilities that they neglect their own ambitions. Time alone to center, regenerate and re-focus is of paramount importance. They must be objective about how the people and things around them make them feel. Nostalgic, subjective Cancer is always tempted to wander off and live in the past, especially when coupled with Gemini's sharp mind and memory. But while Memory Lane is sometimes a nice place to stroll, too much sentimentality can leave these people motivated more by yesterday than the here and now. There needs to be a healthy balance between their mind and their emotions. These Geminians hopefully learn to savor and learn from the past without leaving themselves insecure and inhibited, unable to partake of today's opportunities.

With a thrifty-nickel Cancer personality, these people are not quick to spend their hard-earned money, and their Gemini gets scattered just enough to misplace their loose change, so they're usually not the types to spontaneously spring for snacks. But Geminians born shortly after dawn are generous with their time and energy, and their information, too. With Gemini glibness, they're great on the phone. And with Cancer's fondness for public places, they're the clerks who know every aisle of merchandise like the back of their hand. And, of course, they'll be eager to personally escort you to the exact item you're looking for. And how common is that? So as long as these folks remember to nurture themselves, they'll stay interested, healthy, and happy in life.

Gemini Born Mid-Morning:
Gemini with Leo Rising

These are the well-informed people who inspire your confidence and hold themselves responsible for their deeds. They're not as prone as other Geminians to gloss over things and miss the point. And with their cordial open-mindedness, they are always willing to listen to objections. What's not to like? When we mix Gemini's "smart aleck" with Leo's attention-getter, we might end up with a real character. These folks are quick-witted and entertaining.

With mid-morning magnetism, Gemini geniality, Leo confidence, and Leo rising's striking appearance, especially regarding the crown of the head, this combination usually results in an impressive person. These Geminians are romantic and demonstrative with their affections, and they've that wonderful Leo generosity. Very impressive indeed! Just pay them a compliment and see how they react. Their intelligent, well-read Gemini is usually front and center on current events and almost any other subject you might care to discuss; and if you thank them for their intelligent input, they'll love you forever. Leo is a show-off at heart, but Gemini provides a playful quality. So flaunting their knowledge while watching *Jeopardy* is mostly "no harm done." But if they do become arrogant and obnoxious, they compromise their Gemini congeniality. They need to avoid arrogance so as not to obscure their judgment, coming up with brain-dead opinions. Too often, Gemini knowledge is just superficial information, not a good foundation for a knowledgeable person seeking respect and recognition.

Geminians with Leo rising are inspiring networkers, and probably flirtatious. Oh, yeah! There's lots of fun to be had here! They're great schoolteachers, promoters, entertainers, or spiffy clerks behind the front desk of a posh hotel. They're responsible and take their work and relationships seriously, but they still love to be noticed. Anyone in love with one of these people is well advised to give them lots of attention because they move along pretty quickly in the face of neglect or disrespect. They know from their life's experience that a new and inspiring opportunity might not be too difficult to find.

Gemini Born Around Noontime:
Gemini with Virgo Rising

These are the busiest minds on the planet. These people are world-class analyzers with an insatiable curiosity. When Virgo's natural helpfulness and productivity combine with Gemini's Mr. Nice Guy approach, an extremely modest and well-intended person is likely to emerge. Their helpfulness is second to none. Both Virgo and Gemini hold intelligence in the highest regard, so Geminians with Virgo rising usually have a wealth of information with which to solve problems and fix things. They ferret out inconsistencies, compute the figures, analyze the data, and serve up the results to whomever requires them, with enough explanation and annotation to make the information useful. Whether they're bookkeepers in the back room; efficient, multi-tasking medical assistants; or discerning retailers who know just how to display their merchandise, they never miss the details.

But they're always trying to figure out this or that, dismissing their feelings as womanly nonsense, and, of course, this leads to misguided judgments. Knowing our will and using our intelligence are the two ingredients to "smart," but smart does not equal wise. Smart is in our heads, but wise is in our deeds. If we don't act responsibly in accord with what we know, our wisdom is lost. And if we don't add our intuition to what we want and think, our judgment can't progress from smart to wise! Our feelings always need to be considered because sometimes the wisest option won't make logical sense. Seeing themselves relative to others doesn't usually pose a problem for these Geminians, due to their noontime birth. But introspection might be a lot more challenging. If Virgo, the Worry Wart, leads these Geminians down the path of fretfulness and insecurity, they can become a bundle of nerves, second-guessing themselves into a major migraine. They need to zero in on what's happening inside, as well as see themselves in context, relative to their surroundings. Rather than creating problems for themselves by focusing on the little things, turning mountains into molehills, and micro-managing to the nth degree, these Geminians do better when they overcome the temptation to nitpick and allow themselves the freedom to engage in the kinds of thought and behavior that make for a more relaxed experience.

Gemini Born Early Afternoon:
Gemini with Libra Rising

These are some delightfully nice people! When Likable Libra's obliging people-skills adorn Gemini's natural chattiness, personal interaction is practically recreational, and everyone gets their fair share. Geminians with Libra rising usually know how to say just the right thing at just the right time; they're genuinely interested in the people and things around them, unusually aware of how they're being received, and willing to meet others more than halfway. Their Gemini curiosity might get them inquiring about things that aren't any of their business, but people usually succumb to their charms and reveal themselves because these folks are so obviously well-meaning; there's rarely any phoniness here, and no underhanded conniving going on, either. They simply revel in helping people. And the benefit of all this charm is that the process of "who they know, not what they know" puts them in the seat of opportunity every time. They benefit from the resources of others while adding their own element and improving circumstances for all concerned.

However, because Geminians born early afternoon are so characteristically obliging, they usually need to learn to be fair to themselves. Sometimes it's too easy to get the best of them. If they align themselves with people who aren't compatible, their greatest strength becomes their downfall. If their key relationships continually present obstacles to their progress, they need to pull away and move along—but they find it miserably difficult to do this, even when it's in their own best interests! They've a lot of "I don't wanna be alone" in their motive, so they need to avoid people who are not supportive and maybe even jealous of their pleasant nature. They'll find themselves being controlled with negative words and nasty comments that erode their self-esteem. They always need to expect a fair return on their heartfelt effort.

There's a premium on considerate fair play here, and an emphasis on ethics that equips these Geminians for the judiciary. They're good teachers and honest salespeople. They might have a legginess and physical grace that greatly benefits their presentation. And although they might find themselves spread pretty thin in their quest to be all things to all people, if they're well-connected with compatible people who appreciate them—no problem! Their next opportunity is bigger and better, and just around the corner.

Gemini Born Mid-Afternoon:
Gemini with Scorpio Rising

Now this is an odd combination! Secretive Scorpio coupled with chatty, informative Gemini is a strange fit at best. These people focus better than other Geminians, but their secretiveness works against them. They need to learn how to trust. If they over come their aversion to feeling vulnerable and possess enough courage to risk rejection, they do much better.

Geminians with Scorpio rising are always informed. Gemini's curiosity motivates endless inquisitiveness, and Scorpio never bothers to ask for permission to find out anything. So these people are usually willing to rifle through drawers and shake the hedges to find that missing piece of information; they probably have no license to gather it, but they'll help themselves just the same. And unlike other Geminians, these won't reveal their purpose or their source. They dispense information on a need-to-know basis. They snoop around, looking for clues, reading the books, and consulting the maps and charts, piecing together answers that remain opaque to others. They do this all so thoroughly that, vocationally, they make excellent tax auditors or superb mortgage closers. Their informed Gemini knows all the fine-print regulations and the hidden fees. An hour or two in the library spent tracking down some obscure manual for all the answers is never a waste of time for these folks. With Gemini's affinity for transportation and Scorpio's inclination toward money-lending, Geminians born mid-afternoon make splendid managers at an auto lot; and with Scorpio handiness they might even like to tinker with the machinery themselves.

Scorpio's "do it now and think about it later" impatience makes for a great deal of energy and gusto in this combination. Most Geminians are inclined toward mobility and exercise, and are often found walking or jogging through the neighborhood, cordially greeting neighbors and passing along some community tidbits, but these Geminians kick it up a notch: Bicycling or speedwalking might be more their style, and with a more intense purpose, they might not stop for extended chats. Also, with Scorpio gusto comes avarice; Gemini's inclination toward superficiality can possibly set a trap here, creating a person with a narrow life perspective who is all work and no play: just money, money, money. Gemini's friendliness and chattiness really need to be emphasized. It's important for these Geminians to not let their Mysterious Scorpio paranoia obscure their natural sincerity. Sometimes, Scorpio loves to fly beneath the radar, sight unseen. So with native intelligence and a dose of greediness, they might be tempted to engage in underhanded tactics, finding themselves, ultimately, in big trouble. It's always in tricky Gemini's best interests to keep things on the up and up. If they're truthful and straightforward when they're backed against the wall, their Gemini sincerity will always pull them through.

Gemini Born Around Sundown:
Gemini with Sagittarius Rising

Great combination! Sagittarius is the smiley-face Pollyanna of the zodiac, Sagittarius is the wizard of winning ways, and with a sociable dinnertime birth bestowing people skills galore, these Geminians are popular, well-connected conversationalists. Even when their Happy-Go-Lucky Sagittarius foot-in-mouth syndrome kicks in with Gemini's scatterbrained chattiness, they're likely to come off as charming and harmless. They're well-rounded, well-informed, and fit for many enterprises, but, in particular, travel agent, cruise director, or time-share representative. They're always in a hurry, with things to do, places to go, and people to see. They enjoy the good life, and might work as entertainers, politicians, or college professors. But no matter where they are, there's apt to be a bit of a celebration.

Geminians born around sundown are often drawn to horses and wagering so, high-rollers that they prefer to be, you might find them at the track, trying their luck with the ponies. However, while this particular pastime is a harmless diversion for most people, Geminians with Sagittarius rising are so prone to an "It's okay, we'll do better next time" outlook, that no matter how much they're losing, they might try, try again. And this, of course, leads to compulsive behavior. So these Geminians can often become willy-nilly wild things, habitually leaping before they look. They're too easily inspired and are often willing to go for broke without double-checking their facts. And because Sagittarius is acutely aware of the power of a promise, they might be living in their tomorrows. This is the proverbial working man who promises the missus a fat paycheck but blows it all on the gray #8 horse in the #2 race.

False promises are a nemesis here and must definitely be avoided. These people can afford to promise only what they can deliver. They need to always be true to their word and avoid spreading themselves so thin they leave friends and colleagues hanging. If they steer clear of these pitfalls, all is well. Their sweet demeanor and winning smile need to be free to work their magic without being hindered by recurring disappointments.

Gemini Born Early Evening:
Gemini with Capricorn Rising

There's much more orderliness here than with other Geminians. This is a responsible personality coupled with a quick and efficient ego. So "do what's expected, plus!" is the name of the game. As children, these people act older than their years, taking a serious approach to most things and happy to be helpful. They're in good stead with their teacher and their parents because homework and chores always get done without anyone asking twice. They have the air of the boss about them. They're not impressed with intensity, raised voices, a lack of punctuality, or any hint of disrespect or carelessness. They're truly the "keeper of the keys." But the big issue here is attitude. Sometimes the conversational Gemini is all but absent in this overly serious Capricorn personality. With a yearning to be productive and a "business is business" demeanor, Gemini with Capricorn rising is a bona fide manager. Given their likes and interests, these Geminians might work in the pharmacy or in the parts department of an auto shop. Their quick-minded Gemini teamed with Capricorn rising swiftly finds whatever items are needed to fill the order. With the sardonic cynicism of the Wise Old Goat and their characteristic Gemini glibness, they might be stand-up comics or comedy writers who turn life's bitter ironies into a knee-slapping feast.

Geminians born early evening are quick-minded and informed, but their personality might be too authoritative. Their bossy demeanor can become a real pain if they don't lighten up and maintain a sense of humor. With their "I'm the boss, so do it because I said so" mentality they run the risk of alienating people and making things more difficult than they need to be. And a reserved, unapproachable Capricorn on display makes it difficult to read them. If they avoid an overly official posture, they get better results. Even when they have a lot on their mind and a full docket of important business to attend to, they're well-advised to openly invite the thoughts and suggestions of the people around them. If others know that the door is always open—and the mind is, too—they'll warm to these Geminians, giving them the cooperation and cordiality that all good businesses thrive on. Whether in the workplace or the family room, Geminians with Capricorn rising are well-served to relax a bit and let a little Jitterbug Gemini the Nice Guy shine through.

Gemini Born Mid-Evening:
Gemini with Aquarius Rising

Here we have a friendly and humorous conversationalist. Aquarius' magnetism is a good complement to Gemini's quick-mindedness. So with a good attitude, these people are informative and willing to share what they know—often with a hilarious delivery. The alert awareness of Aquarius rising gives depth and enlightenment to Gemini's sometimes superficial understanding. And these Geminians are team players, well-trained, thoroughly disciplined, and in good standing with their peers. They've read all the manuals and passed all the tests. They're prepared for any emergency and ready to rise to the occasion, tip-top and shipshape. They're not as personally congenial as some other Geminians, but they firmly believe in and enjoy a community effort; they show up for every meeting, and revel in active participation. They arduously hold to the Musketeers' motto, "All for one and one for all!" Even when their peers don't know them well personally, they're still familiar to everyone and generally recognized as an indispensable part of the group. With their sharp Gemini mind and plugged-in Aquarius perspective, they're always in the know.

There's a lot of magnetism here. Geminians with Aquarius rising take quickly to any regimented environment and might hold military posts. Their interests usually involve technology, speed, flight, and environments in which danger is close at hand and emergencies are par for the course. As a work environment, the airport, train station, and bus depot are ideal. But whatever their vocation or pastimes, Geminians born mid-evening will enjoy the team concept and camaraderie that these circumstances provide—and sometimes so much so that they neglect their home life. While the stiff-spined, on-deck, at-attention quality of Aquarius can be tempered by the Gemini ego's more flexible approach, these Geminians might still end up lacking warmth and dismissing every hint of sentimentality. Emotions are a bit of an enigma to them; they much prefer logic. If it's not in the handbook's list of regulations, they might not recognize it as valid. It's not that they don't think of their spouses romantically or that they aren't genuinely fond of their children; it's just that they give so much of their time and energy to their stressful career, their associations, and their softball team that they're simply too often late for supper, arriving home still preoccupied by some important issue from earlier in the day. If Aquarius' Electric Light Bulb will glow more warmly for those closest to their hearts, and if they'll be a bit more generous with hugs and kisses, they'll experience a warmer life—without ever giving less of themselves to their commitments.

Gemini Born Around Midnight:
Gemini with Pisces Rising

These people are unassuming, and they aim to please—but they're a tad secretive. Peaceful Pisces' "don't rock the boat" mentality has an interesting effect on chatty Gemini. The non-combative, unassuming qualities of Pisces the cosmic traveler blend pretty well with Gemini's sincerity. These Geminians avoid disagreement and disapproval at all costs; they keep their mouth shut and their ears open to a much greater degree than most other silver-tongued Geminians. They're intelligent listeners who not only comprehend the information they've gotten; they follow up by emotionally absorbing the deeper meaning. Their intent is to avoid intensity, so they cooperate and assist. But Gemini does love to chat, so Geminians with Pisces rising are more free with their words in less public circumstances, such as intimate telephone conversations or in the online chat room where they're physically unseen and feel more secure. They're always willing to stay on the phone with a far-flung family member, listening to their difficulties and hoping to be helpful. They're sharp-minded quick learners, and they love to be home alone with a good book. They're often drawn to photographs and illustrations, and are sometimes adept photographers themselves. They've an eye for imagery, and are sometimes fascinatingly photogenic.

The compassionate nature of these two signs often leads Geminians born 'round midnight to vocations that allow them to help the unfortunate. Hospitals, mental health facilities, prisons, or even the Humane Society are institutions that give them an opportunity to care for living things. They're acutely aware that God puts us here on earth to enhance life however possible.

Pisces' vivid imagination can aid Gemini's busy mind in many instances, but sometimes these folks get scattered and find themselves confused or misunderstood, wandering far from reality, overprotective of their children and tempted to withdraw into their own safe harbor to appease their insecurities. They're well-advised to not blow things out of proportion; they need to stay grounded to be able to discern which people truly appreciate them and which do not. These Geminians have a somewhat delicate psyche that often leads them into marriages and partnerships with strong-willed individuals who penalize them for any misjudgment, no matter how trivial. Already delicate by nature and apprehensive of confrontation, Pisces reacts by silently withdrawing, and that's no complement to Gemini's need for productive communication. They still benefit from—and take pleasure in—communicating, so a state of cowed reticence doesn't work well and it never fulfills them. They're wise to take courage and stand up for themselves.

Gemini Born in the Wee Hours:
Gemini with Aries Rising

Here's a childlike conversationalist who probably talks faster than anyone you've met in weeks. They're full of ideas and questions, and they've an unusually disarming charm. We open up to them because they're interested in everyone, and very non-threatening. Their honesty is second to none: They tell it like it is—or at least how they see it! They might display a lot of willy-nilly, but chances are they really didn't miss anything. It's just the flit-around impression they leave. Geminians with Aries rising are straightforward, trustworthy, and on the move, with no time to waste. However, there's a nervous impatience here that can waste a lot of time and energy without accomplishing much; they love being on the move and need to avoid becoming mindlessly "busy dizzy." They feel sinful if they sit down to relax or just do nothing. They'll "do it now and think about it later" until their eager beaver earns them a righteous reputation for doing more than their fair share, time and time again. But their patience level wanes, to say the least.

These Geminians have a sit-up-straight attitude that usually gives them great posture, good muscle tone, and an urgent, sometimes nervous quality that makes for a Mighty Mouse physical trainer or an energetic sports coach. With Action Aries rising, they just can't wait! They might be drawn to NASCAR or drag racing, or fulfill their need for communication and instruction in the kindergarten classroom, where they can be physically active while giving instruction. There's always an anxiousness about Aries, and with Gemini's come-and-go, they leave others to wonder where in the world they've come from. Gemini's quick-minded, but sometimes flighty, "Hi! How ya doin'? Where ya from? I've been there! See ya later!" demeanor is in high gear when Aries rises.

Geminians born in the wee hours need to think before they speak, so as not to put their foot in their mouth. They're honest and usually charming in their innocence, but ideas that are extremely superficial and not well thought-out are sometimes better left unspoken. An Aries personality is likely to go charging in where angels fear to tread, so these urgent-minded Geminians need to think things through and look for the bottom line before they jump to conclusions. Heaven forbid they come off as willy-nilly nitwits when they're otherwise so charming and adored!

Gemini Born Pre-Dawn:
Gemini with Taurus Rising

These are the most focused, determined, articulate Geminians of all, and unlike most Geminians they prefer to slow down and bask in the sensual—or even stop to smell the roses. They love beauty and their animal comforts. And their clever minds conjure all kinds of ways to treat themselves better. If they like you, you're welcome to all they possess; their generosity is limitless, rooted in Gemini's airy perception of life. Taurus can attract beautiful things, but Gemini is in tune with the pleasures of sharing. So it's quite an awesome combination.

The Taurus personality obscures much of the Gemini ego, in both positive and negative ways. Taurus, the Banker, provides stability to Gemini's hummingbird flightiness, but can also make Gemini stubborn and much more demanding. An important issue here is how deliberate these Geminians are. If they think things through before they commit themselves, all is well. But the flit-around quality of Gemini can make a big mess with a Taurus, the bull, personality. They're focused, intense, and articulate, but mindless behavior can bring devastating consequences if these folks don't use Gemini's light touch. It's very important that these Geminians keep an open mind because their tendencies toward superficiality can leave them locked up in materialistic bull-headedness. But when these Geminians' minds are empowered with a focus on worthwhile information, they're unusually well-equipped to deliver that information impressively. Geminians with Taurus rising might be adept orators or memorable lecturing professors. Not that they're unhappy in the cab of a Mack truck, which allows them to simultaneously fulfill their Gemini wanderlust while their sedentary Taurus stays seated for hours at a time: They can travel a thousand miles without ever leaving their seat!

Taurean practicality is indispensable to them in their workaday world. But they'll improve their personal lives if, after work, they broaden their horizons with art, culture, and a plethora of different viewpoints. An extended worldview will expand their mind and give them opportunities to exercise their generosity. Generosity is one of their most useful tools and endearing qualities, and the more true friends they acquire, the more instances they're afforded to graciously pick up the tab. As intently focused on material accruement as they are, and reveling in their worldly comforts as they do, they usually enjoy an abundance from which to share.

THE CANCER SUN SIGN
AND ITS RISING SIGN PERSONALITIES

THE CANCER SUN SIGN
June 22–July 22

Cancer is the Mother Goose of the zodiac, and a maternal sensitivity and nurturing spirit are two of Cancer's most endearing hallmarks. Cancerians understand that we humans are put here on earth to care for living things and have a green-leaf effect. Their acute awareness of the need for life's necessities drives them to diligently provide food, shelter, and clothing not only to their nearest and dearest loved ones, but also—depending on the scope of their awareness—to almost anyone else in need. Though they're naturally thrifty, with a tendency to make do with less, and a proclivity to clamp down mightily on whatever they're holding, they're not so much selfish as security-minded. If the situation arises, they'll feed everyone on the block. Wherever we find Cancer, we'll find strong doses of nostalgia and imagination, and a great deal of subjectivity.

Emotion is Cancer's middle name. The crab's instrument panel doesn't include keen eyesight. So Cancerians navigate their world through feeling, shuffling and scuttling sideways, quickly withdrawing when they sense danger. And they *always* sense danger! Unable to peer sharply into the distance, Cancerians exercise vigilance, testing the waters for hazards. But Cancer's caution and sensitivity is their aegis of protection. They rely upon wily insight, shrewdness, and tact to avoid danger and maintain their safety. But these qualities are most useful and beneficial when they're not embedded in moodiness and festering resentments, the all-too-common products of an overly emotional, and highly imaginative, approach to life. Some rising signs will serve to mitigate Cancer's emotional subjectivity, providing a much needed objectivity and a broader perspective. But others will fuel the fire, making Cautious Cancerians even more susceptible to their greatest weaknesses, including living in the past, holding on too tightly to past hurts, and falling prey to the manipulations of people who indiscriminately place blame on others. Without objectivity, Cancerians find it difficult to understand that, while they're responsible for their own actions, they're not responsible for the sins and shortcomings of the world. No other sign in the zodiac feels the weight of the world more than Cancer, the dutiful custodian. When they diligently heal, help, and labor out of a healthy concern for living things, Cancerians are the willing workers, greatly appreciated and, hopefully, well-rewarded. But building their house upon a foundation of unreasonable guilt, shame, wrath, and remorse is always a recipe for disaster.

Cancer Born Around Dawn:
Cancer with Cancer Rising

Cancerians with Cancer rising are doubly cautious and subjective, but with a sunny morning time disposition. They're unusually sentimental people who feel a lump in their throat at the mention of loved ones or memorable days gone by, and they reach out with emotional support to anyone in arm's length with a broken limb or a broken heart. The mothering instinct is tremendously motivating in double Cancer. These folks are family-oriented, love their homestead, and, with a fierce pack rat tendency, they hold on dearly to family heirlooms or scrapbooks, sometimes stuffing the attic with so much memorabilia that it's hard to make a path to the window. Still, family members are always welcome, if they can just find an uncluttered place to sit!

These Cancerians are boundless workaholics, self-starters who are never finished. In fact, they'll feel guilty for not doing a better job when, in reality, they're doing twice the work of everyone else. They just don't stand off and look at things objectively! This is especially true when their emotions get the best of them. If they're not vigilant, they can succumb to rollercoaster mood swings and a mired-in-the-past point of view that leaves them nursing old wounds. In the manager's seat, they can be quite the slave driver, feeling hampered by underlings who simply aren't as motivated as they are, or micro-managing an employee who made an honest mistake a year and a half ago. Whatever their vocation or relationship, they need to remember to step back and try to see things in context. Cancerians born at dawn are naturally drawn to property management, real estate, and construction and renovation. They're also effective in settings where their presence might be required from dusk 'til dawn, such as restaurant management or farming. But they'll be most successful when their boundless effort is complemented by the maintenance of a reasonable perspective and an eagle's eye for golden opportunities. Though they never benefit from ill-timed and haphazard fits and starts, these Cautious Cancerians can be a bit too cautious, sometimes finding themselves reticent even when opportunity presents itself and is obviously well within their reach.

Cancer Born Shortly After Dawn:
Cancer with Leo Rising

Now here's a Cancer with a gangbuster personality demanding attention—but always with a sunny disposition. With Leo the Lion at the helm, these are no reticent crabs. They're courageous and fully ready to make their wishes known, push for what they want, and let the chips fall where they will. A Lordly Leo personality, with its competent and confident, "I can handle it, give it to me and I'll show you how to do this" demeanor, brings the industrious crustacean an opportunity to stand up in front of the crowd and shine. After all, Leo is the consummate showman.

This is a powerful blend of Cancer's do-it-with-feeling diligence and Leo's do-it-right-the-first-time competence. If the walls need painting, these Cancerians apply a coat in record time with their "do it now and think about it later" approach; then, with the housework completed, they step out into the limelight, expecting gratitude and respect. If they'll keep one eye on their audience, constantly gauging how they're being received and adjusting their performance to suit their audience's tastes, they'll likely get a standing ovation. Willing-worker competence always prevails over emotional bluster; if Cancerians with Leo rising are blinded by the stagelights, too self-centered to notice even the front row's reactions, they'll probably end up playing to an empty house. Perspective and objectivity are the key to allowing Cancer's diligence and Leo's courage to work in tandem, complementing one another and producing marvelous leadership qualities. But blind ambition and self-indulgence can lead these Cancerians into terribly obnoxious behavior: Suddenly they're unable, or unwilling, to meet others halfway, and they attempt to get their way by issuing ultimatums. The "my way or the highway" approach works only when "my way" is magnetically attractive and tempered by everyone's needs. If Cancerians born shortly after dawn will objectively assess their situation, they'll be thoroughly effective when they're put in charge, whether they're elementary school teachers or heads of state.

Cancer Born Mid-Morning:
Cancer with Virgo Rising

Modest and helpful, with an intelligent wanderlust in their eyes, these people wish the world were perfect and they'll use every bit of elbow grease they have to make it that way. When the industrious, unassuming ego of Cancer combines with Virgo's helpfulness and productivity, the result is an extremely unassuming, self-motivated worker; these Cancerians are the kind of people who project an always-useful volunteer spirit at the Chamber of Commerce, the PTA, or whatever other community efforts they might join. Beyond their Cancer diligence lies a profound awareness that what they give to others they also give to themselves. They're always modest and usually very caring people. In fact, they're sometimes so caring and so unselfish that they're easily taken advantage of. They're well-advised to wisely pick and choose how, when, and where they apply their helpfulness, or they'll end up with others heaping added responsibilities onto their shoulders, leaving them to do everyone else's work as well as their own. Fair-minded peers and colleagues hold these Cancerians in high esteem, but if the goldbrickers get wind of these people's willingness to offer unlimited favors, the moochers will form a parasitic line out the door and around the block. But these folks rarely complain. Oh, they might fuss and pick about inconsequential details in typical Virgo style, but their willing worker helpfulness remains intact no matter what. Being fair to themselves doesn't always come easily to these Good Samaritans. They're usually very humble. As employees, they show up at work no matter how sick they might be; and as the boss, they sometimes allow underlings to offer illegitimate excuses for unacceptable results. Virgo's affinity for the underdog and Cancer's tender heart leave these Cancerians preferring to "understand" and let people off the hook. But, sometimes, this only leads to their becoming enablers rather than helpers. Cancerians born mid-morning need to give heed to their best counselors, be aware of their subservient tendencies, and refuse to always pick up the slack.

Virgo, the Worry Wart, often creates some undue anxiety over health and weight issues, and Virgo's neatness coupled with Cancer's emphasis on house and home creates an intolerance for dust on the furniture or litter on the floor. These Cancerians' houses are neat as a pin, and all their knickknacks are well-placed and orderly. On the job, they're super retailers with what might be the most beautiful display windows in town. They're also fabulous make-up artists; genuinely caring and wonderfully efficient nurses; or, with their ability to tie up loose ends at the very last moment, they might be highly dependable payroll clerks.

Cancer Born Around Noontime:
Cancer with Libra Rising

These people start out trying to please everyone, and they stay in everybody's face! They're more aware of the people around them than almost any other combination in the zodiac. They're sociable, obliging, and interested in everyone within earshot.

Cancerians born at noontime are ambitious overseers who willingly put in as many hours as necessary to get the job done. They have managerial objectivity and, with an eagle's eye for what's fair, they want to keep every team member happily involved and enthusiastic. With their Likable Libra personality and sensitive Cancer ego, they foster consideration and cooperation among their co-workers, clients, and customers. They never ask others to do more than they're willing to do themselves. It's in their nature to be aware of everyone else's reactions, and, at their best, they gauge their own effectiveness through the positive responses and cooperation they receive from others. In a way, they love themselves through the people around them. When they've earned the seat of authority, they're keenly aware of the contributions of each employee; they don't overburden their staff, but neither do they tolerate laziness. These Cancerians are effective property managers and, with their obliging Libra personality, they're often highly successful wheeler-dealers; but if their susceptibility to avarice leads them to want more than their fair share, they can suddenly find themselves undermining their own best qualities. They really need to keep the green-leaf greediness of Cancer in check. They're also highly visible restaurateurs, attentive to their customers, obviously happy to see their friends again, and enjoying moving from table to table to make sure the meals are satisfactory and the room temperature is just right.

Whether on the job, at home, or out in the neighborhood, Cancerians with Libra rising have all the tools to be productively diplomatic. Already blessed with the patient willingness to "wait and see" when the chips aren't falling where they prefer and no single option seems inspiring, their noontime birth enables them to understand that tomorrow's another day and "what goes around, comes around." The Cancer temptation to live in the past is mitigated in this combination; there's less tendency to bemoan yesterday's misfortunes or to be controlled by past mistakes. Their acute awareness of the people and things around them, and the enjoyment they reap from their interactions, tends to keep them living in the here and now. These Cancerians do well to follow their inclination toward an enlightened patience, allowing things to develop in their own good time. They benefit most when they leave the door propped open, so opportunity can return when the time is right.

Cancer Born Early Afternoon:
Cancer with Scorpio Rising

Ambition, passion, energy, and a "grab the handle, we're outta here!" gusto characterize these Energizer bunnies. These are highly active, emotionally motivated Cancerians. They're handy, sexy, and totally focused on whatever they've chosen to accomplish, whether in the home or out in the workaday world. But their green-leaf greed and "I'm goin' broke" insecurities usually lead them to want more than they've already accumulated, leaving them with no clue that "more is never enough." The engine's always running here. Fortunately they possess a natural stamina or their constantly revving engine would wear itself out in no time.

Cancerians with Scorpio rising are in tune with the processes of perpetuating life: Conception, mothering, and nurturing are innate parts of their personality. They're successful breeders of puppies, or gardeners with remarkably green thumbs, possibly so proficient in these areas that they can make a vocation of them. And with Cancer's penchant for real estate and Scorpio's inclination for lending, they're often very knowledgeable mortgage brokers. The blending of other Cancer and Scorpio traits can also lead them into banking, insurance, home renovation, and the healing arts. Mysterious Scorpio always has an uncanny ability to see around corners and under rocks, and Cancer possesses a heightened sensitivity, so, whatever their profession, Cancerians born early afternoon are rarely caught by surprise. They're usually adept at comprehending the hidden meaning. They've a sixth sense that makes for marvelous instincts. But their weakness might be found in their Cancer tendency to be too thin-skinned, getting caught up in their emotions. When their feelings get hurt and they harbor resentment, they have the capacity to become quite vindictive. They've a potential for ruthlessness that can leave their adversaries wounded and suffering. Cancerians with Scorpio rising are wise to avoid imagining insult where none was intended, or disloyalty where it doesn't exist. They need to avoid purposely surrounding themselves with people who are less aware than they, just because they'll be easier to control; eventually these Cancerians will come to resent these very people for their apparent inferiority, even if they're simply being themselves.

If they maintain their objectivity and regulate their ferocity, these Cancerians have the energy, sensitivity, and focus to be successful at whatever they choose to do.

Cancer Born Mid-Afternoon:
Cancer with Sagittarius Rising

Here come the most delightfully inspiring people on the planet. They're caring and benevolent, and so optimistically smiley-faced that there's little evidence of Cancerian caution or apprehension. Oh, it's there somewhere, but it's not obvious. Sagittarius is what's showing here. The willy-nilly, high rolling, Happy-Go-Lucky Sagittarius personality is a wonderful complement to the sensitive, cautious Cancer ego. With supreme inoffensiveness, these people inspire and uplift others with a cheerful ability to say the right thing at the right time. There's an inviting Pied Piper here. The glass is always half-full rather than half-empty, and they present their optimism in a way that never fails to raise spirits. They're fun-loving creatures with winning dispositions who see little merit in crying over spilled milk. They respond to error with an "It's okay, we'll do better next time" attitude.

Cancerians born mid-afternoon find great success in life when they use their Sagittarius personality to put a positive spin on negative circumstances. For instance, if they're tempted to dwell resentfully on the past, which is a common Cancer proclivity, their Sagittarius forgivingness and awareness that "tomorrow's another day" supply them with the tools to put those resentments quickly to rest. "Onward and upward!" is their battle cry. They're always on the verge of rushing in where angels fear to tread. They feel their God within from moment to moment, and they know from experience that the necessities of life tend to work themselves out when they keep a positive attitude. They know that their family loves them dearly, and that people almost always respond to them positively. They're eternally aware that forgiveness always triumphs over bitterness. What's not to like about them?

This nurturing Cancer ego coupled with the benevolence of Sagittarius rising possesses marvelously well-developed people skills, and because these individuals are extremely self-motivated, they often enjoy a successful career in sales or in any other area that rewards them for inspiring others to think as they do. They're very convincing! They might be drawn to selling travel-related wares such as time shares or vacation packages. But the public and celebratory aspects of theme parks and nightclubs are also suitable settings for a happy-go-lucky workplace, as are the wide-open spaces of a family ranch. If they don't allow their Cancer greed to lead them into shifty schemes and a patent misuse of their confidence-building powers, they can find a great deal of personal fulfillment in any number of vocations.

Cancer Born Around Sundown:
Cancer with Capricorn Rising

Tradition and practicality is the name of the game here, but these folks are far too serious for my taste! They too easily become the trolls under the bridge with "somebody's gotta do it" written all over their uninspired faces. A better attitude works wonders! With the cautious sensitivity of Cancer and the calm, cool, and collected respectfulness of Capricorn, Cancerians with Capricorn rising are master manipulators with a fair-minded and nurturing awareness that benefits everyone involved. Their cautious touch and their "goes around, comes around" sensibility are two of their most powerful tools and commendable qualities. Because they're consistently aware that "one hand washes the other," they're hard-working, even-tempered, and inclined to treat employees and co-workers like family. But an overly serious Capricorn demeanor sometimes obscures their deep emotional sensitivity. If they aren't careful, they can develop an "all work and no play" attitude, especially if they succumb to the Cancer proclivity to feel like they're going broke.

Maintaining an objective viewpoint is a challenge for Cancer, but Capricorn is the sign of objectivity. So these Cancerians need to keep things in context and see themselves relative to others to insure that they respond to circumstances as they are, not as they imagine them to be. For instance, they can be so fearful of financial loss that they tolerate controlling or abusive behavior in people whose efforts they mistakenly believe to be indispensable. Or they'll fall into such disabling extremes of caution and pessimism that they can't make decisions, running the risk of allowing a golden opportunity to slip through their grasp. If they step back, gather their wits, and apply some Wise Old Goat practicality, they usually discover that things are rarely as gloomy as they feel, and that the route to success is often clearly marked.

Cancerians born at sundown love a dependable routine. They play by the rules, and "if it's not in the book, we're not doing it that way!" Tasks and procedures that others find boring might well be these people's cup of tea. They like things systematic. And with Cancer's love of family, they're definitely the sort to carry on the family business, making fudge or furniture or widgets and sprockets exactly the way Mom and Pop made them fifty years ago. If they'll be a bit more demonstrative in their affections, they'll be invited to lunch and to parties more often; their peers do genuinely love the willing worker and the sensitive soul beneath the stoic exterior.

Cancer Born Early Evening:
Cancer with Aquarius Rising

A thin-skinned Cancer with an electric "live wire" personality? Now that's a switch—but it works! Aquarius is the Big Attitude of the zodiac, so attitude is key here! A magnetic, friendly demeanor will work wonders, but a subconscious and unrecognized "will to disagree" can be devastating. If Cancerians born early evening are aware of and reasonably uninhibited by their emotions, the friendly, magnetic side of their Aquarius personality will blossom, making them a joy to be around and very "right on" in their perceptions of people and things. But when Aquarius rises there's usually a penchant for strong opinions and a love of defending them. So argument is their favorite indulgence: they think what they want to think, and never mind the facts. Plus, with unrecognized Cancer emotions churning full tilt, they can easily become the sort of people who just won't listen to reason; they disagree tirelessly and pointlessly, basking in egotistical "I'm right and you're wrong" nonsense and coming off as sourpusses with a chip on their shoulder. It isn't that they should disregard their feelings to become cold, unemotional robots; instead, they need to be diligently aware of their feelings to understand how those emotions are influencing their judgment. Their temptation is to keep their emotions separate and to dwell in them entirely without realizing it.

With sufficient objectivity, these Cancerians can use their Aquarius, the Electric Light Bulb, personality to garner success in many fields. They possess the qualities to be excellent promoters, enlightened physicians, or innovative engineers. Aquarius' inclinations and interests almost always make for especially successful firefighters, soldiers, and airline workers. Cancerians with Aquarius rising are gifted at detecting error, and quick to notice the shortcomings and weaknesses in the plans and designs they're assigned to work with. They take their duties seriously, hold themselves highly responsible, and expect the same from colleagues and associates. Cancer has little tolerance for a proposal that won't work, and Aquarius is keenly aware of the dangers of technology or any risky venture, so these folks are always on guard and most comfortable when every precaution is taken, guaranteeing that the project will come off without a glitch. If they see shortcuts being taken, they might well become whistle-blowers. When Cancerians born early evening learn to trust their emotions without being enslaved to them, their professionalism is extraordinary.

Cancer Born Mid-Evening:
Cancer with Pisces Rising

Cancerians with Pisces rising are kind-hearted people helpers who emotionally soak up everything around them. They absorb information like a sponge. But you can't get much out of them. They're too secretive and cautious! Without even realizing it, they leave others feeling left out. But they fit in wonderfully with self-centered people who want to do all the talking and get all the attention! A Pisces personality always makes for a good, empathetic listener, but in tandem with a Cancer ego, Pisces' listening skills are enhanced to the nth degree. With their Cancer too sensitive to risk rejection and their Pisces too delicate to endure disapproval, Cancerians born mid-evening would much rather keep their mouth shut and their ears open. In this combination, Cancer's subjective nature will almost always develop into a sixth sense. These people rarely miss the point and are usually proficient at reading between the lines to understand much more than others think they do. However, it behooves them to show themselves and let people know where they're coming from; otherwise, their taciturn demeanor is misinterpreted. If they're excessively quiet and unassuming, they run the added risk of leaving others to feel that they're purposely excluding them or, worse, that they're hiding something. Because they won't disclose themselves, others grow suspicious; so a lot more "shoot from the hip" and courageous "show and tell" is in order here.

Cancerians with Peaceful Pisces rising have a gentle and artistic spirit. Though they aren't usually motivated by promises of fame and fortune, and don't always feel comfortable in the limelight, they approach everything with an enormous depth of feeling. Because they're so in tune with the vibrations around them, they're often accomplished musicians—and their active imagination, joy in working at home, and tendency to keep late-night hours might add up to a talented writer. They need to be sure, however, that their imagination doesn't get the best of them—and that's no easy matter! They sometimes conjure demons where there aren't any, so if these Cancerians aren't careful they find themselves forever battling irrational fears. Already inclined to hold their tongue, they can be so apprehensive of rejection, afraid of disapproval, and averse to criticism, that they run away and hide. They need to remember that even a clam opens its protective shell from time to time.

Cancerians with Pisces rising are often quite successful as teachers, nurses, dental hygienists, or mental health providers. They're security guards who see around corners and under rocks. They're nightclub owners who love the nighttime clientele. But whatever venture they choose, their ticket to success involves more courage, forthrightness and, above all, objectivity.

Cancer Born Around Midnight:
Cancer with Aries Rising

These people are charming and sensitive, with more courage than most wimpy Cancerians. They're cautious about important things, but ever so spontaneous! Though impatience is always an Action Aries pitfall, the innate caution of Cancer works well to temper its intensity in this combination. A sensitive, "do it with feeling" Cancer ego combined with a childlike, eager beaver personality results in a delightful blend of willing worker and trustworthy nurturer who makes things grow with consistent diligence. These Cancerians are temperate and sensitive enough to know when they're pushing just enough, so they rarely overdo it. As long as they allow their sensitivity to remain apparent, the childlike charm, honesty, and inoffensiveness of Aries will serve them well.

Cancerians born around midnight enjoy life. They're happy, sexy, and flirtatious, with a healthy feeling of well-being. They appreciate family and look forward to spending time with loved ones. Aries' love of children and Cancer's nurturing instincts usually make for a wonderfully involved parent. And there's usually lots of physical family resemblance with Aries rising, so Cancer's fondness for family is even more rewarded. Getting the family involved in group projects, whether it's home repair or visiting new places, is one of these people's favorite things—they love having "places to go, people to see, and things to do."

On the job, Cancer's workaholic spirit and Aries' early bird "do it now and think about it later" equip them to be excellent promoters willing to put in long, productive workdays. From dawn 'til dusk, they're bright-eyed and bushy-tailed. There might be intense financial ambitions, but Cancerians with Aries rising are usually so equitable and honest that they're trusted implicitly by their peers; no one fears being taken advantage of. They're great coaches, and major contributors on a construction site. They're highly appreciated by their supervisors because they aren't the kinds of workers who always need to agree with the boss before they'll follow directions and tackle a job: They just want to get things done so they can move on to the next challenge. They love that "good job well done" feeling of accomplishment. When they keep their most positive qualities front and center, and aren't too impatient with those who can't quite keep up, Cancerians born around midnight prove to be a joy and a treasure to everyone they meet.

Cancer Born in the Wee Hours:
Cancer with Taurus Rising

These people are too serious and need to lighten up and be more playful. Sometimes they actually need to learn how to have a good time, because no matter how much money they make, "more is never enough." Whenever Taurus is involved in any combination, there's bound to be a great deal of intensity and a need to be more buoyant, and Cancer with Taurus rising is no exception. These folks feel their disappointments too deeply and aren't resilient enough. With a tendency toward heightened emotions and a thin-skinned sensitivity, their bull-headed Taurus personality can render them angry and unforgiving when they feel they've been slighted. Objectivity is the key: Pouty faced Taurus can make for a real sad sack if there's no ability to see the light at the end of the tunnel. So "lighten up, and move along" should be the name of their game. With sufficient objectivity, these Cancerians can benefit greatly from Taurus' natural generosity and bottom-line focus. They're diligent and thorough, never leaving even the most difficult jobs half-finished, always following up on leads and doing everything possible to close a deal. Taurus, the Banker, demands that time and money be invested profitably, that there's a pay-off for every effort. Coupled with Cancer's avarice, these characteristics can lead to a limitless appetite for money and power. These people rarely understand that "more is never enough," and might well be drawn to financial vocations involving banking or brokering. They love the cha-ching of a cash register. But they're not misers: They willingly share their comforts and show their love and appreciation with material gifts.

Sometimes Cancerians with Taurus rising seem somewhat dull; they appear to have few interests beyond going to work and making money. They're very demanding people, demanding of others and demanding of themselves, and they don't like to be disappointed; their Cancer subjectivity often makes them feel as though the pain and frustration of disappointment will never end. Ultimately, they work so hard to make things fruitful that they run the risk of alienating friends and colleagues. But when they lighten up, they're able to reveal that there's much more to them than meets the eye. They might be quite the history buff or art collector. They're in tune with the aesthetics of wood floors and vaulted ceilings as well as the sublime tastes of gourmet dishes. They even enjoy a simple casserole if it's prepared with attention to the recipe. They might be much more well-read and well-traveled than others suspect. So if these Cancerians will step back; look at things with a calm, cool, and collected objectivity; and allow their natural generosity an opportunity to express itself, they'll always be appreciated by friends and neighbors as more than just a successful businessperson.

Cancer Born Pre-Dawn:
Cancer with Gemini Rising

Now these folks wear their hearts on their sleeve, always ready and willing to ramble on about how they feel and why they feel that way. They're glib and personal. But don't let them get their feelings hurt! They'll give you a gush of emotion in a heartbeat. They're more obvious and naïve than most other Cancerians, and they're often very cute in their demeanor. They give the impression they wouldn't hurt a fly—and they wouldn't! Cancerians born pre-dawn are involved parents and genuinely concerned friends. The sensitivity of Cancer and the inquisitive geniality of Jitterbug Gemini work in tandem to produce a lot of heartfelt concern, often expressed through easy conversation. These people are always willing to share their time and talk to others about their problems, whether it's at the kitchen table or over the telephone. Their door is always open, and friends and family members who need a place to stay can count on their homespun hospitality for a bed and breakfast.

The Cancer ego mitigates some of Gemini's less positive qualities. Quick-minded Gemini often causes shallow thinking and some lack of tact, but Cancer's sensitivity provides a feeling for the deeper significance of any issue at hand. Cancer's caution also puts a bridle on Gemini's tendency to ramble. Cancerians with Gemini rising are well-suited to a multitude of vocations. Diligent and hard-working, expedient and affable, they're naturals when it comes to customer service. With a penchant for instruction and learning and a genuine willingness to cooperate, they're often marvelously adept elementary school teachers. Actually, any career requiring a good memory and a pleasant demeanor will present these Cancerians with numerous opportunities for advancement.

Cancer's emotions, however, can sometimes be a bit draining, rendering these people needy in romantic relationships. They might be easily wounded, and very quick to remove themselves from attachments in which they feel even remotely used, slighted, or unappreciated. And later, in the quiet after the storm, their Cancerian nostalgia might move them to reminisce and idealize a tad too much: They're deeply touched by all of their emotional experiences. What they need is a friend as true-blue as they are. Just as they're always willing to lend a shoulder to cry on, Cancerians born pre-dawn shouldn't be embarrassed to ask for some emotional support every now and then.

THE LEO SUN SIGN
AND ITS RISING SIGN PERSONALITIES

THE LEO SUN SIGN
July 23–August 22

These are the people at the front of the crowd, volunteering instruction and insisting everyone pay attention. With their "do it right the first time" attitude, they're adept at displaying their wares and inspiring confidence. They're naturals at telling people what to do, and they're terrible at doing what they're told. No one in the zodiac dislikes obeying a command like Lordly Leo! Their ego gets in the way BIG TIME. But competence and confidence are cornerstone qualities here. Fearless and lion-hearted, Leos are courageously willing to roll the dice—without any nagging insecurities. They're ready to take the lead; they're the type to say, "Stand aside, I'll show you how to do this," and they don't suffer much from stage fright. They thrive on center stage because Leo is the consummate showman.

No one knows how to leave a big impression like these people. But what kind of impression will it be? And to what end? Well, this much is true: To be pleased with the results, Leos need to behave in ways that make them proud of themselves. Throughout their life, on the job and at home, they respond well to positive recognition, expressions of gratitude, and generous genuflections, so they need to know if their rising sign personality complements their regal ego. Does their personality elicit the sorts of responses that fulfill them rather than frustrate them? If they're unwittingly inviting people to ignore them, to take them entirely for granted, or, worst of all, to question their competence, they're on a collision course with misery. And it's because they've lost sight of others, being too selfishly focused on themselves. Leos need to keep themselves in context and be aware of their audience if they're going to facilitate, rather than obscure, their most attractive traits: their innate generosity, their demonstrative affections, their adoration of children, and their magnanimity towards the weak and needy. However, Leo's temptation is to get lost in the glory of the stage and become completely wrapped up in self. There's no doubt that when the show is over there will be a lot of talk. Leos never go unnoticed. But the real objective for Leos is to present themselves in such a way that their competence and magnanimity come to the fore rather than retreat toward self-importance and egotism. The reviews are inevitable; so why not make them raves?

Leo Born Around Dawn:
Leo with Leo Rising

These people give new meaning to "gangbusters!" They stand out in a crowd, and they love to be noticed. They usually don't need as much sleep as the rest of us because they're so robust. As children, they insist they aren't sleepy at naptime, and they run circles around their playmates. In adolescence they usually give their superiors a run for their money because they're fearless and unafraid to test their luck, always trying something new. Hopefully, they develop better sense later in life. Even though they're gentle-hearted, they've an "out of my way!" demeanor. In double Leo, the sunny disposition and stamina of Leo are impossible to ignore. They have a full-blown, eight-cylinder constitution reminiscent of the Energizer Bunny. The Leo crown of the head is doubly pronounced: There's usually something about the forehead, the hair, or even the beard or mustache, that stands out. They might even be bald. But a noticeable crown is likely.

As in all dawn births, the sun sign traits are more obvious. Leos with Leo rising love to take the ball and run with it, and usually they do so by invitation. Their peers have learned that they know what they're doing; they've the competence and confidence to handle the most difficult challenges. Vocationally, they work well with children. They're trustworthy police officers, maybe involved in police youth programs. They thrive in almost any kind of work that puts them on stage. But in the course of dancing in the spotlight, these Lordly Leos need to be extremely wary of becoming overly intense and coming off as too full of themselves. They're "do it right the first time" deliberate in everything they do, but they might miss the point in a conversation while they're mentally rehearsing their next line. Sadly, they're not the best listeners. And it's not anxiety; it's studied competence—but it's self-absorbed, nonetheless, and it causes them to lose sight of their audience, which is a fatal error for any showman. The more oblivious Leos with Leo rising are about how they're being received, the greater the chance they'll be remembered for the big Leonine mess they make rather than their magnanimity, generosity, and competence. Taking a step back to see themselves in context is a strategy they need to employ continually in life.

Leo Born Shortly After Dawn:
Leo with Virgo Rising

These people aren't easy to identify as Leos. They don't obviously resemble much of what we've talked about as typical. They're more self-conscious and stay in their own place better. They'll give you the best seat and not complain. Virgo is the antithesis of confident Leo; these folks check and re-check themselves constantly. Leos born shortly after dawn are characteristically big-hearted and robust, but their personality is more modest and helpful than in other combinations. And like all after-dawn births, they need to be alone sometimes to regenerate themselves. They benefit greatly from intermittent moments of solitude—as long as those moments don't last forever. There's a fierce independence here that might require these Leos to migrate to relationships and vocations where they're not micro-managed, although a really good manager will recognize their Leo no-need-for-supervision "willing worker" pretty quickly. They thrive in work that helps others to make a good impression, perhaps some sort of consulting or image-making. Leos with Virgo rising might be especially conscientious—but potentially over-confident—physicians.

The nitpicky, helpful, and productive Virgo personality is a great fit for the "do it right the first time" element of the Lordly Leo ego. Virgo, the Worry Wart, ensures that all the t's are crossed and the i's dotted, allowing them to come off as all the more competent. And unlike some Leos, these folks don't need ticker tape and fanfare. Because of Virgo's modesty, they're often more comfortable with a firm handshake and a quiet "thank you" off to the side. This isn't to say that they don't thrive on attention and gratitude. After all, they're still Leos. So when people comment favorably on their youthful appearance, their stylish apparel, or their keen intelligence and sharp wit, their attention-getting Leo ego loves it. They just prefer the applause to be a bit more subdued.

On the other hand, these Leos don't usually take well to criticism. When their delivery is critiqued or their knowledge questioned, they're likely to take it as a belittling of their competence and might not respond very gracefully. They need to be open to correction when it's warranted. Ultimately, however, before they muster their Virgo attention to detail and their Leo ego to fearlessly tackle a task, they need to ask themselves if they'll be sincerely rewarded or if they're just being used and abused again. Are they being tapped for their confidence and competence, or is it that they're simply available and always willing to be helpful? Time invested in work that isn't appreciated is always time poorly spent for any generous and Lordly Leo.

Leo Born Mid-Morning:
Leo with Libra Rising

Talk about impressive! These are some people-pleasing winners! Polite Libra makes these Leos extra willing to share themselves and be considerate of others. And they're wonderful to their closest friends and loved ones. They'll do anything to keep people happy and entertained. Their mid-morning birth gives them a friendly magnetism, and their Likable Libra personality delivers a lifetime of powerfully successful associations; and if they play their cards right they'll reap a fruitful harvest of personal happiness and professional advantage.

Rewards are a given when these well-connected Leos stick to the goals they've set for themselves and embrace the opportunities that friends and colleagues provide, as well. They instinctively know that it's neither necessary nor ultimately beneficial to unfairly use or manipulate people, and they're masters at keeping everyone pleased by making fair decisions. They really love to be "all things to all people." If they invest in people wisely and remember that "one hand washes the other," their naturally demonstrative affections and obliging demeanor will earn them the good will they crave. These folks really want to be liked, so they give generously of themselves, and their recipients give right back. However, it behooves Leos born mid-morning to keep a handle on their Leo ego along the way. It tends to inflate itself, and when these Leos get so proud of their conquests and achievements that they see nothing else, they're liable to leave themselves a long line of disgruntled individuals who initially loved their style but eventually came to feel as though they weren't treated well. Someone so adept at making friends is poorly served making enemies. But their fearless and determined sun sign is well served by behavior that demonstrates genuine concern.

On the vocational front, stand-up comedy and other forms of showmanship might be very suitable, and the political arena, too, is a natural setting, especially when these Leos can be up close and personal with constituents. They have a wonderful knack for personal exchange.

Leo Born Around Noontime:
Leo with Scorpio Rising

Lighten up! And stop controlling everything! It shows no faith in life. These people take themselves and everything else too seriously. Honestly: If there's anyone in the zodiac who needs to tone it down, it's Leo with Scorpio rising! These people are too intense and they push too hard. The combination of Leo and Scorpio results in a "grab the handle and we're outta here!" gusto, an absence of insecurity, a great deal of impatience, and a "do it now and think about it later" mentality that rarely takes a break. They're like silent locomotives. They might be highly successful physical trainers with a peacock attitude, or "let me show ya how to hold that bat" PE teachers. Any profession that leaves them in charge suits them just fine. A career in law enforcement might be ideal. They're comfortable in a great many roles that allow them to take the lead and get the job done with vim and vigor. They always rise to the occasion.

If Leos born at noontime encounter difficulties in life, it will be due to intolerance, impatience, and a controlling, overly demanding manner. They erroneously see the world in black and white. And there's an element of the drastic here that breeds results more extreme than they've intended. When they take to the weight room, they don't leave until they're totally pumped. When they look for a hobby, they tend toward the radical. They might end up in leather and chains, with tattoos and piercings, and seated on a roaring Harley-Davidson. When they exact revenge, they leave their adversary severely wounded, or even lifeless. True, there's no error in a buff body or a nice bike, but unnecessary severity is never recommended.

Mysterious Scorpio is naturally suspicious, so when people stare at their awesome image, rather than taking it as a compliment, these too hostile Leos are apt to react with paranoia, receiving the attention as though it's an unspoken affront. They create a cycle of "Look at me! But don't you dare look at me!" that confuses people and frightens them away. And, unfortunately, some of those fleeing individuals might have made great friends and useful colleagues. These Leos need to know that if someone is really up to something, they'll spot 'em a mile off. There's no chance Scorpio will miss a thing! So Leos with Scorpio rising need to have their full-throttle fun without taking it all so seriously.

Leo Born Early Afternoon:
Leo with Sagittarius Rising

Now here's a person that's fun to be around! They prance around with a sweet smile and a glowing warmth; they dance and sing and put on a really good show, the absolute life of the party. They're inspired, positive, and tolerant of error. The warm glow of the sunny Leo ego is well-served by an optimistic, forgiving, Happy-Go-Lucky Sagittarius personality. These Leos are great company when they put their best foot forward, and they almost always do. But watch out for that Sagittarius "foot in mouth"! Leos born early afternoon are inclined to say things without thinking, though they usually mean no harm. That's why all is forgiven if they'll show just the tiniest smidgen of innocent, good-natured repentance.

Leos with Sagittarius rising tend to feel better when they're outdoors. Being in nature bolsters their faith in life and leaves them feeling at one with God. These people are explorers and adventurers. They might feel right at home as forest rangers or nature tour guides, sea captains or cruise directors, or in vocations that allow them to care for animals. With their ability to inspire others, they're highly effective in leadership roles and might be excellent coaches or politicians. But it's also here, in the realm of inspiration, that these people can create their own undoing. Leos born early afternoon feed on inspiration. It fuels their fire. So out of desperation they sometimes look for inspiration in questionable activities or unprofitable pursuits, believing in things that promise more than they can deliver. Their winning ways will probably enable them to make a living with their minds and people skills rather than hard labor, leaving them with lots of seemingly free time on their hands. And if they latch on to some folly and get overly excited about it, their determined Leo ego has a hard time letting go—even after it becomes obvious that they're completely wasting their time or, worse, getting themselves into trouble with some con game. There's nothing wrong with treating oneself to a little diversion, but these Leos need to be very careful that they don't wind up making fools of themselves.

Leo Born Mid-Afternoon:
Leo with Capricorn Rising

These people are the folks in charge and the "keepers of the keys." They have "I can handle it and do what's expected, plus" written all over their calm, cool, and collected faces and vouched for in their resumes. With Leo's pride and

Capricorn's unyielding sense of responsibility, a good job well done is all but guaranteed. Leo's competence and confidence are just what the doctor ordered for an ambitious Capricorn personality. If these people show up punctually, being respectful and orderly, they'll end up in charge of the entire block. They're absolutely masterful! But they might need to be more light-hearted. They're too sober about everything. They need to smile. If their Capricorn, the Wise Old Goat, will lighten up enough to let their sunny disposition shine through, they'll not only earn accolades for how well they've handled the project or account, they'll also inspire confidence in others, ensuring a quick climb up the ladder of success.

A Capricorn rising sign always signals a tendency to be overly serious or sour and much too business-like when it's time to lighten up and relax. But a Leo ego provides the ability to be jovial and affectionate if a conscious effort is made. The proof is in these folks' intimate relationships. Leos born mid-afternoon are wonderfully loyal romantic partners! They love to do things for their beloved, whether it's washing the car, folding the laundry, or picking up a take-out dinner as a nice surprise. And when gratitude is expressed for these little favors—watch out! These gestures will become their thoughtful routine.

If these Leos avoid being excessively demanding, they're superb management people. They're tremendous organizers. But no one starts at the top, so Leos with Capricorn rising need to be careful not to step on too many toes during their ambitious climb to the coveted corner office. There's a proclivity towards competition and jealousy here, and these Leos need to be careful not to react with bitter resentment when colleagues are rewarded for their achievements. Instead, they should be genuinely happy for them. Leos love to be alone on the stage, but there's always a need for good help in a successful business. The establishment of a good rapport, the cultivation of congeniality, and the willingness to be a team player are essential. Remember: Doing a damned good job isn't always enough to earn the promotion, especially when diplomacy has been thrown out the window.

Leo Born Around Sundown:
Leo with Aquarius Rising

Watch out for these argumentative stress bags! They tend to be negative. It's not all logical. It comes from their uptight, unrecognized emotional nature. If you pay close attention, you'll hear them say "no" to something, and then explain "yes" without a clue as to what they're doing. So here again, a better awareness can work wonders. As children, they laugh when they're disciplined because they're too stressed *not* to laugh. It releases their tension. They are strong-minded, big-attitude characters who can be a joy with their sharp sense of humor, but a nightmare with their argumentative and contentious reactions. Remember: Aquarius is the sign of attitude. A good attitude wins these folks the world with good-humored magnetism and an "all for one and one for all" approach, but underlying this loads-of-laughs exterior is a powerful "will to disagree" that can manifest itself at any moment. Leos with Aquarius rising often think in terms of right and wrong when there's really only a difference of opinion, so they're likely to dismiss as "absolutely wrong!" anything they disagree with or don't easily understand. An open mind is the key here. An open mind enables them to see that different ideas aren't necessarily wrong. With the blending of Leo's egotism and craving for attention and uptight Aquarius' Big Attitude, arguments are liable to follow these people around the corner and down the street on a really bad day. When they hear themselves saying, "but I didn't say anything!" they need to realize that their attitude was showing like a neon sign. If they can harness this natural contentiousness and maintain a level of self-awareness that allows them to keep from being too unreasonable, they can go the distance as highly successful trial lawyers, controversial talk radio personalities, or in any other vocation in which debating skills are crucial or bickering becomes an art form. But without self-awareness, there's the potential here for terribly closed-minded, boulder-on-the-shoulder, "the answer is always no" sourpusses for whom every trip to the supermarket is a potential ulcer because they can't help scolding the child who pushes his mother's shopping cart a little too fast or arguing with the cashier over trivial words she meant only as chitchat.

No one is well served by alienating others, especially Leos born at sundown. They sometimes tell themselves that they can be happy all alone in the boss's office or the spare room where they can tinker with gadgets, but the silence soon becomes unbearable and they seek out an audience—or an audience comes to them!—and they suddenly remember how fulfilling it is to hear others laugh at their jokes and compliment their achievements. The truth is that they *love* to be around people! And the cultivation of people skills will allow their Aquarius, the Electric Light Bulb, personality to illuminate the entire house with generous good cheer.

Leo Born Early Evening:
Leo with Pisces Rising

Who would've thunk it? Low key Leos with a delicate disposition, and all too will-ing to surrender the stage just to keep the peace and retain their serenity? The secretiveness of Pisces is an unlikely blend for the showmanship of Leo, and it creates both positive and negative results. The key is allowing showy Leo's ego and Pisces' yearning for serenity and isolation to complement or temper, rather than overwhelm, each other. For instance, in this combination, the scaredy-cat Pisces personality can be heartened by Leo's confidence. When these people are tempted to turn tail and run, they do well to remember there's a lion's heart beating within them. They have the ability, if they'll exercise it, to be more reasonable in the face of seemingly daunting circumstances. But Pisces rising never wants conflict!

These Leos' mid-evening birth instills some very humanitarian values, qualities always useful to people who pride themselves in their contribution. They're marvelous in people-helping vocations. But their Leo competence and confidence will very likely be cloaked in a sometimes delicate Peaceful Pisces "don't rock the boat" demeanor. They don't require fanfare, on the one hand, and they don't seek out confrontation, on the other; but they're still Lordly Leos, and the displeasure that Pisces takes in disapproval ensures that they'll find a way to set the record straight if their unassuming, "don't mention it" contributions are belittled or taken for granted. Still, their difficulties are often rooted in their Pisces tendency to be too secretive and unwilling to reveal themselves. This attitude is very useful for developing better listening skills, but it's not so effective at building trust. To top it off, they often enjoy working late at night or spending time alone to reflect and regenerate, so they're drawn to ethereal callings and Florence Nightingale pursuits or vocations that demand so much of their time and heartfelt attention that their loved ones feel alienated and left out. This is rarely rewarding for Leos. They need to share themselves! If Leos born early evening find themselves wondering why friends and family aren't providing the attention, gratitude, and congratulation all Leo's crave, they need to ask themselves if it's because they've made those friends and loved ones feel excluded with excessive silence. Spreading around a little more Leo sunshine might well be their most effective strategy.

Leo Born Mid-Evening:
Leo with Aries Rising

Now these are some childlike, good attitude folks, who put on a hell of a show with an up and at 'em, no time to waste, ask-me-I'll-tell-ya, all around good disposition. Aries' childlike impatience and Leo's sunny ego are a sure sale. The charming, refreshingly honest Aries personality tempers the Leo ego's tendency towards self-involvement without compromising its competence and confidence. Leos always leave a big impression, but Leos with Aries rising are more equipped to leave a delightful impression than most other sun sign/rising sign combinations. They adore children, inspire confidence in others, and are so expedient in handling their responsibilities that they're not insulted by supervision—the job is always completed properly, and long before deadline! The boss grows to love them for their efficiency. Action Aries keeps Leos born mid-evening a step or two ahead of the game. Their forte is vocations that require activity, whether chasing children around a playground or zipping all around town for UPS. They're valued employees because their forthrightness impels them to let management know exactly what their department needs, even when it's not what management prefers to hear. Aries never forgets that honesty is the best policy. And once these folks have scaled the company ladder themselves, they become gifted supervisors. They're natural leaders. They might be adept at working with their hands and drawn to hobbies like motorcycle-riding that give them the opportunity to both tinker in the garage and zip down the highway. They might also find a rewarding career in the military.

If they have a fault, it's probably rooted in their Aries impatience. Leos with Aries rising can be a real bother, so much so that they're rarely willing to wait for friends and colleagues who just can't keep up. Their friends arrive on time but knock on the door only to find that these Leos have already left, ten minutes earlier than planned. They just couldn't wait any longer! This can leave people frustrated and insulted, and if these Leos come off as self-serving and inconsiderate rather than merely "I just couldn't wait!" impatient, the offense they create will make problems for them down the road. At their worst, they run over people, sometimes the very people whose company they might most enjoy. The remedy is self-awareness, with healthy doses of Leo magnanimity and Aries charm. Letting up on the gas pedal every now and then will allow others to get ahead of them occasionally. And wouldn't that be generous and charming?

Leo Born Around Midnight:
Leo with Taurus Rising

Here come some intense people who need to lighten up and not deal with life as though everything is black or white. They're too much "my way or the highway" and have too little willingness to compromise—and both Leo and Taurus are fixed signs, so they feel their disappointments too deeply. Leo's pride and Taurus' determination make for a particularly dependable, focused person, but these folks are entirely too serious about everything. They're dignified but sometimes aloof. And they're resistant to change, wanting to hold onto the status quo. They need to move along to avoid becoming unapproachable sad sacks. Leos with Taurus rising are confident and competent enough to do just about anything they set their mind to, but they're at their best and most satisfied in practical pursuits—unless they find a way to exploit their potentially beautiful, articulate, baritone voice. They're proficient in vocations that revolve around banking or real estate, but will probably be most happy when they're self-employed. They might flourish when they're running a small business and calling their own shots, but their challenge is to avoid being too demanding of their employees, chasing them away with a bullish intolerance. Their most positive traits, from their Leo magnanimity and generosity to their Taurus bottom-line practicality, can be compromised if they go overboard with the pouty faced, stick-in-the-mud, grumpy stump side of their Taurus personality. And with Leo's tendency toward self-involvement, this sort of thing can easily happen if they don't stay flexible, open-minded, attentive, and accommodating to their moods. Although open-mindedness and flexibility are sometimes near impossible for them to maintain!

Leos born around midnight aren't easily impressed with anything. They demand excellence both as professionals and as consumers. They insist on a quality effort from employees and colleagues as well as from themselves. They can actually be quite hard on themselves, even when they're doing a better job than everyone else. But if these Leos can temper their intense seriousness and use their generosity as a basis for growing their people skills, they'll become the most valued members of the team. On the other hand, if their demanding ways become little more than blatant intolerance, they'll find themselves considered too difficult to work with. Taurus, the Banker, likes to keep things simple, but while "keep it simple" is practical and useful, it's not all that celebrative. So these Leos need to remember to go with the flow, to enjoy the party and have a good time. If they'll lighten up and move along, they just might end up enjoying themselves!

Leo Born in the Wee Hours:
Leo with Gemini Rising

Here are some "icing on the cake" congenial people with warm, sunny dispositions. They're unassuming and accommodating but well aware of what needs to be done and ready to give intelligent instruction. These people pour on the Gemini chatty-faced charm to get the attention they prefer to satiate their sunny Leo ego. They're masterful at putting others at ease by showing an interest in them. These Leos have a naturally inquisitive, spry, flit-around demeanor that's very entertaining—a pure joy to behold. They move gracefully from person to person at parties and conventions, and their voice itself might be distinctive, whether through a leisurely southern drawl or a willy-nilly, thinly-toned prattle. In fact, they might make their living with a microphone, whether at a radio station or a dispatch office. They're naturals at ventriloquism, comic monologues, and college auditorium lectures, though other sorts of career choices can be just as rewarding, including physical training, writing, and package and mail delivery. These Leos might even drive a school bus—and love every minute of it! Going here and there and being with children are two of their favorite things to do.

The level of success they achieve will be defined by the level of their awareness of self and circumstance. If they see themselves objectively, they'll live a happy life and make a substantial contribution. Jitterbug Gemini is sometimes superficial, and if this becomes the norm with a fixed, self-aggrandizing Leo sun sign, frustration is likely because people won't respond in the ways they prefer. Friends and colleagues will become evasive, making excuses to avoid them. Gemini doesn't mind taking flight from a hopeless situation and finding some other place to be, but Leos don't do well with the knowledge that someone has found them less than delightful. If they aren't careful, they can find themselves repeatedly insulted by reactions that, if the truth be known, they've created themselves. But on the other hand, with intellectual depth, these Leos can be both competent and confident and a whole lot of fun, as well. These are the sort of people who are so light and limber at a gathering that people are flabbergasted to discover they hold an incredibly responsible position in a multimillion dollar corporation. Leos with Gemini rising just need to avoid being labeled shallow or scatterbrained. Their Leo mastery, coupled with their Gemini glibness, gives them the best of both worlds.

Leo Born Pre-Dawn:
Leo with Cancer Rising

These are the sensitive, competent workaholics of the zodiac. Cancer feels dutiful, while Leo takes pride in a conscientious effort. So these people never need anyone to motivate them. They already feel like it's their responsibility to make the grass green! To say the least, they're not too objective. They feel the weight of the world when it comes to their duties and obligations, whether it's business or personal. They often have two spouses: their partner and their career. But marrying their career can lead them to a very limited perspective of life if they aren't careful.

Leos with Cancer rising are determined and diligent and well-equipped to run their own business. As a matter of fact, self-employment is probably the best vocational fit for them because Leos usually lack flexibility when it comes to being told what to do, and their stubborn streak will sometimes get them into trouble with the boss. If they can be farmers or real estate brokers, or if they make substantial profits as landlords, they're apt to feel like they've died and gone to heaven.

Leos born pre-dawn are affectionate, generous with their concern, and always willing to offer a shoulder to cry on. They'll happily whip up a hot meal for a down-and-out friend. But as understanding as they are, they need to grow an objective eye through which they can view themselves in perspective. Leos can be so self-involved and prone to obsess on things that they become oblivious to their surroundings, and Cautious Cancer is very susceptible to emotional confusion. It's not uncommon for these Leos to find themselves in personal relationships that seem to hold no promise for improvement. Emotionally dependent, fearing being alone, resistant to change, and nostalgic for the past, they stay in hopeless circumstances where they're more a servant than a partner. They just need to fill their lives with responsible activity and pay their partner no mind. And they need to avoid indiscriminately unloading their emotional disappointment on sympathetic ears wherever they can find them. That's no way for Lordly Leos to fulfill themselves: Before they know it, they'll come to resemble that cowardly lion with too little heart, cramped in a steel cage in a roadside carnival. Leos with Cancer rising need to apply more objectivity to their view of life. They can be objective for others in a nurturing way, but seeing themselves in perspective isn't so easy. Once they understand what they really want in life, all they have to do, with their Leo competence and confidence, is simply get to it.

THE VIRGO SUN SIGN
AND ITS RISING SIGN PERSONALITIES

THE VIRGO SUN SIGN
August 23–September 22

Here come Mr. and Ms. Fix-It, the intelligent problem solvers of the zodiac. If you're emotionally distraught, they want to fix it. If you've a production problem, they'll tinker their way to a correction. Helpful, productive, sometimes stylish Virgoans derive great satisfaction from contributing to a job well done and cooperating in ways that are practical and useful. They're very willing workers whose intelligent analysis is always on the mark. They make their diligent contributions with an unassuming modesty that differentiates them from people who live for the glory and fanfare. Their virtuous modesty is one of their most endearing traits. But there's more to usually pleasant, always busy-bee Virgoans than rolled-up sleeves and an "aw, shucks" attitude. They're incredibly complicated human beings, and these complexities originate in an intelligent, analytical, often skeptical mind that can lead to successful and satisfying careers in vocations that require critical thinking skills and proficiency with numbers. On the other hand, they can be prone to Virgo, the Worry Wart, insecurity that can be terribly crippling. They try to get all their judgments from their head, without consulting their emotions enough. They really need to pay closer attention to what their emotions are telling them. But remember: How this all works out depends largely on their particular rising sign.

As intelligent and aware of details as they are, Virgoans sometimes become nitpicky types who fixate on seemingly inconsequential matters and scrutinize them to death. But if they're aware of themselves, they can come to terms and channel it into more productive behavior. They're awesome with their Fix-It stuff, zeroing in on the tiny component that everyone else missed precisely because, at first glance, it seemed so inconsequential. But with too little self-awareness, analysis becomes their be-all and end-all. They'll forget that feelings and emotions, as illogical as they can be, are an integral part of what it means to be human. If everything were purely logical, life would be a piece of cake! They'll coldly frustrate family and friends with endless criticisms, or more likely, they'll turn these criticisms in on themselves. They'll focus on every little blemish or flaw, every little vulnerability or weakness. And in an insecure attempt to hide those blemishes and weaknesses, they'll parade around the one thing they trust—their intelligence—with trickery or flippancy that's intended to make themselves look smart but only creates a bad impression. This is the sort of behavior that Virgoans need to avoid. They're too genuinely caring and helpful to defeat their better qualities with misguided doubts and insecurities.

Virgo Born Around Dawn:
Virgo with Virgo Rising

There's no boredom here! These people can stare at a blank wall, and find something interesting about it. Talk about busy-minded tree squirrels! They're usually youthful in appearance, and often stylish cuties. And, oh my, are they picky. Virgoans are always buzz-saw productive, but these Virgoans are doubly so. And as Virgoans are analytical and helpful, these Virgoans are doubly analytical and helpful. But they need to apply their extraordinary helpfulness and productivity to practical ends, to problems that really need to be fixed and tasks that really need to be accomplished. Earth signs need practical rewards for their efforts, but these Virgoans forget to ask for them. At home, they're probably neat freaks in at least one particular way: It might be an impeccably organized kitchen, or precisely displayed knick-knacks on well-dusted shelves. But they'll need a better outlet if they're going to avoid becoming obsessive, and this is where a compatible work life comes in. As health professionals or computer troubleshooters, they're right in their element; they can spend their days analyzing problems and malfunctions and figuring out how to fix them like the busy little rodents they love to be. Or they might be contented accountants, hunting down missing funds. And given Virgo's penchant for fashion, department stores and the fashion industry are a perfect fit; they can analyze trends and showcase their sense of style. All of these vocations provide opportunities for Virgoans to do what they love in a way that pays off in green paper with dead presidents. And no matter how successful they become, they still maintain that virtuous modesty that they wear so well.

But if Virgoans with Virgo, the Worry Wart, rising are unhappy and unfulfilled in their work, they become very discouraged. Virgo is more delicate, and sometimes not as sturdy, as some of the other signs. These Virgoans are not only prone to be doubly helpful but may also be doubly insecure. They lose themselves in their surroundings, overwhelmed by challenges that seem insurmountable. They can succumb to that common Virgoan attitude: "Screw you! I've been sick!" They need to write "I CAN handle it!" next to their mirror and somewhere in their workplace, so they can be constantly reminded to sit up straight and take it on the chin; they need to stand up for themselves and avoid becoming doormats. Otherwise, they'll end up attempting to bolster their egos with flippant comments, clever comebacks, and devious schemes, all intended to make themselves appear intelligent, but often resulting in squandering the good will and trust they've worked so hard to earn. People who'd thought these Virgoans were genuine and caring come to suspect them to be gossipy troublemakers. So Virgoans need to be as helpful and productive as they're driven to be, all the while trusting that that's exactly what people appreciate most about them. It's their shining star!

Virgo Born Shortly After Dawn:
Virgo with Libra Rising

Everything depends on relationships with these people. They're so motivated to share and belong that they seldom consider what they're getting in return for their heartfelt help. So fair and considerate partners are key! Compatible partners give them extreme comfort and much easier lives, but incompatible commitments will bring them to their knees. They need a good sense of self, and sometimes they just don't have it. They may be the most loving partners on the block, but it's easy for people to give them less than their fair share because they often border on the obsequious in their dealings. They're the servile hostesses who never get to talk with their guests because they're too busy catering to everyone. Being sociable, obliging, and genuinely likable, they start out trying to please everyone and usually end up doing a bang-up job. They're well aware of the warm feeling that comes from being of help to someone: They love to acknowledge, encourage, and compliment people. With a little backbone, modest Virgoans wear the Likable Libra personality extremely well, resulting in delightfully pleasant friends, neighbors, and colleagues. Diplomacy comes naturally because they're so empathic and aware of the people around them. (On the downside, Libra is the meddler!) They're the sorts of doctors or nurses who are well-known for their personalized care; prison guards who never abuse their authority; corporate tax professionals who are just as at ease with human beings as they are with numbers and expense accounts. Libra creates "people who need people," but there's always that delicate and sometimes subservient quality about Virgoans that makes it easy to be taken advantage of. These Virgoans need to be well-connected with people who treat them graciously and repay their help and consideration with gratitude and respect. They're uncomfortable asking for things, and, truth be known, they shouldn't have to ask for a well-earned "thank you." People who are too proud to say "please" and "thank you" need to be avoided, if at all possible.

As is true of many people born shortly after dawn, these Virgoans need some time alone to center and regenerate themselves. There's often a spiritual side to Virgoans with Libra rising that can be wonderfully enhanced with such a routine. They might take naturally to prayer or meditation. It's in these moments, away from people, that they contemplate their circumstances and put everything into perspective, especially their involvements. Investing themselves with mutually helpful individuals allows them so much more happiness in life. They feel better about themselves, and their lives become easier and more fruitful, a virtual cakewalk. But if they're all tangled up with losers and abusers, they'll feel like they're walking on broken glass.

Virgo Born Mid-Morning: Virgo with Scorpio Rising

These people are more "grab the handle" and "out of my way!" than most other Virgoans. They behave as though they're on a mission, with no time to waste. But they're not likely to tell you where they're going or where they've been. A Scorpio personality gives them that full-blown, eight-cylinder, trademark Scorpio gusto! And they're always thinking ahead. They set goals and plan a strategy. But they don't rush or do a shoddy job. That sort of behavior would never please a Virgo ego. With their extraordinary energy level and a better focus on the bottom line than other Virgoans, they do a whale of a job—in less time! They have a hands-on involvement with life.

Even though Scorpio rising brings a suspicious nature, these Virgoans are still more friendly, magnetic, and cooperative than many other Virgoans, and they express their friendliness in uniquely unassuming ways. Without compromising their natural modesty, they step forward and get involved with an "all for one and one for all" attitude. They love a team effort. There's not so much insecurity here. But a Mysterious Scorpio personality always brings some sort of intrigue, and in this combination it manifests itself in an ability to honor privileged information. They share information on a "need to know" basis, a characteristic that can be very helpful to friends and colleagues or anyone who has valuable secrets to keep.

However, it's in this respect that Virgoans with Scorpio rising can unwittingly compromise themselves. Scorpio's tendency to be quick to exact revenge, and Virgo's penchant for finding entertainment in mischief and trickery, can create problems. If these Virgoans get wrapped up in a powerful resentment, they might very well act out in ruthless ways, revealing some of those secrets that have been entrusted to them for safe-keeping. They need to remember that, even if they seem to derive some primal pleasure from inflicting pain, it's only a secondary reward and never helpful or productive. If they avoid succumbing to meanness when friction arises, the sky's the limit, both personally and professionally. Among other things, these Virgoans make wonderful physicians, insightful forensic scientists, and highly competent mortgage brokers. And if they've behaved themselves along the way, they'll find people emerging from the woodwork to lend a hand and repay them for all the indispensable contributions they've made.

Virgo Born Around Noontime:
Virgo with Sagittarius Rising

These are some sharp-minded winners who get the picture with their perceptive Sagittarius personalities and never miss the details with their intelligent, analytical Virgo behind the scenes. This is a powerful combination for fun and profit: Sagittarius loves a party, and Virgo's the caterer!

An easy toothy smile and a positive, forgiving spirit are very common in this combination. But what's more, a noontime birth invests modest Virgoans with an "I'm in charge" demeanor that's pleasingly sincere and unassuming, with a wonderful, loyalty-fostering appreciation for their employees. So they're almost always well-respected. Because their purpose is productivity, not self-aggrandizement, they're just not demanding or authoritative. They're in tune with the underdog. They know their employees by name, and their helpful, happy, concerned and forgiving spirit manifests itself daily. If they do falter in any way, it might be that they can be prone to some impatience and can sometimes be too optimistic when, realistically, circumstances aren't all that great. After all, they're used to being lucky, and Virgoans with Sagittarius rising know better than most that winning ways can win the world. So with self-awareness and a healthy dose of objectivity, their winning ways will always deliver functional success, which is good for them and great for their underlings.

Virgoans with Happy-Go-Lucky Sagittarius rising are usually easy-going, jovial people who might even have a bit of Jolly Ol' King Cole in their physical nature. They're naturals at telling jokes and entertaining people. And it's well-received as long as it doesn't come off as high-handed or arrogant. With Sagittarius in the mix, these Virgoans need to avoid appearing holier-than-thou at every turn. And if they'll interject some of that natural humor into their management style, they'll be doubly rewarded. The key is to gratify their Virgo ego by making sure their actions are helpful, their contributions are practical, and—very importantly—their character is on the up and up. It's always possible that once these Virgoans, with their love of trickery, discover just how easy it is to escape punishment—and once they've realized the power of a promise—that they'll resort to misleading people, making false promises, and misrepresenting themselves. Sometimes they need to learn that although con games might seem to pay off in the short term, they're never productive in the long run. Virgoans born at noontime must always enhance their winning ways with benevolence and service to others.

Virgo Born Early Afternoon:
Virgo with Capricorn Rising

These willing workers do what's expected, and then some. With a calm, cool, and collected, business-is-business Capricorn personality, these Virgoans usually know how to deal with authority, whether it's theirs or someone else's. They're highly dependable, always ready to help out by rolling up their sleeves and lending a hand, loyal to the company, respectful to the boss, and business-savvy. They'll increase productivity so much that their climb up the corporate ladder is almost guaranteed. Virgoans with Capricorn rising are generally considered indispensable both at home and on the job: They love being able to sit back at the end of a day and enjoy that "good job well done" feeling. However, it's important that they don't succumb to a totally workaholic attitude that leaves them overly serious and somewhat detached, with a limited view of life. They find it hard to complain about unreasonable circumstances: Virgo's modesty and Capricorn's sense of responsibility make it difficult for them to speak up when they're overworked—even when demands exceed what's humanly possible! They need to learn to draw a line in the sand. It takes a lot to overwhelm Capricorn, the Wise Old Goat, but, after all, these Virgoans are only human, and if they end up getting in over their heads, their Virgo egos are inclined to give way to insecurity. They end up blaming themselves. It escapes their notice that they're doing twice as much as everyone else. So they need to lighten up enough to enjoy life and remember that inspiration, not obligation, is the first indicator of success.

Virgoans born early afternoon are appreciated mostly for their practical, level-headed, responsible approach to life and their love for doing little favors. People seek out their counsel and respect their advice. And the competitiveness of some Capricorn personalities is mitigated a bit by Virgo's modesty. But if they feel their intelligence has been insulted, they might briefly lose their cool, and that's when their bossy, insensitive Capricorn pushiness sets in. They're especially sensitive to indications that their intelligence is being underestimated, and their pride in this respect is easily wounded. They need to be objective and certain they're not perceiving insult where there is none. When their suggestions are questioned, chances are that, rather than expressing doubt, the questioner simply wants to be sure he's understanding them correctly. Everyone knows these Virgoans' opinions always smack of Capricorn's stone-cold-sober earthly wisdom.

Virgo Born Mid-Afternoon:
Virgo with Aquarius Rising

Virgoans with Aquarius rising are electrically charged with a sharp sense of humor and a vivaciously friendly attitude. And they always have an urgent understanding of exactly what to do when the pressure's on and the crap hits the fan. They're ship-shape, with an "all for one and one for all" attitude. These analytical Virgoans' troubleshooting skills are often applied to advertising, electronics, all sorts of technical fields, and sometimes powered flight, so they're often found working on computers, in hangars, at airports, or for high-tech juggernauts like NASA. And when they're in uniform, as Aquarius often is, they tend to wear that uniform in a snappy Virgo style with an officer's decorum rather than a raw recruit's overexuberance. When things threaten to spin out of control and the stakes are high, Virgo's eagle eye for detail ensures that no warning light will blink unnoticed. Even in vocations with less dire consequences, these Virgoans are vigilant troubleshooters, keen on precision. They're good salespeople who respond to their client's every concern, even the little things that might seem trivial.

Virgoans born mid-afternoon probably aren't the type to talk a lot about emotional matters, even in close relationships. It's not that they're uncaring or inconsiderate. It's that emotions lack precision and are therefore undefined and hard to "fix"; emotions aren't easily analyzed or quantified like an accounting problem. These Virgoans believe the helpful things they do for their loved ones are the evidence of their love. And, in most cases, this is understood, as long as their BIG ATTITUDE Aquarius doesn't shift into negative high gear. Of course, Aquarius, the Electric Light Bulb, always poses this risk because, for good or ill,

Aquarius rising projects a big attitude. Still, with their sun in modest Virgo, these people are less inclined to be stiff-minded and argumentative. But their Aquarius "will to disagree" can be triggered if they sense that they've been underestimated. They are fiercely independent and highly sensitive to disrespect. When they're told they're wrong, they hear, "You're stupid." The key for them is to be willing to engage people of opposing viewpoints in real conversation, to talk *with* them rather than *at* them, to hear their explanations, and to explain and justify their opinions rather than clobber people over the head with controversy. If they're on edge and defensive, they'll almost always be perceived as too difficult to work with, and others will fail to see the helpful, modest soul beneath the uptight exterior. The secret to success is backing up their good effort with a cooperative attitude.

Virgo Born Around Sundown:
Virgo with Pisces Rising

Here comes Florence Nightingale—helpful, considerate, always eager to listen, ever willing to cooperate. These people are among the most delicate, concerned, and empathetic individuals on the planet. They're sincere, sensitive, and intelligent; they're unassuming and non-combative. Being short on egotism, they prefer to stay out of the limelight whenever possible, and they're so adept at "don't rock the boat" and "give and take" that they often end up in charge wherever a flexible, "light touch" management style is preferred. Many counselors—vocational, guidance, and emotional—are Virgoans born at sundown. They're found in all sorts of people-helping professions, and with a shrewd, easily adaptable Pisces personality complementing their analytical Virgo ego, their versatility is limitless. They might use their keen Pisces eye to aim a camera or envision a blueprint. Imagery and creativity are cornerstone Pisces traits. And these Virgoans are very in tune with vibrations, whether from people or musical instruments. They might well be accomplished musicians.

There's a go-with-the-flow light touch in both Virgo and Peaceful Pisces, so these Virgoans instinctively and wisely avoid intensity and confrontation. Virgoans born at sundown are proficient escapists: At the first sign of belligerence, they split the scene! And they're nowhere to be found when the crap hits the fan. Because confrontation wears on them, it's important for these Virgoans to be involved with people who accept them for who they are and won't bully them with argument. However, they think the best of everyone and naively convince themselves that a person doesn't really mean it when nasty comments are made. They prefer to ignore the facts if the facts are distressing. They're all too willing to take the blame when it's placed indiscriminately on their shoulders, to acquiesce when they're rudely told that everything's their fault. They're left frustrated, sad, and confused. Better that they leave ill-tempered people to their own devices, and find themselves a place among people who will truly appreciate their helpful, productive, unassuming demeanor. If these Virgoans will surround themselves with compatible colleagues, friends, and partners, they'll get back two-fold all the cooperation they so freely give.

Virgo Born Early Evening:
Virgo with Aries Rising

The charming, childlike quality of bright-eyed, bushy-tailed Aries is a fine complement to intelligent, analytical Virgo. Virgoans born mid-evening are agile and energetic; they show up early because they "just can't wait!" "Do it now and think about it later" is their mantra, so they're always well-received by their co-workers. And they're usually doing more than their fair share without being asked. With Action Aries rising, helpful, energetic Virgoans are usually so productive that they leave people flabbergasted. While Virgo is a willing worker with a buzz saw attitude, Aries is expedient and probably way ahead of schedule. But these Virgoans need to avoid letting "productively busy" turn into unproductive "dizzy busy." They're so enamored by activity for activity's sake that they easily fall into a cycle of "go to first job," "go to second job," and afterward "go sign up for parachuting lessons just to avoid boredom." There's a serious lack of serenity here. These people can't sit down! Of course, there's nothing wrong with staying busy, but, equally true, there's more to life than acting like a chicken with its head cut off. These Virgoans need to slow down just enough to keep things running smoothly without tension or mishaps.

This isn't to say that they should compromise their nature. They're rarely happy in sit-behind-the-desk or stand-behind-the-counter jobs where they can't move around, and they shouldn't force themselves to stay in inappropriate situations. They'd rather zip around town, delivering messages, passengers, or patients; or run back and forth from station to station. They shouldn't be so overly modest and masochistically loyal that they feel guilty for wisely serving their own interests, whether they're escaping a dull neighborhood or a stifling workplace. Often when they find themselves in stultifying situations, their springtime Aries optimism erroneously convinces them that summer's always just around the corner. They constantly tell themselves that things will change just because time passes. Well, sure, but you've got to help the changes along with corrective behavior! Their faith in life is admirable, but it needs to be realistic.

Childlike, charming, generous, honest, and probably well-proportioned and physically attractive, these Virgoans are delightful to be around. But Virgo's nervous insecurity and Aries' impatience will get the best of them if they lack self-awareness. Without some serenity they'll become accidents waiting to happen: Never a good situation for someone whose idea of fun is jumping out of airplanes or whose livelihood is delivering precious cargo! If Virgoans with Aries rising will learn to center themselves and cool their jets, they'll give people time to savor their childlike charm—and still get things done with more ease, in less time.

Virgo Born Mid-Evening:
Virgo with Taurus Rising

These are more dignified and not so approachable Virgoans. They're tasteful and quality-oriented, and they have more focus than some other Virgoans. The somewhat stand-offish Taurus personality keeps their helpfulness from being taken advantage of. Visitors who aren't punctual and interested probably won't be staying long. They're just as helpful as any others, and probably even more productive given their Taurus bottom-line sensibility, but they stand up for themselves in such a way that they're not easy targets for abuse. Vocationally, they flourish in banking and accounting, with a head for numerical analysis, and in management positions they're appreciated for generously providing their workers with whatever backup they need to get the job done—but those workers might be expected to move mountains on a daily basis. After all, that's what the boss does! And on a bad day, these Virgoans' bullish personality might set eyes rolling when their Virgo ego starts nitpicking a minor issue to death, unwilling to just let it go. Taurus can be very dogged and doesn't "lighten up and move along" well.

Virgoans are already inherently stylish, but with narcissistic Taurus, the Banker, rising, they benefit from a taste in fashion that might permeate virtually every area of their life. It's obvious both on their shoulders and their walls that they have an aesthetic eye. They can coordinate a color scheme like nobody's business. They usually prefer tailored clothing and enjoy accumulating attractive things of high quality and value, and they revel in their ability to sniff out a bargain: Finding a form-flattering dress or shirt at seventy percent off sends them to seventh heaven. But it's also in this area of their lives that dissatisfaction creeps in, exposing them to disenchantment with what they've built for themselves. Virgoans born mid-evening tend to forget that, by themselves, material goods are never completely satisfying. There's a spiritual side to human beings that isn't fulfilled by home furnishings, new clothes, or tasteful jewelry. Forgetting that "more is never enough," these people might feel an emptiness at times that confuses them. They find themselves asking, "How can I be unhappy? I have a nice home in a well-maintained neighborhood and a new car in the driveway. And I like my job." The antidote is time spent caring for living things, a return to the helpful, productive activities that drive the Virgo ego. They might discover that offering one of their new neighbors a ride to the grocery store, or however else it is that they exercise their Taurus generosity and Virgo helpfulness, is more fulfilling than enjoying their possessions.

Virgo Born Around Midnight:
Virgo with Gemini Rising

These are quick-minded, chatty-faced people with a lot of bright ideas. And hopefully a few of those ideas will actually work! But even if friends and colleagues have to sort through a whole lot of nonsense to find what's workable, these Virgoans are still a joy to be around, especially in the comfort of their own homes. Virgoans born around midnight are naturally congenial, glib, sincere, and disarming, and if they'll emphasize these positive traits and avoid rambling on, they'll earn the respect and adoration they deserve for their quick-mindedness. The Jitterbug Gemini personality almost always creates a talker, but because midnight births are sometimes quite shy, these Virgoans might prefer one-on-one situations like sitting at the kitchen table or conversing privately over the telephone. They're often more focused on the people closest to their hearts than on strangers they meet at a party. They sometimes feel that their most important duties and responsibilities are those that revolve around their home-life. It's here, at home, that they feel most comfortable, and they take great pride in the appearance of their houses. Don't forget: Virgoans usually have a neat freak hidden in there somewhere, whether it's obvious or not.

These Virgoans love to escape into a good book, or even a sewing machine, that lets them wander off into their busy minds. Sometimes they're apprehensive about venturing out of the house and trying something new, preferring instead to stick with what's familiar in their own workshop or craft room. Virgoans with Gemini rising need to keep a focused eye on their insecurities and not let those insecurities paralyze their willingness to follow their inspirations. On the other hand, they're extremely curious and highly analytical, and in social settings they exercise these traits by conveying interesting information and showing a sincere interest in the people they meet. Their glibness usually gives them wonderful people skills. But if, out of nervousness, they begin blabbering about things well beyond the scope of their knowledge—a typical Gemini pitfall—they're apt to appear scatterbrained. They need to understand that when they feel out of their element, it's rarely helpful to continue rambling on and on without noticing others' reactions. These Virgoans earn high marks for alacrity, efficiency, troubleshooting, and helpfulness, but they need to avoid prattling away the respect they've worked so hard to establish.

Virgo Born in the Wee Hours:
Virgo with Cancer Rising

These people have a wonderful "grow your own," green-leaf quality about them that's a joy to behold. They're modest, helpful nurturers who cultivate people and things and bring them to fruition, whether underlings at work, neatly-dressed children at home, or plants out on the balcony. To anyone who shows up at the house, they offer a drink or something to eat. They're admirably hospitable. Virgoans born in the wee hours are extremely caring, mostly due to close family ties. They're a bit homespun; they're the good neighbors who are always willing to look after the puppy next door while its owner is off on vacation. And whatever they do, they do it with feeling. Analytical Virgoans tend to live in their head, but their Cautious Cancer is extremely emotional, so their Virgo helpfulness is always heartfelt. On the job, they're well-respected for doing more than their fair share. They love to be productive and aren't very good at relaxing, anyway, so they come early and stay late. They're smart, hard-working, and admirably unassuming. At home, they take care in selecting and maintaining their furnishings and, with their own hands, they make the most of their decorations. They love to make their surroundings comfortable, both physically and emotionally, for all the people who live there.

These Virgoans make splendid property managers and medical assistants; they thrive in any capacity where they can demonstrate their "move mountains" attitude and astound others with their ability to do the work of two or three people. However, difficulties might arise if those Cancer emotions wreak havoc on Virgo's tendency towards insecurity. Virgoans with subjective Cancer rising need to learn to stand off and see themselves objectively. They worry about the future, about asking for more than their fair share, and about speaking out of turn. They worry that they aren't welcome. They don't always behave as if they're comfortable with themselves. It's just that they're much too modest! They fret over whether they're justified in asking friends for a favor or the boss for a raise. They fear that the boss will forever remember any unreasonable requests. It somehow escapes their notice that, day in and day out, they work harder than their co-workers and are more helpful than their neighbors, any of whom would feel honored to sing their praises. But even though their fears are unfounded, they remain. So Virgoans with Cancer rising need to grow an eye of objectivity that allows them to see themselves relative to others. These Virgoans need to allow themselves to be rewarded. It might unsettle their modesty to receive too much positive attention, but a little limelight now and then is exactly what they need to help them shed their insecurities.

Virgo Born Pre-Dawn:
Virgo with Leo Rising

Ah! Finally! A Virgo who wants some attention! These are probably the most self-assured and assertive Virgoans of all. They're also more focused and determined than other Virgoans, and they're better at getting to the bottom of things. Blending the intense, robust, and possibly striking presence of Lordly Leo the lion with productive Virgo creates a "do it right the first time" attitude that complements helpful Virgo quite nicely. But it's important for these Virgoans to make a conscious effort to be more flexible. They might not handle disappointment well, finding it difficult to lighten up and move along; and there's likely to be a good deal of pridefulness in their behavior. Nonetheless, Leo's "I can handle it, give it to me" attitude enhances Virgo's productivity. They're always the organization's best bet to initiate a project, and Leo's generosity is a good fit for Virgo's Ms. Nitpicky. They're typically willing Virgo workers, but they also take pride in themselves and love recognition—something not always true of the modest Virgoan. These Virgoans are also comfortable receiving accolades for their achievements. They complete the task in record time, revel in the applause, then go home to enjoy the fruits of their labors and the love of their dear ones.

But Leo's undoing is almost always the tendency to get lost in the spotlight, and Virgo is already inclined to miss the big picture while sweating the nitpicky details. So if these Virgoans don't make an extra-special effort to increase their self-awareness, they find themselves oblivious to their surroundings and growing increasingly unaware of how they're being received. This is not to say they're no longer productive, affectionate, or generous—these core Virgo and Leo traits will always be cornerstones of their makeup. But they occasionally succumb to a tunnel vision that probably focuses on material things and makes them appear more one-dimensional and shallow than they really are. And a decreasing ability to see things realistically is particularly dangerous for them: That prideful, stubborn streak they often harbor makes them resistant to change. Virgoans with Leo rising are caring enough to know that there's more to life than prancing on stage and acquiring possessions—they just need to remember to follow their inspirations and care for living things.

CHAPTER 11

THE LIBRA SUN SIGN
AND ITS RISING SIGN PERSONALITIES

THE LIBRA SUN SIGN
September 23–October 22

Likable Librans are the most "we"-oriented people in the zodiac. They're characterized by "I don't want to be alone" and "One hand washes the other." They put themselves in the other person's shoes more naturally than any of the other signs, and they always see both sides of the coin. They revel in being aware of, invested in, and obliging to the people around them. They're often the deal-makers, diplomats, and legislators in our society, and they've a keen eye for what is equitable because they make a judgment only after they've weighed all their options. So you mustn't get impatient with them if they can't decide yet.

Librans are the people-watchers in the airport, the sidewalk café patrons who enjoy the parade of men and women even more than they enjoy their coffee. And when it's time to connect with people rather than simply observe them, Librans always exercise the principles of "give and take." Throughout their lives, it's who they know, and not always *what* they know that brings them to their next opportunity. Of course, the best relationships are those in which the sum is greater than the parts, the kind that facilitate a snowball effect in which I give two, you give four; I give eight, and you give sixteen. If these Librans are living happy and successful lives, it's usually because they've formed wonderfully supportive relationships that benefit them through word-of-mouth opportunities. And they've set the whole thing in motion themselves with a sense of fair play. People don't forget it when you're good to them! So the key here is coupling their fair-minded and considerate behavior with compatible people to insure that their interactions run smooth as silk. This is Likable Libra's utopia! If they're fair to themselves and objective about their relationships, their interactions are full of fun and profit. No one really benefits from being unfair to others, but for Librans this is doubly true.

Yet don't forget, the particular rising sign personality can either complement or undermine Librans' ability to behave wisely and in their own best interest. Some personality types will make the daily practice of equitable behavior a bit more challenging, while other types will lead Librans beyond interacting, into out-and-out meddling. Still other personality types will obscure their self-awareness in such a way that they'll run the risk of losing themselves in their primary relationships, becoming so afraid of being alone that they define themselves by their partners and compromise their own identities. If they'll accentuate their most positive traits; exercise integrity in dealing with friends, family, and colleagues; and pursue relationships with compatible people rather than stay in difficult situations, Librans will get what they want and enjoy life with surprising ease.

Libra Born Around Dawn:
Libra with Libra Rising

Need someone to do a job for you? These are the people to ask: They can give you a list of competent people. Great referrals and recommendations are in their bailiwick. They're usually so well-connected they seem to always know just the right person for any occasion. And do Likable Librans born around dawn ever enjoy occasions, especially social or productive business occasions. Double Librans are doubly inclined towards the "I don't wanna be alone" attitude that sometimes drives Librans into difficult relationships and, unfortunately, keeps them there. They're also doubly inclined towards meddling; they're so aware of everyone else's situation that minding their own business can be a tall order. But the good news is that with self-awareness, these Librans can tap into the temperance and balance that's an innate part of their consciousness and keep themselves from going to extremes. It's their Likable Libra balance that makes them such gifted diplomats: They're able to weigh the options so precisely that they find the most equitable equation almost every time.

An example of this temperance in action is its potential effect on Libra's characteristic indecisiveness. Librans are well-known for their "eenie, meenie, minie, moe, left or right, I don't know...oh, hell, wait and see" behavior. Yet without proper balance, this habit can become a sort of paralysis, an excuse to *never* make a decision, or, on the other hand, a provocation for Librans to chide themselves as hopeless procrastinators. But when Librans are at their temperate best, their "wait and see" becomes a mantra that almost always works to their benefit. It compels them to look both ways before crossing the street and keeps them from rushing recklessly into ill-conceived projects; it helps them develop patience; it reminds them of the universal truth that everything develops in its own good time, that spring follows winter and won't be hurried along by human restlessness; it enables them to stop and smell the roses as nature takes its course.

Librans born around dawn are fair and square diplomats. They're deal makers par excellence, and they thrive as managers, politicians, and attorneys as long as their indecisiveness doesn't lead them to be less than true to their word. Remember: The best time for changing one's mind is rarely after the deal's been made.

Libra Born Shortly After Dawn:
Libra with Scorpio Rising

Here comes sociable Libra with a mysterious, sexy, "no time to waste" personality. With Scorpio rising, likable, polite Librans benefit from a full-of-gusto, "do it now and think about it later" personality that makes them handy and energetically helpful. They warm up to strangers gradually, but they're amazingly devoted to the people who mean the most to them, and they often express their devotion through practical assistance and thoughtful favors. They're good with their hands in some fashion or another, whether it's playing a guitar, fixing an engine, or applying make-up, and Librans born shortly after dawn will sometimes put these skills to work professionally, using their Libra word-of-mouth to make contacts and spread the word. But Mysterious Scorpio is also a natural detective, so they might excel as private investigators, psychologists, and counselors, too. They've a knack for finding things out, whether it's checking up on suspect credit ratings or potentially unfaithful spouses—but they need to be careful that they don't conjure demons where there are none. Paranoia can be a problem for suspicious Scorpios. With Libra's preoccupation with other people's concerns and Scorpio's tendency toward suspicion, they can sometimes overreact to what's actually an innocent deed or gesture.

And these Librans also need to guard against attracting suspicion to themselves with too much secrecy. There's a touch of mystery about their personalities, and a deep look in their eyes sometimes makes them a bit intimidating. So they need to make a special effort to show themselves, state their case, and let people know where they're coming from. It's important that they have enough courage to take the proper people into their confidence in order to earn trust. They tend to throw themselves heart and soul into romantic relationships but clam up when it comes to letting their partners know what they're thinking or how they're feeling. Partners who are perceptive themselves might notice something's wrong; but otherwise dissatisfactions are left to fester. In business relationships, this Scorpio secrecy can be an asset or a problem. It might make these Librans seem dishonest, as if they intentionally hold back information for selfish gain when it's really just their nature to parcel out data on a "need to know" basis.

Because Libra's bread and butter are beneficial interactions, these Librans need to avoid falling into these unseen, unspoken behavior patterns, and perhaps their best strategy for maintaining self-awareness is regular quiet time, extended moments when they sit and reflect on recent actions and consequences, judging them honestly and objectively. They'll discover that others find them even *more* likable when they're a little more transparent in their daily dealings.

Libra Born Mid-Morning:
Libra with Sagittarius Rising

These people have that good feeling of well-being. They're the most delightful, well-acquainted social butterflies in the zodiac. With a Pollyanna outlook and a spring in their step, Librans with Happy-Go-Lucky Sagittarius rising tend to be all-around happy people whose toothy smiles and winning ways spread inspiration wherever they go. They're obliging and a joy to be around. There's a community-oriented, volunteer spirit here that often leads them into active roles with organizations like the Chamber of Commerce or the PTA, and they might be among the first to volunteer to staff the local polls on election day. Of course, this is very beneficial behavior for any Libran because they benefit most from the contribution they make to the people they know—and the connections they have. These Librans have a special knack for developing fruitful associations with particularly cooperative, friendly, and powerful people.

However, Librans born mid-morning need to be careful that they don't try to please everyone to the point of being two-faced or constantly promising more than they can deliver. More than any other sign, Sagittarius knows the power of a promise, and with Libra's desire to please, these Librans can easily fall into a pattern of delivering assurances that aren't nearly as certain as they make them out to be. They should realize that such behavior is never beneficial, and it's certainly not necessary; it's just that they can't say "no," or even deliver any bad news. But they'll inspire confidence and adoration even if they *can't* deliver the moon. This is especially important to keep in mind for Librans involved in careers where negotiation is a primary function. They have the potential to be marvelous politicians—for as long as they don't make promises they can't keep! And is that a bad politician's trick, or what?

Another area of concern involves being overly indulged as children, leaving them to think that bad behavior is cute and fun to get away with. If the parents were overly permissive and spoiled these Librans as children, some of that sense of privilege carries over into adulthood, resulting in an "I'm better than you" arrogance that can really turn people off. The problem is that if they never grow up, they end up as con men who never deliver! But if they invest themselves with the right people and treat them fairly, these Librans will find that everybody loves them and the sky's the limit.

Libra Born Around Noontime:
Libra with Capricorn Rising

Now here come "the benevolent manipulators," who never raise their voice, and keep everyone happy and cooperating. These Librans are generally able to manipulate circumstances in such a way that everyone ends up satisfied. They return to work day after day, feeling good about their contribution. And never are these management skills more pronounced than when Capricorn, "the boss," rises. Librans born around noontime are so patient over the long haul, and so well-equipped to make do under difficult circumstances, that they're able to ride out just about any storm with a "tomorrow's another day" sensibility. They know that what goes around comes around, so they're masters at staying at the helm and keeping things together. But remember, both Libra and Capricorn are active signs, so their moment-to-moment behavior might be more hurried, impatient, and pushy than their long haul, "goes around, comes around" sensibility. Nonetheless, these Librans bear up under the strain with their Capricorn "somebody's gotta do it," troll-under-the-bridge approach, never losing sight of the need to keep others motivated, or at least accommodated. And the more people there are to keep happy, the more satisfied these Librans are. When leadership needs to be fair and patient, yet firm and authoritative, these people are the perfect fit for the front office. They're never intimidated by shouting or swayed by melodramatic emotions. They'll be fair with their decisions and generous in their judgments, but they'll never accept "I don't wanna do it" as a legitimate excuse for anything. After all, "Somebody's gotta do it!" From their own personal experience, they've learned all about doing what needs to be done, regardless of their druthers.

It's at home that these Librans might meet with some difficulty. One of their most admirable traits is their undying loyalty. As spouses, they tend to be both faithful and dutiful. But they often navigate their family circumstances with an unemotional, Capricorn, the Wise Old Goat, detachment that can leave them oblivious to their partner's disenchantment. They express their commitment by handling their chores with meticulous precision and dependable regularity, taxiing the kids, emptying the garbage, maintaining the lawn or the car or the kitchen with nary a complaint, and probably contributing a healthy paycheck to the running of the household—yet it escapes their notice that, for whatever reason, in the eyes of their partner the honeymoon is over, especially if they've been approaching things with a "look what I do for you" attitude. At least in this area of their life, they'll benefit immensely from being a little less mechanical and a lot more demonstrative. After all, these are the people they're supposed to be closest to. No one's asking them to run up and kiss strangers!

Libra Born Early Afternoon:
Libra with Aquarius Rising

Friendly, intuitive Aquarius fits wonderfully with a Likable Libra ego, to produce the best people skills in the zodiac. These people experience plugged-in, accurate first impressions that guide their judgment and endear them to their peers. And they love to share their humor! Without even realizing it, their high-strung behavior sometimes leads to actions that people find hilarious. But these folks are definitely Big Attitude! And who knows how that attitude will appear? Will it be electric, explosive, friendly and magnetic? Or endlessly argumentative, fraught with a will to disagree? Well, you can count on this much: It'll be powerful and obvious.

When Aquarius rises, attitude flashes like a neon sign, and these Librans usually learn early in life that a magnetic, witty Aquarius, the Electric Light Bulb, attitude is an infinitely better complement to their obliging, Likable Libra ego than a sour disposition. Librans are usually very aware of how they're being received, and Librans born early afternoon are best received when they spice up their daily behavior with big dollops of their friendly good humor and maybe even some heartfelt encouragement. For these people, laughter really is the best medicine. They're wonderful salespeople and successful promoters, especially when their presentation is sprinkled with good-natured jokes and puns and lots of back-slapping. When top gun Aquarius kicks in and leads them into the military, they wear the uniform well, channel their humor appropriately, and elicit favorable comments from everyone that matters. They're willing and able to communicate encouragement or acknowledge a good job well done with a "we're in this together" nudge that's truly sincere and always appreciated.

However, poor taste in associates can be a real problem for these loads-of-laughs Librans. Nothing can bring out their argumentative side more quickly than intensity, and intensity is easy to come by with determined Aquarius in the house. But their Likable Libra just wilts when they can't please and appease just about everyone—they need to understand that not everyone is amenable. And in a Libra/Aquarius combination, uncomfortable relationships might well include their most important commitments. There might be an obstinate or manipulative ex-husband or ex-wife in the picture who's determined to aggravate and annoy. In instances like these, Librans born early afternoon are best advised to take a firm position but keep their sense of humor, to remove themselves as much as possible, and to focus their funny-bone sensibilities on good friends and appreciative colleagues. They'll hopefully realize that the new people they haven't met yet will bring big improvements.

Libra Born Mid-Afternoon:
Libra with Pisces Rising

Peaceful, gracious, and fascinating is the name of the game here! These folks are good listeners with more to add than you might think. They're so prone to continually acquiesce to the people around them that you might never find out what they were going to say. These are among the most empathetic people on the planet. Gentle Pisces with involved Libra always has a genuine concern. There's a bit of a delicate demeanor about these Librans that makes the cultivation of pleasing relationships a top priority. Yes, the Libra ego thrives on connecting with other people, but the Peaceful Pisces personality simply withers in the face of disapproval. So it's a must for these Librans to associate themselves with compassionate, like-minded friends, partners, and colleagues. On the one hand, they might refrain from jumping willy-nilly into unwise relationships because of their Piscean scaredy-cat, "master of avoidance" traits. But on the other hand, if they've been somewhat sheltered for much of their lives and well-provided for by generous parents and loved ones—as is sometimes their destiny—they're liable to put on their rose-colored glasses and succumb to an "I can't do it alone" mentality. They tend to buddy up pretty quickly, out of fear of being alone—but sometimes with all the wrong people. And in these unfortunate instances, they find it very difficult to empower themselves to get out of the situation. So they need to tell themselves, moment to moment, that they can find inspiration and enjoy life, even without someone to adore them.

If Librans with Pisces rising can be both confident and amenable, their lives are apt to be a gentle joy. Due to their peaceful and considerate approach to things, they're considered valuable co-workers, and they might even possess some artistry that's useful on the job. If they're painters or writers or craftsmen of any kind, their likable, obliging, people-pleasing Libra will prosper quite nicely from word-of-mouth opportunities. The key here is for them to remain free to pursue their inspirations and avoid trapping themselves in imprisoning situations that leave them feeling unsupported and too weak to do better. For these Librans, a little backbone will go a long way.

Libra Born Around Sundown:
Libra with Aries Rising

Here comes a bright-eyed, bushy-tailed, "summer's coming!" whipper-snapper. The Aries personality with an obliging "what can I do for you?" Libra attitude is usually a joy to behold—for those who can keep up with their zip-zip, "no time to waste" behavior! If these Librans play their cards right, and they often do, they're some of the happiest critters on the planet. Because of their sundown dinner-time birth, there's an extra dose of polite, obliging Libra here, and with their up-and-at-'em, spry and optimistic Aries personality they show up early and stay late with their sleeves rolled-up, always ready to do more than their fair share. After all, Libra's always looking for approval, and Action Aries can't sit down anyway, so why not leap in, get up to speed, and lend a hand?

With a good feel for who complements whom and a penchant for workable partnerships, coupled with the people skills to make the most of social occasions, Librans with Aries rising might be wonderful party planners or banquet organizers. They're adept at getting good help and making the most of their word-of-mouth advertising; plus, their efficient Aries gives them just what it takes to keep a multitude of people, with varied individual preferences, happy and well-served over the course of an evening. They're attentive to everyone's needs and never let anyone feel neglected or left out. "Slow service" is not in their vocabulary.

If there's a problem for these Librans, it might be their Aries' impatience rushing them into partnerships with people who just don't fit well. And when disappointed in their relationships, they're inclined to get busy dizzy, neglecting their partners while zipping through their lives, and doing everything possible to avoid thinking ahead. There's sometimes a lack of foresight here as well as a dislike for being alone, so an adequate amount of planning for the future and a willingness to be self-sustaining are capabilities that need to be cultivated. Though they're masterful at inspiring others, they need to understand that some people refuse to be inspired. And when that's the case, it's time to lighten up and move along to greener pastures!

Libra Born Early Evening:
Libra with Taurus Rising

Here's a more centered Likable Libra, with a dignified demeanor, who won't be bothered with nonsense. If there's a way to increase rewards while minimizing effort, these people will find it. Their Taurus personality might be a bit stand-offish and "steady-as-she-goes," but once these folks decide they like someone, watch out! Taurus kicks in with material gifts and Libra shows up with concern and cooperation. Deliberate, focused, but make-it-easy Taurus, the Banker, benefits quite nicely from Libra's sociable and attentive ego, but sometimes the bullish side of Taurus can be a problem if it's worn on the sleeve. So Librans born early evening need to be careful they don't overdo the "one-way Wendell" routine that comes so easy for Taurus. "My way or the highway" can create a very lonely road, indeed, and Librans are rarely fond of being alone. If they're perpetually bull-headed, refusing to listen and to consider the other person, they'll undermine the "give and take" that Libra thrives on and sadly end up by themselves, without the partner they prefer.

The Banker is driven by practicality, so these Librans know how to get things done with an easy-does-it approach. They're adept at allocating, whether it's funds or responsibilities, and they take a simple approach that makes things easier for everyone. These qualities make for skilled managers and overseers. If they'll avoid being demanding and intolerant, if they'll just lighten up and be patient with people, they'll discover that "go with the flow" works best. Libra never benefits from a lack of harmony!

Letting things take their course and allowing people to come around in their own time pays off big for these Librans. They need to temper that raging, snorting, overly intense desire to want things their way, especially when the timing isn't right or the object of their desires is inappropriate. When the house is too expensive or the man or woman of their dreams is already married, the key is to back off and let things happen in their own time. This is almost always the wisest course. And they'll know they're handling things correctly when relationships become pleasingly cordial and life gets a whole lot easier. Pretty Venus the night star is the principle of attraction in this galaxy, and she rules both Likable Libra and materialistic Taurus. So when goals are delayed and difficult to achieve, these Librans need to slow down, rethink their priorities, and let things come to them a bit. They need to use their powers of attraction—and just take it easy!

Libra Born Mid-Evening:
Libra with Gemini Rising

What's not to like about a chatty-faced, obliging person who's always interested enough to say, "Hi there! How are ya? Where ya from? I've been there! See ya later!"? Insanely curious about everything that breathes—and more!—Librans with Gemini rising are the sorts of people who are so superb at passing the time with cordial conversation that they're the perfect elevator companions. No uptight, zipped-lip, stare-at-the-numbers, "just get us to the top floor" here. They're glib and interesting people, eagerly offering friends a ride to the airport, and never allowing any uncomfortable silence to fill the air during the trip. Being in motion while chatting up a storm suits their Jitterbug Gemini personality, and keeping people happy satiates their obliging Libra ego. So as long as they don't let their conversation degenerate into rambling nonsense or hurtful rumors, they'll be greatly appreciated. Being as aware of others as Libra almost always is and possessing a penchant for yakkity-yakking as Gemini does, these Librans need to avoid crossing the line between chatting and gossip. Gemini's flit-around nature enhances Likable Libra's ability to earn friends and influence people for fun and profit. But if they get lost, scattered, or mistaken … God help us! It'll take forever to get them back on track. Though, of course, they're so charming there's never any shortage of empathetic workers to get them up and running again.

Youthful in appearance and spry as can be, these Librans make very successful elementary or middle school teachers; they're masterful at keeping their students interested with bright ideas and new-and-improved presentations. They're naturally adept at giving directions and telling people what they need to know. So if it's information you need, these are the people to talk to. Needless to say, they make great dispatchers! In management positions, they're skilled at keeping their underlings informed and feeling considered. But again, there's always a temptation to say more than is necessary or just ramble on about matters that are of no consequence—and if the subject is superficial, they can appear very flighty or shallow. Their mid-evening births are well-served by slowing down enough to double-check their facts. This also helps them avoid those helter-skelter, busy dizzy behavior patterns that make for missed appointments and broken promises. With their curiosity, sincerity, and helpful availability, these Librans have the potential to be more well-liked and deeply cherished than almost any other sun sign/rising sign combination; it's simply a matter of making certain that their interactions with others result in mutual benefits rather than confusion, missed opportunities, and emotional estrangement.

Libra Born Around Midnight:
Libra with Cancer Rising

Here's the obliging nurturer of the zodiac. At their best, these people are won-derfully willing workers, polite and productive, naturally inclined toward rewarding and lucrative careers or ventures involving real estate. They're effective managers whose mothering instincts motivate and equip them to attend to the needs of their employees without patronizing or belittling them. They're also superb deal-makers because they cut all the meat off the bone: The penurious quality of Cancer serves Librans well in helping them to sometimes end up with more than their fair share. They'll generously house and feed their friends as a social gift or just to be helpful, but when it comes to business—you'll need to keep a firm eye on their cagey Cancer stinginess. These Librans can't bear to pay too much for anything!

The potential risk here is that when the obliging Libra ego, so eager to please others and averse to being alone, projects through an emotional, nostalgic, wrapped-up-in-my-feelings Cancer personality, there's a tendency to depend too much on others for validation and, also, a serious lack of emotional self-sustenance. At work, in those previously mentioned management positions, these Librans expect and facilitate diligent effort from every member of the team. But they sometimes unwittingly undermine their authority by becoming too friendly and cozy with their employees when they need to be the authority figure. And they sometimes tolerate too much unacceptable behavior. They might come off as emotionally needy, requiring too much support from their partners, while, on the other hand, offering support to people whose bad habits and lack of motivation require tough love rather than enabling. They have a hard time saying "no," and they justify their lack of resolve with excuses like "just for old time's sake" or "because it's family." And perhaps most dangerous of all, they might even allow their contributions to go unrecognized and uncompensated. It's extremely important that they see themselves and their circumstances objectively. Enhanced objectivity and self-awareness helps all of us to keep our-selves and our experience in context. But the Libra/Cancer combination is more subjective than average, and sometimes it's impossible for them to see beyond their emotions.

Librans with Cautious Cancer rising need to be sure they're getting, and giving, a fair share—without becoming too emotionally dependent on the people around them. If they'll stand up for themselves and steer clear of emotional neediness, they'll run businesses into record profits and earn undying loyalty from legions of grateful friends and colleagues. The choice is theirs.

Libra Born in the Wee Hours:
Libra with Leo Rising

With an attention-getting and sometimes striking appearance and an "I can handle it" attitude, these people might be quite noticeable in a crowd. And even when they don't immediately stand out, their robust behavior grabs people's attention sooner or later.

The generosity of a Lordly Leo personality is a great attribute for generating that "I give you two, you give me four, I give you eight" snowball effect that Libra thrives on. These Librans are great at rallying support for their causes, particularly when they make effective use of their Libra awareness of others. Of course, Leo is masterful at creating big impressions and delivering showstopping performances, so when coupled with Libra's obligingness and desire to be liked there's a best-foot-forward here that's unusually successful at getting what it wants. All they need to do is be gracious in their delivery and let people know that their generosity is motivated by their love to entertain and make people feel better about themselves. After all, a good time among friends is precious, and these Librans know it better than most. When circumstances call for a more serious approach, their Leo competence couples nicely with their "Did I do my share?" Libra. It's just a matter of not letting Leo's "me, me, me" get in the way. When they buy their friends a ticket to an attraction, it needs to be a ticket to their friends' favorite attraction and not a ticket to their own favorite one. If their friends and colleagues feel like their needs and desires are truly being considered, these Librans will be well-received, earn approval, and inspire confidence in others, while getting the attention they crave. What a deal! It's all a matter of keeping an eye on their audience's reaction and avoiding coming off as too self-serving.

But as is usually the case with Leo rising, these people need to have a free rein. They already hold themselves accountable, so they just need their space to do things their own way, and if they make a few mistakes, that's simply the process of learning their lessons. On the job, they need a reasonable amount of independence to feel respected. They don't necessarily mind having a boss, as long as the boss has earned their respect. They want to earn recognition for a "good job well done." Working with children is often a plus because with kids they get to be in charge, and they've often got a "big kid" attitude themselves. Ultimately, if Librans with Leo rising will be pleasingly entertaining in life, they'll bask in all the adoration they prefer.

Libra Born Pre-Dawn:
Libra with Virgo Rising

Librans born pre-dawn have a modest, unassuming, but rock-solid dignity about them and a determined focus that's second to none. They've more fixity than Librans born other times of day. They're not very willing to take a back seat, even though their modest Virgo personality implies that they might. As is true with all pre-dawn births, there's a stubbornness, determination, and focus here, and these are not usually present in either Libra or Virgo separately. Standing up for themselves isn't always these Librans' favorite posture, but their pre-dawn birth qualifies them to stick to their guns when they need to assert themselves to make things fair. Libra loves it when things are fair! Their sense of self-worth allows them to be true to their helpful and obliging nature without ever feeling subservient. When others need a hand, these Librans love to apply their problem-solving Virgo intelligence. With only a few, brief instructions they'll put things together perfectly and be thrilled that they could help. But if anyone takes this to mean that they're easily taken advantage of—watch out!

A nitpicky, analytical Virgo personality allows these sometimes meddling Librans to read people simply by observing their moment-by-moment behavior. They can learn a lot about a person from the way he holds a spoon or the manner in which he signs his name. But this tight focus can sometimes turn into possessiveness in relationships: The insecurity of Virgo coupled with "I don't want to be alone" Libra needs a good deal of reassurance, so they sometimes make their partners feel trapped or constrained.

Librans with Virgo rising are often fashionable, tasteful people who usually experience good fortune when it comes to financial matters. They've a superb eye for value. However, when things take on a slower pace, giving them more time to spare, they need to avoid letting their Virgo, the Worry Wart, rob them of their enjoyment of life. Without people to see, things to do, and places to go, they sometimes turn on themselves, worrying about things that will never happen or that are otherwise totally unimportant. A positive attitude works wonders, and not only when it's applied to themselves but where others are concerned, as well. For instance, when their partners need to adopt more desirable habits, they can be helpful with better ideas, patient "reminders," and consistent "nudges" rather than by out-and-out "nagging." Both at work and at home, these Librans want to be helpful in the most considerate and practical ways.

CHAPTER 12

THE SCORPIO SUN SIGN
AND ITS RISING SIGN PERSONALITIES

THE SCORPIO SUN SIGN
October 23–November 21

These are the sexy, full of gusto, "Grab the handle, we're outta here!" speedsters who whiz past you every day, faster than the speed of sound. Scorpios are the dragsters of the zodiac, ever active, energetic, and highly intense. They're quick to contribute, very deliberate, and motivated to get the job done, so they tend to be very competent workers. Two of their most useful tools are their expedience and their Scorpio insightfulness.

Scorpios are almost always in-the-know. They're naturally suspicious to begin with, and very adept at gathering information, but they're amazingly equipped to do their information-gathering in surreptitious, clandestine, secretive ways. They love intrigue. What's hidden from others is rarely out of reach for Mysterious Scorpios! They see around corners and under rocks. They have eyes in the back of their heads. They often possess a piercing, sometimes intimidating, stare that makes others feel transparent, as though their secrets are being laid bare. And when Scorpios use their uncanny perception to see what's hidden from others, they earn accolades for their effectiveness and indispensability. They're not always the most talkative people, and they tend to dispense information—especially significant, sensitive, or privileged information—on a strictly need-to-know basis. So even if they aren't the ones barking orders, they're most definitely in the driver's seat. They develop a reputation for always knowing the score, whether anyone else knows it or not.

However, it's important for Scorpios to keep things aboveboard and honest. They're so adept at accomplishing things by stealth that they're sometimes tempted to cross the line, peeking into files or peering into windows that ought to be considered off-limits. Scorpios rarely ask permission to snoop around. And while it might not be fair to label them as cloak-and-dagger, trenchcoat-wearing, "Mum's the word" secret agents, they can certainly play the role! But if Scorpios get wrapped up in shrouded secrecy, too suspicious and paranoid to reveal themselves, always loving the intrigue, they'll attract suspicion. People fear the unknown, and if Scorpios hide themselves they spook the people around them and wind up being the ones investigated. Scorpios need to remember that disclosure builds trust. They need to put their best foot forward, remembering their morals and ethics, never turning ruthless or vindictive, which—especially when Scorpios are involved—can result in irrevocable harm. The bottom line is this: Scorpios' power and knowingness always comes with ethical responsibilities.

Scorpio Born Around Dawn:
Scorpio with Scorpio Rising

Double Scorpios function best when they're left alone to do things their own way. And that works, because no one can keep up with them anyway. Plus, they're intensely self-motivated, mostly because their guilt level soars if they don't do the best job possible. So there's really no need to supervise them. The sorts of hands-on management and direction that other people might find helpful or even reassuring is apt to be considered by double Scorpios as needless meddling. They don't take well to what they perceive to be an invasion of their turf. They want enough space and privacy to go about their business in their own unseen way, and when things work to their advantage they use their investigative skills to quickly build a body of knowledge and otherwise hard-to-come-by data that affords them a great deal of job security. What's happened is they've worked themselves into a position where they're absolutely indispensable. They simply know too much, and they've got the goods on everyone. Whether it's at home, at work, or at the PTA, these Scorpios have ferreted out the useful information that everyone else needs—it's an unspoken understanding, and everybody knows it!

But, ironically, with too much intensity, Scorpios born around dawn can turn into the kinds of managers they themselves dislike. They're godawful intense, they don't deal well with disappointment, and because they don't like to share information they have a hard time allocating work; they end up succumbing to the old "do-it-yourself" syndrome. They're apt to be called back to the workplace long after they've finished their regular hours because no one else knows the combination to the vault or the codes for the new filing system. And if these

Scorpios become too intolerant, rigid, and hyper-determined, they'll be totally subjective about everything—and will find it difficult to keep things in perspective. Because they won't lighten up and move along, every little molehill seems a mountain. And, suddenly, everything's a crisis!

It's good for Scorpios with Scorpio rising to blow off steam at the end of the day, to go ahead and spend an extra thirty minutes at the gym if they feel like it helps them relax. They're likely to be good with their hands, and "handy" pastimes such as applying makeup, doing minor home repairs, painting, guitar playing, or woodworking might provide a great release. And in their professional realm, they might use their dexterity as surgeons or professional cellists. They naturally pursue whatever dreams, goals, and aspirations they have, with gung-ho fervor, sometimes willing to show themselves, and intending to use their skills and their knowledge in positive ways.

Scorpio Born Shortly After Dawn:
Scorpio with Sagittarius Rising

Here comes insightful Scorpio, with a bevy of winning ways and maybe some dancing girls to boot! They've a celebrative disposition that sparks enthusiasm and has everyone following merrily along with wild anticipation. It's an easy flow for these people to accentuate the positive, so Scorpios with sweet, optimistic Sagittarius rising can be Scorpio-powerful in an inspiring, winning, and convincing way. We're likely to find them smack-dab in the middle of the winner's circle! They've Scorpio's dogged determination and investigative skill to get to the bottom of things; they're always coming up with that invaluable piece of information that completes the puzzle, solves the mystery, and unlocks the door. But they dress it up and present it with a Happy-Go-Lucky Sagittarius smiley-face that projects a brightness, buoyancy, and cheerful enthusiasm that most other Scorpios find hard to come by. The Sagittarius personality's winning ways are a boon to almost any sun sign, but especially for introspective Scorpios, who otherwise might be too intense, too intimidating, and unwilling to disclose themselves.

As is usual for people born shortly after dawn, these Scorpios benefit from time spent alone, allowing them to regenerate their energy. It's in these moments of solitude that they sort through the everyday chaos that leaves so many of us frayed. Where their peers and colleagues see only hustle and bustle, these Scorpios use their Sagittarius downwind scent to decipher life's riddles. They're apt to enjoy outdoor excursions, maybe even into remote wilderness; these sorts of adventures might also provide the tranquil diversion that Scorpios need to hone their powers of perception. They're apt to be sports enthusiasts and might be first in line at a football game, baseball game, or boxing match. And sometimes there's a bit of the competitor in their character that can easily go overboard. They need to avoid frustrating others with useless competition designed to satiate a desire for self-aggrandizement. They sometimes enjoy testing people, just to see if others can keep up; and they almost always win, but rarely with much grace. Thus, in their meaningless victory, they actually lose—because they've unwittingly compromised their delightful Sagittarius magic that wins friends and influences people, and they've adopted an inhibiting jealousy. No one enjoys a person who wins badly! There might even be some "get out of my way" impatience here that amounts to raw arrogance, undermining all the charm that Sagittarius' winning ways provide the focused Scorpio ego. Scorpios born shortly after dawn need to roll up their sleeves and follow their glad-to-pitch-in instincts without allowing the work to become a contest. And if they cooperate rather than compete, their eternal insight coupled with their inherent ability to find the missing pieces will always make them deeply appreciated and profitably rewarded—because they've delivered the goods with a Sagittarius smile.

Scorpio Born Mid-Morning:
Scorpio with Capricorn Rising

The by-the-book, "trust the system, it works" Capricorn personality brings a respectfulness to the Scorpio ego that allows these Scorpios to toe the line a lot better than most. Even drudgery, something most Scorpios don't easily endure, might be tolerable in this combination—as long as there's a "business is business" reward at the end of the daily grind. Scorpios with Capricorn rising are used to cooperating and equitably manipulating their way to success and approval; they've a masterful sense that started in childhood and continues as adults, and their mid-morning "look to the future" birth enables them to make useful connections with powerful people. They usually see eye to eye with the boss and have a natural ability to contribute as a genuine team player. As business people, they're often the strong silent types but are quite willing to listen. After all, Scorpio always likes to find things out, and Capricorns are naturals at not letting the cat out of the bag. They're often involved in community programs or organizations like Junior Achievement. They diligently do their homework and can produce all the statistics supporting their agenda. They're superb researchers. They jump through all the hoops and legitimately earn a reputation for being in the know.

But Capricorn, the Wise Old Goat, always runs the risk of being too serious and dour, and in tandem with a Mysterious Scorpio sun, this can lead to tight-lipped, sour-grape, power-hungry behavior when there's a narrow perspective and a deficit of self-awareness. They need to remember how to celebrate! Their mid-morning birth always prospers from their networking and joining with common causes. They're humongous contributors, but being too sullen and silent undermines their opportunities. They also need to avoid being vengeful. Because they've often established many valuable connections and accumulated a large amount of resources, they have the power to affect a lot of people; and it's their responsibility to use that power in benevolent ways. They need to remember it's rarely in anyone's best interests to devote precious time, money, and energy to negative issues that are better forgiven. They need to look to the future, focusing on what they can build for tomorrow rather than on what they can destroy to vindicate the past. Working shoulder to shoulder with their colleagues, they can tackle and complete monumental projects from the ground up.

Scorpio Born Around Noontime:
Scorpio with Aquarius Rising

Tightly wound, big attitude Aquarius coupled with Scorpio's suspicious, investigative nature makes for interesting and alert people with an electric light bulb intuition. They've an eye in the back of their head. Because they're always on edge, convinced that "the crap is gonna hit the fan," they're prepared for any emergency. It's Aquarius' electronic vigilance that avoids the explosive consequences of ignoring trouble spots and warning lights, so they're naturals at handling dangerous situations. Compared to everyone else, handling emergencies is a snap for these people. Circumventing danger is "all in a day's work!" So they're often found in cockpits, on battlefields, at the scene of a fire, or anywhere else that requires adrenalin, fast-thinking, and a knowledge of safety procedures. In tandem with a Scorpio sun sign, the Aquarius personality is as competent and "on the ball" as ever. But these Scorpios need to avoid letting their suspicions rob them of their serenity and leave them stressed-out and unable to relax. Their "Halt! Who goes there?" posture sometimes amounts to a very unhealthy paranoia. If they can separate intuitive insights from uptight anxieties, they become masterful detectives. But that's no easy task. On a bad day, they'll check the locks over and over, not quite believing everything's secure. The bottom line is that Scorpio's investigative instincts are extra useful when they're plugged into Aquarius' computerized, World Wide Web awareness. Properly integrated, the possibilities are endless. With objectivity and a communal purpose, they're wonderful police officers, alert and ship-shape, part of the team, and adhering to the rules as true believers in the system. As engineers, they notice the flaw in the blueprint before it ever works its way into the production line. The key is employing their insight positively, producing practical benefits, rather than succumbing to unproductive paranoia, leaving them totally unable to put anything into perspective—including themselves. If they steer the positive course, everyone on the block will admire their fully-prepared team-player attitude and actively seek their advice on matters from Community Watch programs to finding government regulations on the Internet.

If these energetic, highly motivated Scorpios temper their insight and alertness with tolerance, humor, and a lighten-up-and-move-along attitude, they shine like the Electric Light Bulbs they were born to be. They'll earn the respect and cooperation they deserve for their conscientious approach to life. If they'll just relax and be a little more trusting and accessible, they'll be pleasantly surprised by the improved reactions they get from people.

Scorpio Born Early Afternoon:
Scorpio with Pisces Rising

Here come the peacemakers with an insightful solution! With their delicate gentility, Scorpios with Pisces rising are really not good at confrontation or intense exchanges. And they really don't need to be; their shrewd eye for circumventing hostilities works every time, and they'll be long gone before the trouble starts. They know instinctively that contention is a waste of time. They just love their serenity and are usually very empathetic, so they're real Florence Nightingale types, compassionate, gentle-hearted, and maybe a bit angelic, the Scorpios who truly understand that we're placed on this earth to care for living things and are always on the look-out for ways to do so. When a critter finds its way into the neighborhood pond, and the authorities plan strategy to kill it, it's often a Scorpio born early afternoon who shows up to intervene, able to find the poor, displaced creature a proper home back in the wild where it belongs. Peaceful Pisces enables these Scorpios to overcome the ruthlessness and vindictiveness that can often spell trouble for other Scorpios. And remember: Whimsical, peacemaking Pisces is the sign of forgiveness, so it softens up intense Scorpio in appealing ways.

Scorpios with Pisces rising are greatly valued by their co-workers because they do their work in an unassuming manner, rarely expecting fanfare or recognition. They go about their business self-motivated to contribute rather than out of a need to hog the limelight. They prefer to do their job and be left alone. And though they're not necessarily invisible, they're sometimes hard to find. Still, people usually understand that they have valuable information—after all, "still waters run deep"—so they're often sought after for what they know. And their modesty puts them in an even better light with the people in charge.

However, these Scorpios do need to be careful that they don't withdraw too much. Pisces can't bear disapproval, and Scorpio's inclination to hide anyway can put them so far back in the cracks and crevices that people have a hard time knowing them at all. They're secretive and not likely to announce their intentions, so from time to time their peers and colleagues misconstrue their motives—and if they don't speak up to clarify things, they can easily find themselves misunderstood and isolated again. Plus, if they're too comfortable in their solitude, their relationships suffer terribly. What happens if their ability to be helpful is compromised? If they'll be courageous enough to risk rejection and disapproval, overcome their shyness, step up to the plate, and let people know where they're coming from, they just might find someone eager to join them in creating more heaven on earth.

Scorpio Born Mid-Afternoon:
Scorpio with Aries Rising

Here comes a bright-eyed, bushy-tailed Road Runner—zipping through life with a childlike smile! With no time to waste and not a hint of patience, these Scorpios are always "up and at 'em." They're charming and expedient, but they can be a bother with their refusal to sit down and wait. Talk about hard to keep up with! The attraction of taking it easy completely eludes them.

Scorpio already runs on eight roaring cylinders, and when the Scorpio ego combines with a zip zip, "I can't sit down" Action Aries personality, the result is a full throttle operator who's way out in front. When they're in their element, Scorpios with Aries rising are the types of people who talk fast and walk even faster. They take the lead, often with a friend or co-worker trailing a step or two behind, trying desperately to keep up with both the pace of the footsteps and the flow of information. And if Aries' impatience is in full bloom, there'll be no sympathy for stragglers. People who can't shift into high gear when the situation demands it are in deep trouble with these people.

Nonetheless, they tend to be quite well-received: their boundless energy results in a huge contribution; and their shoot-from-the-hip honesty gives them great rapport with the people around them. Women with this combination often prefer the company of men, explaining that they find men to be more to-the-point than women. There's also a lot of interest in things traditionally defined as masculine, whether it's sports, or hunting, or auto mechanics. And whatever they're involved with, they're likely to be quite passionate about it, especially romantic relationships. Sometimes Scorpios born mid-afternoon are blessed with a good deal of freedom in life to pursue their interests—they often enjoy a lot of protection when it comes to cash flow and life's necessities. They aren't necessarily wealthy, but in relative terms they often benefit from good fortune in money matters, sometimes from the generous planning of others, allowing them to avoid scrimping and saving for lunch money. And in the course of their lives, they're sometimes destined to come by secrets and other privileged information, satiating their Scorpio curiosity and love of intrigue. It's not uncommon to find these Scorpios working for adoption agencies, brokerage firms, or other institutions where inside information is accessible. And as always, it's useful information, among other things, that makes Scorpios so valuable to others. But it's the responsibility of Scorpios with honest Aries rising to always share that information ethically, never abusing their privilege and never betraying trust.

Scorpio Born Around Sundown: Scorpio with Taurus Rising

This is an obliging dinnertime birth with focus, determination, and a very definite purpose. Scorpios with Taurus rising know how to stand their ground without budging while considering everyone else's position. Now that's a trick! And, with undying persistence, they usually get what they want. So they tend to be the kind of people whom everyone wants on their side. But there's likely to be a heavy dose of avarice when Scorpio's materialism meets Taurus' hunger for satiating the senses and accumulating things. These Scorpios appreciate the finer things in life, whether it's the feel of fine leather, the bouquet of a fine wine, or the delicious taste of a well-prepared meal. They're protective of their personal comforts, and they tend to amass a good deal of personal property. And being deliberate and diligent enough to get what they want, they usually enjoy a comfortable, and maybe even affluent, lifestyle. But if they aren't careful they'll fall into a "me, me, me" mindset that isolates them from people who resent what appears to be—and often is—selfishness. Plus, they sometimes accumulate so much that everything they acquire ultimately owns them, leaving them to say in their last breath, "I'da seen the world, but I had the farm." They need to broaden their scope, however possible.

There's also an "I don't want to be alone" yearning for companionship here that can only be fulfilled by true-blue friendship. However, that isn't to say that these Scorpios like a multitude of people around them. They often settle instead for a small inner circle, fearing that too wide a circle brings the unknown and might invite problems. The old Scorpio paranoia is alive and well, with a touch of Taurus' closed-mindedness. But all dinnertime births, no matter the sun sign, are destined to learn how to share and how to be fair with the people they interact with. And for these people the rewards of learning fairness are stupendous!

Taurus, the Banker, rising can lead these Scorpios to success in careers involving financial institutions. They're good at getting a foot in the door and masterful at closing a deal. They often do well in real estate. They're a bit narcissistic and usually understand the importance of "dress for success." In their professional lives, as well as their personal lives, they smack of tastefulness. And they're loyal to the people closest to them. If they'll exercise their loyalty and be fair enough to "spread the wealth," they'll make things easier and more rewarding for themselves and the people they hold dear.

Scorpio Born Early Evening:
Scorpio with Gemini Rising

Here come some insightful, focused Scorpios with an inquisitive, chatty-faced personality that people open up to automatically because they're so non-threatening. People end up sharing their life story before they know it. These Scorpios show a sincere interest in others and ask questions constantly. They love their information hot off the press and, whenever possible, straight from the horse's mouth. The light and lively Jitterbug Gemini personality provides the Scorpio ego with tolerance, youthfulness, and flexibility, which are all very effective tools for an in-the-know Scorpio. Innately sincere and unassuming, they're usually considered to be very easy people to work with, getting things done before they're even asked. And with a reputation for being extra-cooperative, they receive a lot of consideration and favor from the people closest to them. They enjoy any kind of work that requires efficient behavior with frequent changes of direction. They're masters of communication, whether in a classroom or on the road, though doing research and gathering data are easy and fun activities, as well. They're usually not that fond of the limelight. But whatever their job, they expect to go home with a sense of accomplishment, maybe poised to curl up comfortably with a good book, perhaps a Mysterious Scorpio whodunit. But the key here is managing yet another tool that the Gemini personality provides, which is the gift of gab.

Scorpio's curiosity and natural insight usually leads these people to valuable information that's quite marketable. So knowing what to reveal, and when and how to reveal it, greatly benefits Scorpios born early evening. Wielding information as a weapon or using it to bait people rarely puts them in a good light. And neither does playing a "do I, or don't I know?" game for the sole purpose of amusing themselves with their cagey secretiveness, leaving people to wonder what they're up to. Discretion shouldn't be confused with deceptiveness. They do better to make themselves available to friends and colleagues, cultivate a reputation for offering up helpful insights, and do whatever they can to lend a hand. If putting a Scorpio "this is just between you and me" spin on things complements the relationship, no harm done, even when information isn't as privileged as it's made out to be. And allowing others to share secrets of their own builds trust. But no one's trust should ever be betrayed. The key is sensitivity. When relationships go sour the temptation will be to spill the beans, but what's to be gained by doing so? These Scorpios need to do their best to take the high road—it's the surest way to preserve the adoration they've earned with their tolerance, flexibility, and generous contributions.

Scorpio Born Mid-Evening:
Scorpio with Cancer Rising

Here's "still waters run deep," for sure! Cancer's "feel my way along" blends well with Scorpio's "look for the hidden meaning." There's a lot of introspection and uncertainty here. These people keep most of their emotions under wraps. They hold onto their experiences and aren't quick to share what's on their mind.

When the Cancer personality's willing-worker is fueled by Scorpio's full-blown gusto, extra hours studying accounts at the office or planting extra rows of crops in the field are second nature. They can barely stop themselves from showing up early and staying late. Cancer often gravitates toward public places, so these Scorpios might be naturals at running restaurants, stores, or small businesses that deal directly with consumers. They're wonderful hands-on managers, and unlike some sun sign/rising sign combinations they cooperate with authority figures in the workplace. But that "hands-on" Scorpio quality, as well as Scorpio's innate fertility, might lead them to vocations that involve direct contact with the earth, and if Cancer's "down on the farm" inclinations lead them to some aspect of agriculture, they'll find success growing corn, breeding rabbits, or other such ventures. When these folks are gentle and well-meaning, everything grows green and strong. Scorpios with Cancer rising accumulate things—oh, my do they love to accumulate things! Antiques, family heirlooms, children, grandchildren, cats, dogs, you name it. And they are never ever wasteful. There's an avarice in both signs that often expresses itself through holding on to property. These Scorpios might hold the deeds to several parcels of land; they might be collectors; sometimes they're like human magnets. But whatever accumulates, the Cancer personality maintains and nurtures it. If it's breathing and hungry and crosses their path, it will get fed—and it might not ever leave. If it's a car or a computer, it will be maintained impeccably.

Cancer's emotional subjectivity, however, can stir up trouble for these Scorpios if they're too thin-skinned and inclined to hold everything in, hanging onto emotional hurts until they grow into long-time resentments. They feel the weight of the world and responsibility for everything. They need to lighten up emotionally. Talking about things openly is always helpful and often necessary, but they're usually not inclined to do so. Mysterious Scorpio and overly Cautious Cancer can't allow themselves to feel vulnerable: holding things in and not talking about them is so much easier. A better strategy for Scorpios born mid-evening is to learn from, but not cling to, the past and move forward, accumulating friends and earning adoration for the helpful things they do in the course of a long, industrious, productive day. It's always their positive contributions for which they're treasured.

Scorpio Born Around Midnight:
Scorpio with Leo Rising

Now these people are attention-getters! But they don't usually prefer it. They're afraid it'll blow their Scorpio cover. Things aren't always what they seem with these folks. There's a robust nature here that usually prevails and walks away with whatever it came for. Scorpios with Leo rising always have an agenda, and they don't handle disappointment well. They can be severe with people who don't measure up. Their Leo pride is sorely injured when people take things from them without permission or question their authority—but they don't take such "disrespect" lying down.

A bold and assertive Leo personality enables Scorpios to leave a big impression, but they need to avoid overkill. They're terribly intense. Flexibility needs to be cultivated. Trying to control everything shows no faith in life and creates big problems with the people they need the most. But when they've learned to lighten up and "go with the flow," they're greatly loved and appreciated and their lives become a joy. Lordly Leo covets respect and authority, and these Scorpios certainly possess the dignity to earn just that, but an uplifting "it's okay, we'll do better next time" goes a long way. Too much "my way or the highway" leads to resentment from others—whether in business, social, or family settings—coworkers shying away, friends distancing themselves, the spouse and kids coming up with excuses to make themselves scarce. If these Scorpios see themselves losing rapport with the people they love most, it's a sign they need to loosen up and release people to their own good judgment.

If Scorpios with Leo rising learn to use a lighter touch, they'll amaze everyone with their confidence and competence, their fully motivated willing-worker, and their courage. They rush in where angels fear to tread, but most of the time their competence returns them unscathed. Their sunny disposition provides a charming capacity for working with children. The pride they take in a good job well done and the single-minded focus and determination they display in completing a project on time are the things that create Leo's "big impression" for Scorpios born around midnight. These qualities guarantee that authority will be earned and granted. But when their anxieties get the best of them, they attempt to usurp authority in some overly intense, self-aggrandizing fashion and do themselves no favors. Like Samson of old, this is truly a case of extraordinary power requiring objectivity and wisdom to shine with a warm, generous glow that will illuminate the way for others.

Scorpio Born in the Wee Hours:
Scorpio with Virgo Rising

Scorpios with Virgo rising are often very stylish creatures with a relatively youthful appearance, but there's always more to them than meets the eye. Beneath the exterior, their minds are always at work, analyzing, investigating, and discerning. When they blend their intuition and sensitivity with their intelligent understanding, their judgment is superb, and they end up as "the keeper of the keys" when it comes to privileged information. Virgo seldom misplaces anything, and Scorpio hides things well out of sight; they're able to tuck away their secrets in a place that's very private, but also right at their fingertips. Scorpio's "need to know" merges with Virgo's "need to know MORE," creating a person who learns early in life how to glean a mountain of useful information from very small clues. In the way a woman folds her napkin or the manner in which a man jingles his keychain, these Scorpios can read a lot about a person's character, background, and motives—and they usually derive a sense of personal satisfaction from figuring out such things. But more than an entertaining diversion, this sort of investigative insight is extraordinarily useful when it's aimed at solving problems and effecting improvements, and that's exactly what these Scorpios do best. They're extremely industrious, and they love to be helpful. Whatever their vocation or trade, they tend to do very heady work that requires a good eye for details: As carpenters, they might be known for their familiarity with unusual architectural styles; as physicians, they might specialize in generally unfamiliar fields. And their neat-as-a-pin Virgo personality guarantees that in each and every project, the minor details will not be overlooked.

A modest intelligence is a good fit for investigative Scorpio. They find out what they want to know come hell or high water, so if you're trying to hide something—watch out! They'll render you dead in the road on that deal! However, these Scorpios need to steer clear of letting their Virgo, the Worry

Wart, fuel their Scorpio suspicions to the point of unfounded fears. Excessive fretfulness sometimes makes for a highly imaginative novelist, but there aren't many other practical uses for paranoia. Objectivity is necessary here to abate the anxiety level. Ferreting out the source of problems is one thing; conjuring demons where there aren't any is quite another. And, in this regard, it's worth mentioning that male Scorpios with Virgo rising need to guard against over-analyzing everything to the point of losing the forest for the trees and paralyzing themselves with uncertainty.

Beyond these potential pitfalls, the Scorpio sun sign and the Virgo personality tend to complement one another quite well. For instance, some Virgo personalities are extremely critical, but with a Scorpio ego they're more prone to keep things to themselves. While they'll make their displeasure known, they usually do so in more discrete ways. In the end, if they'll keep a leash on their unrealistic fears and suspicions, they'll make their mark as both insightful and impeccable in all they do.

Scorpio Born Pre-Dawn:
Scorpio with Libra Rising

Now here's someone who would love to know your business. These people welcome the opportunity to help others solve their problems, and they're indispensable to their friends as insightful sounding boards. Perceptive and investigative, with a wonderful ability to put themselves in the other person's shoes, these Scorpios are usually obliging, sociable people, superb at ingratiating themselves with people for fun and profit. More than most other Scorpio types, they enjoy the company of others; Scorpios sometimes desire isolation, but that's rarely the case here. Not that they don't have their Scorpio secrets—but these Scorpios know just what to reveal and when to reveal it in order to build bridges of trust and good rapport with friends and associates. People quickly learn that Scorpios with diplomatic, obliging, Likable Libra rising have valuable insights to offer and aren't necessarily averse to sharing them; so they gather around, hoping for a tidbit, and it isn't long before their undivided attention is rewarded with the inside information they were looking for. At their best, Scorpios born pre-dawn are determined, generous, and typically more secure than some other Scorpios because they're more aware of what everyone else is up to. And their fair-minded willingness to please usually brings a happy ending with a good, firm handshake.

It's deal making, after all, that these Scorpios do best. They know more about "one hand washes the other" than other Scorpios. They're also blessed with an ability to envision a make-over, giving them a sharp and shrewd eye for what new twists will look good, have good value, and work pleasingly for everyone. For instance, when it comes to real estate and land development, they seem to know instinctively how things operate. They're wonderful at getting everyone on board and making it work. They see the promise in regeneration where others see poor location or hopeless decay. And their plans are not fairy tales! Given how smoothly they make things work, they may seem heavenly, but the results will be earthly practical. They simply have a sixth sense for restorative possibilities. They can renovate houses and regenerate love affairs like nobody's business! Libra's tendency to "wait and see" is helpful in this regard, also. If applications or contracts or groundbreakings need to be put on hold to accommodate someone else's legitimate need, these Scorpios don't necessarily see it as a negative. They simply move things around until everyone is appeased, and life goes on.

The key here is wisely chosen associations and compatible relationships. With Libra involved, there's always a danger of "I don't wanna be alone" tendencies leading these Scorpios into incompatible situations just to avoid feeling lonely. They usually know who they're getting involved with, but if they slip up, it may take them forever to extricate themselves; they sometimes stay put long after the love and respect have left, trying to salvage what's innately flawed. It's very costly in time and energy. They need to lighten up and move along in these circumstances. So for associations that begin with promise but for some reason go south, the best strategy is to just let them go, break loose of any negativity, and move on to greener pastures. For these incomparably likable Scorpios, there's never a lack of new—and legitimate—associates eager to extend their friendship.

THE SAGITTARIUS SUN SIGN
AND ITS RISING SIGN PERSONALITIES

THE SAGITTARIUS SUN SIGN
November 22–December 21

Sagi-magi-ragi-ttarians are the "hop, skip, and jump" winners of the zodiac. They're optimistic, forgiving Pied Pipers who inspire everyone with their winning ways and their Pollyanna spirit. They're immune to disappointment. Where some people would throw in the towel, these happy-go-lucky folks skip away merrily with an uplifting gleam in their eye and an "It's okay, we'll do better next time!" attitude. They're range-roving, freedom-loving wild things, reveling in the outdoors, and given to short moments of stomping frustration like a horse in a corral, but their frustration passes quickly—they see no promise in negativity. They're flat-out inspiring with oodles of good luck, making everyone feel as though they'll miss an opportunity of a lifetime if they don't jump on board. They earn compliance and cooperation with a promise to share the wealth. And, boy, do they know the power of a promise!

This is what makes or breaks Sagittarians: knowing how important it is to make a promise—and follow through! If they promise only what they can deliver and deliver what they promise, they're beloved by all. But at their worst, Sagittarians are the embodiment of the silver-tongued devil, becoming bogus "tomorrow's another day" con men, promising the moon but never delivering. Usually, they're completely well-intentioned, not purposely deceiving or misleading, but they do find it easy to exaggerate the possibilities. Their undying optimism gets in their way and overshadows their realism, leaving them with over-inflated expectations. Much depends on how firmly their feet are planted in reality. If they keep it real, all is well. But their eternal optimism is a tempting mistress! We all feel better when the outcome looks promising. When their objectives are practical and their promises are within reason, Sagittarians are at their best, able to earn cooperation—and sometimes adoration—and never lacking for a multitude of volunteers eager to ride with them to the winner's circle.

It's usually early in life that Sagittarians develop their wonderful feeling of well-being. They feel their God-within early on, usually fueled by an adoring parent or—even more likely—a doting grandparent, who serves to bolster their already-vigorous self-esteem. And herein lies another pitfall for these well-intended people. If these adoring adults don't rein in bad behavior and end up becoming overly permissive, Sagittarian children develop a very inflated opinion of themselves. They become spoiled and grow up to be arrogant adults, thinking they should go to the front of the line without ever learning the rudiments and earning their spot. Even though they're sometimes lucky enough to do just that, discipline and respect still need to be taught in the formative years. With a little humility and an acute awareness that it was their kind deeds in times past that laid the groundwork for their good fortune and privileged place in the sun, they are beloved by all.

Sagittarius Born Around Dawn:
Sagittarius with Sagittarius Rising

Even when they're big and round with a Jolly Old King Cole demeanor, these people trot on the balls of their feet! It's nearly impossible for these "saddle up" folks to hold their horses, even when they hear a chorus of "whoa, Nelly!" from the peanut gallery. Anyone who's willing to love these Sagittarius smiley faces, while allowing them all the freedom they crave in life, will be loved right back in the most delightful ways.

Double Sagittarians are double Pied Pipers, always ready to follow their inspirations and to inspire others to go along with the plan. With vivid dreams and a love of the outdoors, these Sagittarians are light and lively, with the best attitude in the room. They've a downwind scent for danger, and with nimble agility they sidestep problems and bound on downrange unscathed. Where some people run and hide, or attempt to fight fire with fire, double Sagittarians find the silver lining, turn on the charm, and go with the flow. They've learned that it's hard to argue with someone who radiates felicity and refuses to frown. Sometimes they've a redness to the hair or skin, with a smiley-faced, long-legged *I Love Lucy* demeanor, but with Sagittarius' propensity for a sweet tooth, big, round, and jovial Sagittarians are not uncommon. Either way, their wacky Happy-Go-Lucky enthusiasm inspires a successful outcome.

However, Sagittarians with Sagittarius rising usually need to slow down, look before they leap, and avoid arrogance at every turn. Hopefully they learn that holier-than-thou behavior simply leaves missed opportunities and bad impressions. Their good luck and optimism should engender benevolent deeds rather than arrogant attitudes. But coming out on top time and time again, snatching victory from the jaws of defeat, can over-inflate almost anyone, and these Sagittarians are no exception. If they're overconfident and high-handed, always testing their luck with a "catch me if you can!" attitude, they'll alienate people who otherwise would be their loyal comrades and compatible partners. Opportunity is always chased away by arrogance and conceit. So the key for double Sagittarians is realizing that their winning ways are not an end, but a means. Living up to their aspirations and benefiting others as opportunities arise increases the positive energy that's already so abundant for these winners of the zodiac.

Sagittarius Born Shortly After Dawn:
Sagittarius with Capricorn Rising

These people are truly double-edged swords! Sagittarius is sweet and positive, but if they're not careful, Capricorn can be sour and negative. Taking care of business comes easily here, but keeping a positive outlook while giving the devil his due is essential. If these people are heavenly kind in their attitude and earthly wise in their deeds, they end up being in charge and beloved by their underlings. But they're the two-sided coin personified, sometimes bouncing back and forth between positive Sagittarius and negative Capricorn. The sweet demeanor of Sagittarius is tempered and challenged by the dour, calm-cool-and-collected approach of a stone-cold sober Capricorn personality. A responsible approach with a winning attitude is the road to happiness here. They're usually very effective at managing people and things, but keeping it positive might be more difficult. If they'll put a positive twist on a sensible explanation, they accomplish the most monumental projects—because they think big!

Still, Sagittarians with Capricorn rising might always dance back and forth between the sweet and the sour, and, if so, all is not lost. The earthly stabilizing effect of Capricorn lessens the willy-nilly tendencies of leap-before-you-look Sagittarius, so these folks are much more dependable than other Sagittarian types. Capricorn, the Wise Old Goat, always feels the burden of responsibility, but Sagittarius knows to keep it light. They feel the tug of war between work and play, but if they can take a break to center and regenerate their energies, and look at their lives objectively, their Sagittarius perception enlightens Capricorn's practicality, and the result is a masterful administrator with a vision for the future. This is why they're usually found out in front of the wagon train, giving direction with an inspiring smile, and waving the wagons forward.

Sometimes these Sagittarians climb so high on the ladder of success that they lose touch with the little people. It's important that they remember their beginnings and give support and encouragement to people with less authority. How they treat their underlings is the key to their character. After all, Saturn, the boss, Mr. "take it on the chin" of the zodiac is Capricorn's ruling planet, and forgiving, benevolent Jesus Jupiter rules Sagittarius. So character is what these people have come to learn in this life's destiny. They mustn't forget to support the underdog. Their confidence in others is apparent in their ability to allocate. They show themselves to be masterful administrators by trusting their underlings to get the job done, and they're less prone to the "do-it-yourself" syndrome. Though the Capricorn exterior can be dour, their Sagittarian hearts definitely know what it is to be kind to animals, share a soothing word, and care for living things. If they'll smile, loosen up, and let their Sagittarius show, the sky's the limit.

Sagittarius Born Mid-Morning:
Sagittarius with Aquarius Rising

Here comes the Pied Piper with a friendly, magnetic "Gee! I kinda like that guy!" personality. These people are inherently able to put their best foot forward. Their grinnin' and grippin' skills always elicit a positive response. How do you argue with a winning attitude that makes you feel like you're part of the team? With other sun sign combinations, the Big Attitude Aquarius personality might be argumentative, but a sweet Sagittarius sun sign negates much of that. Sagittarians always know the power of a promise, but Sagittarians with Aquarius rising have a knack for delivering on their promises in razzle-dazzle Electric Light Bulb style. They're in tune with the promise of tomorrow and the opportunities that lie just over the horizon; their perceptive Sagittarius envisions a completed project before it's begun, and they're superb at inspiring others to climb on board. These are the people who rally the community. With invaluable magnetism, they join organizations and associate well. They excel in many vocations, but find particular reward in management, athletics, and the military.

As is true with all mid-morning births, these optimistic Sagittarians live in their tomorrows. They'll readily sacrifice today's reward for tomorrow's promise, so they don't usually have a lot of hang-ups. They always look at problems or disappointments with a "Let bygones be bygones, tomorrow's another day" attitude. They always feel like tomorrow's where the fun is! Where's the pleasure in griping, brooding, or moping? Sure, they might get a bit down now and then—after all, they're only human. But there aren't many snags that can burst their bright, high flyin' Sagittarius bubble. The one thing that can rile their stiff-spined Aquarius is a one-way power junkie, a "Me! Me! Me!" all-take-and-no-give glory hog. These Sagittarians' "all for one and one for all" team-player outlook and spread-it-around-evenly awareness prohibits such nonsense. So they need to sidestep these people buoyantly and bound on downrange. Time spent in needless confrontation is always better spent in the company of delightful friends and associates, planning the next project or kicking up their heels in full party-mode. And these Sagittarians born mid-morning know it!

Sagittarius Born Around Noontime:
Sagittarius with Pisces Rising

If forgiveness is heavenly and leads to earthly peace, then freedom-loving Sagittarius with delicate, kind-hearted, and whimsical Pisces rising is a good match. This is the winning disposition tempered by the peace-making "cosmic traveler." Pisces is delicate, gentle, and devoted to caring for living things—the Florence Nightingale of the zodiac. And with a happy-go-lucky Sagittarius ego, the Pisces personality reaches out in compassion to lend a hand without any unflattering "Look at all the good I'm doing!" showiness or "Nobody noticed!" poor-me martyrdom. These Sagittarians are often inspired to create beautiful things and are wonderful at producing lovely, graceful images whether it's in the floral shop, a photograph, or maybe even the motion picture industry. But even when they're hard at work in less glamorous vocations, there's still a "movie star" quality in their manner, from a photogenic aspect in their physical presence to their charity towards those less fortunate. Any career affording them a people-helping purpose usually suits them just fine. They're wonderfully motivated to create a green-leaf effect.

Sagittarians born around noontime have a bit of a golden-horseshoe, four-leaf clover good timing in life, but their delicate Pisces personality usually responds to recognition with an endearing humility. Their manner is unassuming and empathic. They're wonderful listeners, genuinely interested and concerned. However, as is inevitably the case with heavenly kindness on the "no pain, no gain" planet earth, it always comes with unfounded earthly fears. There's an anxious fretfulness deep within these Sagittarians that leads them to seek security wherever they can find it, leaving them vulnerable to overly controlling people who promise a safe harbor but deliver a prison. There's a bit of Chicken Little's "the sky is falling!" anxiety in them. A Pisces personality needs to take heart, show courage, and, above all, be objective. Their lives are all about learning how to keep the peace without caving in. The typical Peaceful Pisces aversion to confrontation is at high tide here, and in tandem with Sagittarius it serves them quite well—they learn to align themselves with people who are willing to set aside personal differences for the greater good. And this is exactly where these Sagittarians need to be: in a circle of associates or a line of work that allows them to devote their energies to doing God's work, creating a bit of heaven on earth.

Sagittarius Born Early Afternoon:
Sagittarius with Aries Rising

Happy-Go-Lucky Sagittarius with a bright eyed, bushy tailed Aries personality: the two brightest smiles in the zodiac! There's apt to be a charming physical appearance here and a trustworthy childlike honesty. What's not to like about a forthright, nothing to hide, "show and tell" attitude? Sagittarius with Action Aries rising usually creates an interest in sports and sometimes these Sagittarians are superb athletes. But even if they're not on the playing field, there's a bit of the agile athlete in the way they go about their day. They're not easy to keep up with! However, though their anxious demeanor keeps them racing against the clock, their honest, inspiring, and completely disarming nature makes them a joy to be around.

Still, an "early bird catches the worm" Aries personality can over stimulate Sagittarius, resulting in half-cocked and clueless leaps and bounds. Staying centered, focused, and deliberate can be a real challenge for this combination. Sagittarians born early afternoon need to avoid jumping to conclusions and putting their foot in their mouth. Slowing down long enough to let people make their point is a necessary strategy here. Aries almost always brings impatience, and with a "raring to go" Sagittarius ego there's never any time to waste. They literally feel sinful for sitting down to relax. Go figure! But there's never a rude motive here. When they show up early in the waiting room, to avoid being a bother they'll simply wander off a bit willy-nilly down the hallway to find something interesting—and eventually someone will need to go fetch them. So it's important for these Sagittarians to be realistic in their planning and scheduling. They try to cram too much into any given time slot, attempting to be all things to all people. They're too optimistic about how much they can get done, so they exaggerate the possibilities. Of course, this is merely a reflection of their boundless zest and zeal, but they do themselves and others a disservice when they spread themselves too thin. Forgetting that Rome wasn't built in a day, they end up keeping people waiting.

"Early to bed and early to rise" is often in these Sagittarians' bailiwick. They get the job done in the cool of dawn and dole out the day's workload with a smiley-faced "good guy" attitude. As long as they refrain from promising for tomorrow what can't be finished until next week, they'll succeed in any vocation.

Sagittarius Born Mid-Afternoon:
Sagittarius with Taurus Rising

Here's the winning "We'll do better next time" attitude of Sagittarius with some sensible "stop, look, and listen." Taurus, the Banker's, patience is a good complement to impetuous Sagittarius, while Sagittarius' "tomorrow's another day" attitude brings an invigorating optimism to Taurus' stick-in-the-mud pouty face. The Taurus personality becomes less intense, and Sagittarius becomes more down-to-earth. So these people have more focus and persistence than other Sagittarians, making them more adept at getting what they want. They're determined and deliberate, with the sure footing of the Beast of Burden, while Sagittarius' spryness and good timing remain fully intact. They don't promise more than they can deliver, and they don't zip off chasing exaggerated dreams, but the wind is still at their backs as they race toward the winner's circle. All the Taurus appetites are present here, and they're usually satiated: These Sagittarians often accumulate enough resources to adequately indulge themselves and maybe even live high on the hog.

It's their "up against the wall" resolve and their "When the going gets tough, the tough get going" attitude that makes these people so formidable. Others see how often their perseverance is rewarded and are inspired to climb on board. And Sagittarians born mid-afternoon are able to explain the mechanics of a project with Taurus' nuts-and-bolts clarity, so no one on the team is ever left behind or turning to the wrong page. Simply put, they're just darned good at making things work. And being in the right place at the right time never hurts, either. They're often well-connected in life, with an uncanny ability to enhance other people's resources while benefiting themselves. It's a "one hand washes the other" snowball effect where I give you two, you give me four, I give you eight, and so on.

Everything goes swimmingly for Sagittarians with Taurus rising as long as they don't sabotage their own good fortune with heavy-handed intensity, which is always a danger zone for Taurus. "Lighten up and move along" is the message, and get-over-it Sagittarius is the perfect antidote for bull-headed stubbornness. There's a fun-loving, easy-spirited sun sign ego here, but the personality can get intense, so letting their Happy-Go-Lucky Sagi-magi-ragi-ttarius shine through is essential. If they lack objectivity, they get arrogant and demanding without ever recognizing their lost opportunities. And if they aren't careful, they'll end up sitting in the boss's seat, oblivious, wondering why everyone's looking at them. It's a complete surprise to them when the error of their ways receives correction because they're always so well-intentioned. If there's any mid-afternoon objectivity here to make them aware of how they're being received, all is well. Taurus the Bull stamina on swift Sagittarius hoofs should bring them across the finish line far ahead of the competition.

Sagittarius Born Around Sundown:
Sagittarius with Gemini Rising

Sweet, optimistic Sagittarius, born at obliging, "I don't wanna be alone" dinnertime, with an "icing on the cake" Jitterbug Gemini personality. What's not to like here? These are among the most pleasant, "people pleasing" individuals on the planet. They're always aware of how they're being received and are magicians at adjusting themselves to whatever situation is at hand. With a youthful appearance and a spry, quick-minded intelligence, they flit like hummingbirds from person to person and place to place, and from one quickly conceived idea to another, leaving people charmed by their unassuming good nature. They're genuinely interested in the people around them, and it shows! People usually give them the benefit of the doubt because they're so harmless and obviously well-meaning. Even when they mindlessly ramble with Gemini chatter, they're found to be entertaining rather than annoying; and when they ask for information that's none of their business, people seem to open up like blossoming flowers. They're apt to be especially interested in sports, from fishing to football, and in subjects with philosophical or religious overtones. They read up on the subjects that interest them and are always willing to share whatever information they have. Boy, are they willing to share WHATEVER information they have. (Oops. I hope we're not describing a loose tongue.)

These people are gifted journalists, professors, counselors, and chaplains. Their philosophical Sagittarius and their quick-minded instructional Gemini give them a natural ability to inspire people with their intelligent information and enlightened ideals. They can be found wherever there's information to exchange. They excel as librarians, writers, and long-distance truck drivers who play the silver-tongued devil on the CB radio. There's probably a love of the outdoors here as well, and if their work doesn't take them outside, they'll probably be there in their leisure.

But there's a need for more serenity. These folks are so high-strung that a rest-easy "all is well" faith in life is all but totally absent. Their insecurities run deep. They need to sit back, relax, and not overdo it with their short-term attention span and their tendency towards no-focus, willy-nilly behavior. Yes, they're sincere—and, sure, they're charming—but everything has its limits. They need to avoid letting their loquacious and convincing manner be misinterpreted as fanaticism. And they need to be deliberate and do their homework when circumstances demand focus. If it's important to read the handbook before coming to the meeting, then they need to do just that, rather than show up unprepared and ready to b.s. their way through. If they're up to the challenge of being well-prepared, these Sagittarians almost always persevere to victory.

Sagittarius Born Early Evening:
Sagittarius with Cancer Rising

Sagittarius' downwind perceptiveness blends terrifically with Cautious Cancer's feel-your-way-along. These folks have a graceful gentility about them that's simply awesome, and an uncanny ability to merge their perceived understanding with their subconscious "women's intuition" to come up with the most helpful insights about people and things. And there are other Sagittarius qualities that blend well with Cancer's emotion. For instance, Sagittarius' "straight as an arrow" approach is appealingly tempered by Cancer's cagey wiles, creating a bit more caution and a lot less impetuosity. Where some Sagittarians put their foot in their mouth, these Sagittarians benefit from Cancer's prudence. Where some Sagittarians want to frolic and play, unwilling to buckle down, these Sagittarians are the willing worker; they're not only lucky, they're happy to do even more than their fair share—Cancer's diligence blends superbly with Sagittarius' zip zip "flick of the wrist" expedience. And where some Sagittarians succumb to arrogance, these people understand that the climb up the corporate ladder starts with the bottom rung. But it's important that they learn to say what they mean and mean what they say. Pretentious insincerity is all too easy for their "la-tee-da" Cancer personality. Saying things in an affected or facetious way is their favorite unattractive behavior, so they need to remember that pretentiousness is unkind no matter how it's worn. Otherwise, these Sagittarians are genuine treasures. After all, if insincerity is your greatest sin, what's not to forgive?

Cancer's attraction to public places makes for ideal sales clerks, if they're allowed to move around. And Sagittarius' attraction to wide open spaces can result in very successful farmers and ranchers. They're apt to own property of some sort, whether it's a time-share or a tract of valuable acreage, and sometimes they acquire these properties through Sagittarius' good fortune. It's not uncommon for these people to find themselves included in the will of someone they befriended and maybe cared for in a time of need.

With a Sagittarius sun sign, Cancer's highly developed sense of nostalgia often manifests itself in an interest in history, perhaps the history of religions or the history of faraway, exotic kingdoms. They might also be interested in tracing their genealogy. But they inherently know that caring for living things is life's highest calling. It's their green-leaf understanding of life that makes them so beloved.

Sagittarius Born Mid-Evening:
Sagittarius with Leo Rising

Now this can be a severe case of overkill! These people rush in where angels fear to tread. Though their striking appearance, robust behavior, and obvious enthusiasm are always noticed, and they have a "good time Charlie" presence, people nonetheless wish sometimes that these Sagittarians would just tone it down and cool their jets. They're full-steam-ahead locomotives, energetic and powerful, and they roar into the station with, "Look at me! Here I am!" blast-the-horn behavior that always makes a big Leo impression. Sagittarians with "I can handle it, stand aside, I'll show you how to do this!" Leo personalities are near impossible to rein in and manage. They insist on doing things their own way and almost never seem to wear down. They want to start at the top, and if they "do it right the first time" like only Leo can, their Sagittarian good luck guarantees that they'll get there soon enough. After all, when didn't the doors of opportunity open to a winning disposition backed up by competent behavior?

The real key here is to complement their smiley faced, happy-go-lucky Sagittarius ego with a sunny Lordly Leo disposition. Warmth, courage, confidence, and independence make these Sagittarians very convincing, enabling them to sell their ideas and get all the right people on board with an appealing Pied Piper style. Their striking appearance and fondness for jewelry often grabs people's initial attention, and their ability to entertain and sometimes mesmerize ultimately puts them out in front or up on the stage. They're natural leaders of the pack.

But keeping themselves in perspective without coming off as self-centered and inconsiderate is a real challenge. They mustn't let their successes go to their head. There's a fine line between justifiable pride in "a good job well done" and outright boastfulness. If these Sagittarians cross that line, they alienate the very people who would otherwise be their best allies. Like all good entertainers, they need to keep an objective eye on how they're being received: If they've put on a good show but their audience is still turning away, it's probably because there's too much egotism in the brew. There's no benefit in an obnoxious impression! All that's necessary is a grace and kindness in their purpose. And how can that be difficult with warm, sunny Leo so prominent in sweet Sagittarius' makeup?

Sagittarius Born Around Midnight:
Sagittarius with Virgo Rising

Now here are some low-key, "Oh, something's on my mind" Sagittarians. Or did you not know they exist? A modest, helpful Virgo personality is a good complement to a sweet, optimistic, forgiving—but sometimes high-handed—Sagittarius ego. One reason is that Virgo's modesty tempers Sagittarians' easily inflated opinion of themselves. These Sagittarians are usually held in high esteem by the little people and never lose touch with their underlings. They also never forget to keep an eye on the details, so they're not as prone to leap before they look. Because they require a reasonable period of time to analyze things before they commit, they don't drive off the cliff like some other Sagittarian types. These folks are unassuming smiley faces! They're well-intentioned, eagerly willing to lend a hand, unenvious of the spotlight, and so "live and let live" in their approach to life that they're not likely to clobber people over the head with some wacky, fanatical philosophy. Their ability to maintain a healthy level of modesty while enjoying Sagittarius' success and benefiting from all of this sign's good luck is a real virtue.

On the flip side, Sagittarius goes a long way in mitigating some of Virgo, the Worry Wart's, puniness. Virgo's tendency to fall into a self-defeating "poor me, I just can't handle it" attitude is nearly negated with a happy-go-lucky Sagittarius ego. There's no moping around! It's "Saddle up, we're outta here!" These Sagittarians can always find something that interests them, so they're rarely bored. Their minds are sharp and active, and they love to dissect things. On the job, they're expert problem-solvers, and in their leisure they might enjoy crossword puzzles, quiz shows, or anything else that stimulates thought. They simply love to look for, find, and then have the answer! You might find Sagittarians born around midnight expectantly analyzing the racing form, totally convinced they've picked a winner. Their Sagittarian optimism is alive and well.

The key to successful problem-solving for these people involves finding the bottom line. They sometimes go off thinking what they prefer or jumping to unfounded conclusions, but rushing through information and glossing over things is a never-ending maze. If, instead, they'll let their perceptive Sagittarius do some intelligent Virgo analysis, an accurate understanding will almost magically appear. With their undying enthusiasm coupled with their never-ending willingness to help, they're much beloved by the people most affected by their effort and good will.

Sagittarius Born in the Wee Hours:
Sagittarius with Libra Rising

There's rarely a better mix than the politician and the diplomat! These people have an obliging concern and limitless energy that are cornerstones to their character. They're people-pleasing sweethearts who'll openly share what's on their mind—or if someone else wants to pose a topic, that's fine, too! Likable Libra's obliging consideration for others tends to curb Sagittarius' temptation toward arrogance, and that's just one way these two signs complement each other. The interest these Sagittarians show in people is obviously genuine, andin tandem with Sagittarius' optimism and winning ways it leaves peoplespeaking well of them long after they've left the room. They've a knack for making good friends, and they often enjoy a close relationship with one or more of their siblings.

The diplomatic, "one hand washes the other" Libra personality makes these glib Sagittarians expert wheeler-dealers. They're able to strike a bargain that benefits everyone equally. A major influence here is Libra's "wait and see" mentality enabling them to overcome the Sagittarius impetuosity that otherwise might lead them to go off willy-nilly, thinking what they prefer, never mind the facts. So people willingly climb on board after these Sagittarians make it clear that there's a fair share for everyone. And what's not to like about a people-pleasing winner anyway?

Sagittarians born in the wee hours are superb schoolteachers. They're naturals at disseminating information, whether it's in a control tower or a dispatch office. And they're usually interested in journalism because they love to get the scoop on people. Their curiosity is insatiable! Sometimes meddling is a favorite pastime—it affords them the human interaction they crave. But these Sagittarians need to avoid letting their "I don't want to be alone" Libra mentality and their "just keep tryin' to please" demeanor lock them into relationships that aren't supportive. It's so easy for them to give people the benefit of the doubt that they end up accepting an empty "I'm sorry" for a legitimate apology that promises correction. They need to remember that actions speak louder than words, and that people who say "I'm sorry" but never make improvements are best left alone to their "I can't help myself" routine. If these Sagittarians involve themselves in compatible relationships, they'll stand in the winner's circle with a bevy of friends and supporters applauding them.

Sagittarius Born Pre-Dawn:
Sagittarius with Scorpio Rising

A Sagittarius ego fueled by Scorpio's grab-the-handle, get-up-and-go gusto is fully stoked! These folks are a full-throttle blast—if you can keep up! There's never any time to waste: An endless list of things to do, places to go, and people to see keeps them hopping. And if they've Sagittarius' good judgment and Scorpio's insight, their lives are an eight-cylinder delight. They know what they want—and they get it! And the green-leaf effect of Scorpio adds fruitful stability to "leapin' Lizzy" Sagittarius, but it's anybody's guess as to how obvious these traits will be with a mysterious, internalizing Scorpio veneer. Yes, there's a lot of energy here, but these people aren't likely to be seen prancing across a stage or whirling and twirling in the spotlight. They're still Pied Piper leaders of men, but they tend to inspire their followers and earn their loyalty in less obvious—and many times unseen—Mysterious Scorpio ways. Sagittarians born pre-dawn are shirt-off-their-backs generous. They're always willing to share. But that doesn't mean they're pushovers. To the contrary, they're usually pretty quick to extricate themselves from unproductive situations. If things aren't going well and there's no plan for improvement, they'll remove themselves zip zip to pursue their "tomorrow's another day" destiny. And if their goal is well-chosen, there's no reason they shouldn't go for the gusto. *Carpe diem!*

Sometimes there's an intense look in their eyes, and with dark hair there's often a stunningly attractive red sheen. They do need to watch their weight, however. Scorpio is sometimes susceptible to weight problems that can be exacerbated by Sagittarius' Jolly Old King Cole sweet tooth.

With ears open and mouth shut, Sagittarians with Scorpio rising are born detectives; they absorb information quickly, and they love intrigue. When they're journalists, they seek out purveyors of inside information and corporate or governmental whistle-blowers. Scorpio likes to get up close, feel things out, and experience life first hand, but remember: Biting off more than you can chew can be deadly. Sagittarians with Scorpio rising need to count to ten before they commit themselves.

CHAPTER 14

THE CAPRICORN SUN SIGN
AND ITS RISING SIGN PERSONALITIES

THE CAPRICORN SUN SIGN
December 22–January 19

Here come the objective overseers of the zodiac. Their calm, cool, and collected "take it on the chin" attitude and their natural understanding of responsibility and authority usually lead straight to the boss's office. And if they've an objective Capricorn eye for seeing things in context, they almost always accomplish great things. Even when they don't own the company—and they often do!—they're masterful at managing people and things, and if they've tuned into their best Capricorn qualities they treat people above and below them with respect, which earns them adoration from all. They're people who can be counted on, and the bosses know it. Capricorns are by-the-book believers-in-the-system, "the keepers of the keys," and at their best they perform their duties with complete diligence and extreme loyalty. They show their love and respect by physically helping the people they care for, whether it's maintaining the car or improving the home life. As teenagers they usually act older than their years and carry out their chores responsibly; as underlings, they're trustworthy in the boss's absence; as managers, they follow corporate protocol and never skim the books. And they're never reluctant to say, "The buck stops here."

Objectivity is cornerstone to achieving earthly wisdom, and Capricorns sometimes understand this from childhood, never forgetting that time marches on. They see the natural order of things on this cold-as-stone, "spring follows winter," "goes around, comes around" planet earth. From early on, they learn to give the devil his due and "render unto Caesar what is Caesar's," and this understanding of the ways of the world brings business-is-business profitability. They're master manipulators, and if their manipulation is equitable, everyone gets a paycheck. But Wise Old Goat Capricorns need to avoid getting so wrapped up in their sober purpose that they develop a sour, dour demeanor fueled by a roiling pessimism. If their total existence is filling orders, reviewing paperwork, and making money hand over fist, they'll probably start barking orders, bullying underlings, and succumbing to a tendency to compete with people uselessly. This sets the stage for discontent within the ranks and denies them the favor and cooperation they might otherwise enjoy. And how can things run smoothly if there's no cooperation? They really need to avoid making things more difficult than they need to be.

With objectivity, respect, and self-discipline, the sky's the limit for these people. They're so respectful of people and things that their well-maintained automobiles last an extra fifty-thousand miles and their friends and associates always receive some recognition and gratitude for their friendship. If they'll keep those negative attitudes at bay, success and accomplishment will walk straight up to their door.

Capricorn Born Around Dawn:
Capricorn with Capricorn Rising

As with all dawn births, the sun sign characteristics—both positive and negative—are more obvious and somewhat intensified here, making objectivity indispensable. If they deviate from the principles of respect, responsibility, loyalty, and trustworthiness, these Capricorns almost never succeed. Their destiny just doesn't allow them to cut corners. It's when they're organized and competent that they impress the boss and get what they want—and Capricorns are supposed to know that! Whether they're children obeying their parents or local managers satisfying the big boys at corporate headquarters, the rewards come more easily if their behavior isn't undermined by insensitivity, pessimism, or an overly sour disposition.

No matter the assignment, Capricorns with Capricorn rising almost always deliver a completed project that soars far above everyone's expectations. They do what's expected plus, and up they go again, to the next rung on the ladder. But they need to remember that winning ways work and delivering the goods with a smile beats a frown hands-down, any day of the week. Otherwise, their overly sober demeanor can lead them to be passed over for promotions in favor of less accomplished co-workers who happen to have a positive outlook, a winning personality, and a whole lot more friends to help them along. If this occurs, rather than respond with resentment and jealousy, the trick is to lighten up, learn the lesson, and move forward. Sour grapes never get us anything.

These Capricorns go by the book, whether it's the Holy Bible or the NASA manual. They work well in any business-is-business environment. They believe in rank and file and they march along accordingly, which serves them well for as long as they don't go overboard, appearing callous and a bit of the slave-driver. They need to remember that flexibility and compromise are functional. Whether they're managing a plant, teaching in a classroom, or manning a Navy destroyer, consideration and cooperation are always better strategies than jealousy and opposition. If they remember this, their chosen loyalties and willing underlings will work together to put them in the front office with a calm, cool, and collected, widely recognized mastery—with a wall of honorary plaques and trophies to boot.

Capricorn Born Shortly After Dawn:
Capricorn with Aquarius Rising

First impressions are paramount here! The funny-bone side of the Big Attitude Aquarius personality doesn't always come bubbling out with a calm, cool, and collected Capricorn ego, but if these people will allow their satirical sense to see the light of day, they'll earn more favor and end up getting what they want with a lot less effort. Not that they're short on effort! But a friendly, satirical sense brings good company to share it with, making it all the more enjoyable. Life's just easier for people who make other people laugh, and a humorous comment with a cynical tone just might be the way these Capricorns put their "best foot forward." There's a lively electricity here, so once they've learned to step out of ego and cooperate with their friendly, "Gee, I kinda like that guy!" Aquarius personality, these Capricorns always end up in very good favor.

Capricorns with Aquarius, the Electric Light Bulb, rising are plugged-in and technologically savvy. They're generally not stuck in the Stone Age like some modern-day Luddite resisting computerization for all he's worth, and this makes them especially successful as business managers or big-project engineers. They've a head for business and usually a flair for engineering: They know where to find the forms and how to fill them out, and their business intuitions are usually right on target. Unencumbered by overwhelming emotions and other useless inhibitions, and usually seeing eye to eye with the boss—providing he's earned their respect—their promotion is all but guaranteed. They understand the system and navigate it quite effectively.

So the key here is learning to relax and keep a sense of humor. It's all in the attitude! It's imperative that these people keep their sour grapes under wraps.

With Capricorn negativity they can develop a dangerously recalcitrant attitude in disagreement with all authority—and with Aquarius' liking for things that go BANG!, whether it's the Chinese New Year or a firearm—they need to cool their jets, relax, and lighten up. They mustn't be stiff and unreasonable. They need to remember that we're all in this together: They should always aspire to be the kindly driver lending her cell phone to a stranded motorist. With a more flexible, benevolent, enlightened spirit, and an "all for one and one for all" attitude, their accomplishments might be astronomical.

Capricorn Born Mid-Morning:
Capricorn with Pisces Rising

There's more watery emotion here with gentle Pisces rising, and a sensitive Pisces personality provides the Capricorn ego with a light touch flexibility that many Capricorns lack; these people are both respectful and peaceful, with an unassuming attitude. They're richly talented, sometimes delicate, and highly multi-faceted, and their ability to listen makes them superb administrators. They're the bosses with an open-door policy. Their underlings are always free to speak their minds, though they might not always get a response; they're likely to walk away scratching their heads, saying "I wonder what SHE thinks!" Yet even though they don't always react or share their thoughts on matters at hand, Capricorns with Pisces rising are still pretty easy to work for. Their silence means they're happy with the work. They believe in the people they've hired, and they give them a long leash as well as the space they need to get the job done their own way. And their strategy works because these Capricorns possess such a sensitive radar that they detect troublemakers and avoid hiring people who will fall down on the job or make unnecessary waves. That's why they're in good stead with their superiors!

Capricorns born mid-morning have an admirably unselfish humanitarian streak. They're often involved with people-helping agencies and institutions or church-sponsored charities, either on a volunteer basis or perhaps even as a career. They really do care about people and are often deeply admired for their Florence Nightingale spirit. But they don't often toot their own horn: With Capricorn way up in the boss's office and Pisces yearning for some solitude, there's not much "Look at me!" here. They periodically prefer quiet, so they can hear their still, small voice within. Often, Capricorns withhold information because "it's no one else's business," and Pisces never wants to risk disapproval. So all of this leads to some serious "walk softly and carry a big stick" savvy behind their "I'm in charge," hard to get to, way-up-above-the-tree-line exterior. These Capricorns bide their time for the most propitious circumstances.

But it's Peaceful Pisces' fear of disapproval that might cause problems here. As long as they keep an objective eye on themselves, all is well. They'll diligently carry out their responsibilities, remaining in good stead with their superiors, asking for only a modest reward. But the key is confidence. There's no real reason for these people to be pessimistic about their ability to impress the board of directors. Yet some fear always lingers: That's delicate Pisces, the Cosmic Traveler. Even though they're not the boss and probably don't want to be, they still understand what the boss expects—and they're responsible enough to deliver every time.

Capricorn Born Around Noontime:
Capricorn with Aries Rising

These are the die hard, "get ahead" competitors always muscling up and trying harder. But there's a bit of a dichotomy between the impatience of Aries' and Capricorn's "goes around, comes around" sensibility. Capricorn understands that things take time—and this helps to mellow Action Aries' restlessness, but there's still a massive dose of "no time to waste" get-up-and-go and maybe even some "butting my head against the wall." No one likes to get ahead like these overly competitive characters, so when it comes to staffing their crew, slackers need not apply. These Capricorns avoid sluggish people like the plague; their impatience and intolerance can make for heated exchanges. They're the sorts of businesspeople who are out on the golf course in the early afternoon—but not because they're shirking the day's work! To the contrary: They were at the office before dawn, got things humming immediately, and allocated work to their employees when they arrived. Beyond that, sitting in the office with their feet on the desk just isn't their style. They can't sit down, they can't wait to compete, and they usually hit the road early. They've always got to be doing something.

With good character, these Capricorns are successful and beloved. They're on deck, at attention, eagerly looking for the next opportunity. Their diligence compels them to do what's expected plus, and in typical Aries fashion they'll never ask an underling to do what they themselves aren't willing and able to do. This impressive respect for the people who work for them earns trust and loyalty. Capricorns born around noontime are quick and impulsive, thrive in hands-on positions, and, most of all, they tell it like it is. They'll willingly knock on doors to sell a product, and they're usually quite accomplished salespeople because of their Aries honesty and charm.

Still, these Capricorns aren't quick to relinquish information that could diminish their control—so they don't necessarily "tell all" in the course of a conversation. Sometimes this is wise, but at other times it springs from less positive motives. They need to scrupulously avoid useless and self-aggrandizing competition. They sometimes get preoccupied with the notion that someone's trying to get ahead of them and snatch their next promotion. If paranoid, they can be rather cruel and might unwittingly end up provoking the perfect assistant to either respond in kind or leave for greener pastures. Turning excellent help into a needless rival is never an effective strategy! So to avoid sabotaging themselves, these Capricorns need to cooperate and encourage rather than uselessly compete. If they've learned this lesson, the sky's the limit.

Capricorn Born Early Afternoon:
Capricorn with Taurus Rising

These people are a composite of the practical businesswoman and the common sense banker who sagaciously knows where to put his money. And that's always a powerful combination for success! They build things that last! If it's functionally practical and potentially profitable, these people are front and center, giving coherent explanations and clear directions. Even though the personality is aloof Taurus, they benefit from an early afternoon birth that provides some spryness and flexibility, as well as an eye on the future that brings things to fruition. And Taurus' "easy does it" helps to negate some of Capricorn's "make everything difficult" competitiveness. They inherently know how to "cut the bull" and find the bottom line. Taurus, the Banker's, "Keep it simple, stupid" approach gives these people an extreme resourcefulness, so there's apt to be less pessimism here than with other Wise Old Goat types. But they're still too serious.

They need to keep a handle on their sometimes overly sour demeanor. Grumpy stump Taurus and "it's all going to hell in a hand basket" Capricorn can create some hell on earth if they don't lighten up. They need to look for inspiration wherever they can find it. Why not let people off the hook and move along? They need to remember, "To everything there is a season." There's a time to work, but also a time to play. There's a time to stand firm, and a time to yield. There's a time to frown, and a time to smile. These Capricorns need to avoid "all work and no play" tunnel-vision, especially regarding authority. Two of Taurus' greatest strengths are determination and focus, but when these Capricorns take an "I'm in charge" attitude, making authority and power their only motive, they alienate people right and left. They appear pushy and insensitive and, worst of all, completely ungrateful for the help given them. These are the pitfalls that lose them the cooperation they need so badly from their peers. After all, who ever liked a bullish and jealous power-junkie?

So Capricorns born early afternoon need to objectively survey their goals in life and carefully observe the amount of favor and cooperation they're getting.

If they're constantly frustrated by hostile resistance and water-cooler warfare, they probably need to examine their attitude, lighten up a bit, and gauge the fairness of their actions. If they always emphasize their calm, cool, collected Capricorn demeanor, they'll end up with all the success and recognition they could hope for.

Capricorn Born Mid-Afternoon:
Capricorn with Gemini Rising

An "icing on the cake" sincere and glib personality is a fine fit for these Wise Old Goats; they become more disarming and approachable, with lots to say. These Capricorns are those wonderfully communicative people who are always willing to share the reasons behind their decisions, leaving no room for confusion or resentment. There's an open mind, open dialogue, and open-door policy at work here. Being Capricorns, they still love to be the boss and they're always in charge, but Gemini brings more flexibility and a willingness to hear others' ideas rather than rule with an iron fist. Jitterbug Gemini's chattiness makes these people a lot more open than other Capricorns—everyone stays on the same page because there's more sharing, and that improves the team effort. In this way, these Capricorns endear themselves to their underlings and overcome a good deal of that make-everything-difficult negativity that often accompanies their sun sign. As a matter of fact, they're often adept at using words to create a favorable impression. They know the power of benign misinformation, and they're skilled at using it in the most fortuitous circumstances without letting on that they're following a calculated Capricorn plan. And no one's the wiser—and there's no resentment!—because everyone's purpose is served. How's that for win-win silver-tongued Gemini slickness?

These people are great schoolteachers; their Gemini instruction and Capricorn discipline work wonderfully in the classroom. They communicate openly with their students, helping them make the connection between their classroom education and the ways of the world. As managers, they do the same, making it clear to their underlings how today's behavior will affect tomorrow's outcome. These people prefer to be in charge of their own domain. They don't respond well to being positioned under someone's thumb. They want authority for themselves as well as the opportunity to put their own thoroughly thought-out ideas into practice, knowing that they're usually right on. They're also apt to be great salespeople, peddling their wares with a productive glibness. And, finally, many self-employed truck-drivers who love the back-and-forth, here-and-there nature of their work are Capricorns with Gemini rising.

But as is true with many Capricorns, they need to be careful not to let their Capricorn negativity run wild. They mustn't run off at the mouth only to hear themselves talk, especially if their talk is insensitive; it's hurtful and leaves a hare-brained impression. But with good character and a healthy dose of objectivity, these sorts of problems will be few and far between.

Capricorn Born Around Sundown:
Capricorn with Cancer Rising

Are you ready for this? It's a Capricorn with a sensitive touch and an obviously obliging concern for others—and on a good day, they're even nurturing! These Capricorns are as in-charge as ever, but they have Cancer's feel-their-way-along home and hearth quality that keeps them in good favor with a tightly-knit circle of family, friends, and colleagues. These fiercely loyal Capricorns are custodial towards the people that mean the most to them rather than endlessly competing with them or constantly chasing them with a big stick. Unless they're dealing with a slacker: Their workaholic Cancer coupled with their "I'm paying attention to you" sundown birth makes them painfully aware of everyone's contribution, and they've no truck with laziness. But they've a sensitive touch and a visible willingness to be fair, especially with people who make a legitimate contribution and pull their own weight. Cautious Cancer is helpful and non-confrontational, and their dinnertime birth gives them the ability to see others as equals. They're ideal bosses for productive workers.

These sentimental Capricorns remember the kindnesses shown them by others in days gone by, and look forward to the opportunity to repay every favor. But Capricorns with Cancer rising need to avoid being overly loyal to people who aren't gracious, and they need to put the brakes on involvements that don't bring back gratitude and respect. They feel disloyal freeing themselves from negative bonds, but, like everyone, they've the right to their pursuit of happiness. They need to determine what's fair by keeping their perspective and seeing themselves in context, relative to others. After all, "To thine own self be true." There's no gain in allowing themselves to be taken advantage of.

As always with Cancer, there's a full-blown thrifty-nickel here, and possibly a constant nagging feeling that they're going broke even when their finances are healthy and their cash-flow adequate. They easily get extremely preoccupied with their career responsibilities, especially if they like their work—and that takes their eye off the bottom line. This is when their unfounded fears about finances creep in. They're practical in their outlook and not notably adventurous in spirit—at least until their financial security is intact. They won't be going out on safari until this month's books are tallied and next month's schedule is completed. But as long as they broaden their perspective and identify and pursue their larger interests, they make themselves happy and successful, and with their obvious awareness of and concern for friends and loved ones they're beloved and appreciated by all.

Capricorn Born Early Evening:
Capricorn with Leo Rising

Now here's a sober Old Goat with enough showmanship to leave an impression. These Capricorns are usually way out in front, looking for ways to display their competence, and if they've any objectivity in their judgment and wisdom in their deeds, they move mountains on a daily basis. With their keen sense of responsibility bolstered by Leo's fearlessness, these Capricorns can easily become the most confident, competent, and inspiring people on the planet. Yet, catch this: Their early evening birth gives them much more modesty from within than shows on the confident Leo surface. So what they expect in return for their generous effort might be considerably less than anyone anticipated. They're robust and courageous, and given Capricorn's responsible approach, they do their homework and come prepared. And, of course, this guarantees a masterful outcome. But while they display rows of trophies, their sincere and endearing attitude is "Aw, shucks, it wasn't nothin'!" These people do enjoy the respect and recognition they earn, but their generous Leo personalities make them more than willing to share the wealth.

However, that inward modesty, especially when it's strengthened by Capricorn's reserved attitude, can be interpreted as a cold aloofness, so it helps to put their best foot forward and show the sunny warmth and generosity of Lordly Leo. This is a great advantage in up-close, one-to-one exchanges. If these Capricorns get up front with their affection rather than stand off sternly uncommitted as some Capricorns do, they'll be beloved as well as respected. This is important for Capricorns with Leo rising to remember. Otherwise, Capricorn's axe to grind and Leo's self-serving purpose might lead to steam-rolling over people, resulting in long-term resentments—an extremely unfortunate turn of events considering how loyal and true these Capricorns mean to be. They know the importance of other people's contributions and they mean to be good to those who've played a role in the team's success, but if they're so wrapped up in their own performance that all they see is themselves, they undermine the team's morale. All they need to do is show some gratitude and be encouraging. How difficult is that? Objectivity is key here, with attention given to how they're being received every step of the way. When friends and colleagues seem to be pulling away or resisting, it's probably time to radiate a bit of that Leo warmth.

Capricorn Born Mid-Evening:
Capricorn with Virgo Rising

When it's time for Plan B, call in Capricorn with Virgo rising! These people are understated and conservative, but their shrewd, analytical, and calculating approach always figures a way to play the angles, solve the problems, and get the job done. The unassuming Virgo personality pays close attention to the details, and, with objectivity, the ability to see and organize the little things makes calm, cool, and collected Capricorn a powerful problem solver. These people don't miss much. Capricorns born mid-evening are the managers who know how things work and love to get into the nuts and bolts of keeping it running. They're respected and appreciated for their willingness to step out onto the assembly floor with rolled-up sleeves, ready to analyze the problem and apply the solution, even if it means tightening a few screws themselves. They probably enjoy better rapport with the plant workers than with the board members, anyway. Their modest Virgo isn't likely to disregard the team; a deep appreciation for the help they get is more their style. And they're often sought out for their advice because they've a shrewd intelligence that can figure out a workable solution pretty quickly. As a matter of fact, there's apt to be a real thrifty-nickel here. They can always make it happen for less, but their penny-pinching ways just might become an obsession because they just love to save time and money.

Capricorn's by-the-book approach to management pretty much nullifies Virgo, the Worry Wart's, "I just can't handle it!" and bolsters confidence. Even if there's a delicate physical constitution, they're still tough enough to see the job through. They take great pride in their work ethic. And don't forget Virgo's neat freak: There might be a real intolerance here for individuals who litter their space, whether it's the workplace or the kitchen floor. But life with these folks definitely has its upside! They're probably the most loyal and vigilant helpmates in the zodiac. The one-time favor they offer ends up being the helpful deed you can always count on. They never let their loved ones down. What a delight!

But these Capricorns do need to avoid being smug about their analytical powers and their Wise Old Goat wisdom. It's one thing to take pride in their problem-solving skills, but it's quite another to taunt others with their intellect. A little humility has a better effect. Especially for these high and mighty mountain goats who so competently play a vital role in smoothing out the kinks in our day-to-day operations. Remember: They've already earned the respect and cooperation they're asking for.

Capricorn Born Around Midnight:
Capricorn with Libra Rising

Like few other combinations, Capricorns with Libra rising know how to take care of business and keep things humming while everyone's treated equitably. All parties are satisfied, happy, and coming back for more. They start out trying to please everybody and do a better job at it than any combination in the zodiac. Likable Libra's best foot forward warms these Capricorns, giving them social skills and an eye for what's fair, so their compromise leads to a profitable bargain every time. They're superb dealmakers!

Capricorns born around midnight are benevolent manipulators, able to lead people and guide projects toward a successful outcome that fills the bill for all concerned: They've the uncanny ability to control business situations without appearing dominating. Keeping a Capricorn control with obliging, people-pleasing Libra behavior is a rare skill—but at their best, these Capricorns pull it off wonderfully.

Their midnight birth also adds a home and hearth quality that serves to take the starch out of their brusque Capricorn attitude, so as overseers they're less high-handed and more hands-on; Libra enjoys mingling at all levels. They make a good impression with friendly—but right-on-target—small talk and a tasteful appearance. There's a lot of patience here, too, though not the kind that allows a person to sit calmly in a waiting room for hours on end. These folks are energetic, but they do understand that Rome wasn't built in a day. They've a "tomorrow's another day" sort of patience that allows them to bide their time during a corporate turnaround or wait for the best loan rate when purchasing a car. Their Capricorn "goes around, comes around" gives them that sensibility. But in their personal lives these Capricorns need to avoid being too long-suffering with people who don't affect their lives in a positive way. Libra's "I don't want to be alone" tendencies get in the way here, and they sometimes put up with bad behavior beyond reason. As managers, they're slow to dismiss unproductive employees, especially if they did the hiring themselves. In these cases, they feel that the employee's shortcomings are a poor reflection on their Capricorn good judgment; they wonder why they didn't see the problem coming from the beginning. This is usually an erroneous self-criticism, but even when it's legitimate it's still water under the bridge. They need to cut their losses and move along. When the people they presently depend on let them down time after time, they need to deal with it and welcome new faces. Their respectful consideration will certainly earn them their success, but to expedite the process they may sometimes need to be less forgiving and move on when situations are not beneficial.

Capricorn Born in the Wee Hours:
Capricorn with Scorpio Rising

This might be the most reserved and mysterious sun sign/rising sign combination in the zodiac. These people are exceedingly tight-lipped and often "all-knowing." And there's a hell-bent fearlessness in these "take it on the chin" Capricorns that equips them to handle unreasonably demanding jobs that others avoid. You can find them doing a remarkable job teaching and mentoring developmentally challenged children or underprivileged or at-risk youngsters. They'll fit almost any place where their authority is never questioned. Capricorns with Scorpio rising are especially adept in these types of roles because, among other things, they're fiercely protective of people who depend on them. They're just not the sort of individuals to shirk their responsibilities or let people down; the guilt factor always plays a big role with Scorpio.

Capricorns born in the wee hours have a good eye for profitable investments; they love to investigate and find out what's happening behind the scenes, so they always do their homework. And their interest in business often leads them to careers related to insurance or lending. They enjoy jobs that allow them to handle confidential or privileged information and excel in positions that require the selective dispensing of sensitive data. However, they sometimes go overboard with their secrecy. These Capricorns just don't feel that they owe anyone an explanation, so they attract suspicion to themselves by refusing to let people know what they're up to. Once again, it's the old Capricorn game of making things more difficult than they need to be. When their Mysterious Scorpio paranoia kicks in, they start treating even the most innocuous information like Top Secret files. They really need to put their cards on the table. After all, how else can they earn trust? Another Scorpio quality that might create havoc with responsible Capricorn is their intense desires that can build to ravenous cravings. Scorpio loves to overdo things, and that doesn't sit well with Capricorn's temperance. These full-throttle achievers can actually over-motivate themselves and end up with an intense, pushy avarice.

Finally, there's probably some mechanical skill or artistic talent here, and tinkering with small engines or skillfully applying paint might come naturally for these creatively handy people. And with business-is-business Capricorn as their sun sign, owning their own business is never out of the question. There's a lot of business savvy here, and a great deal of ambition to boot. This combination makes for a "do what's expected, plus" attitude.

Capricorn Born Pre-Dawn:
Capricorn with Sagittarius Rising

It's a ying and yang lifetime for these people! Positive, sweet Sagittarius is the antithesis of sour, sober Capricorn, so these people bounce back and forth between positive and negative thoughts. But remember: Sagittarius brings heavenly kindness and Capricorn brings earthly wisdom. So with good character and a productive blend of their divergent qualities, these Capricorns enjoy meaningful, successful, fulfilling lives—if they follow their inspirations better than Capricorns usually do! More than any other rising sign, sweet, optimistic, Happy-Go-Lucky Sagittarius gives a spring-in-the-step and a bright-eyed buoyancy to the dour old goat. Capricorns aren't known for their dazzling smiles, but these folks can brighten a room on a good day. Though not every day is a good one! Positive thought is the key, and letting their Sagittarius shine through is essential. A big help here is their pre-dawn birth, which gives them focus and determination without the self-serving intensity that usually accompanies these traits. Always respectfully aware of protocol, they give others their space. They're Capricorns! But when they settle on an objective, they mean to see it through to fruition. They earn a lot of respect with their never-say-die resilience, and if they put a little icing on it as they achieve their goals, they're much loved. With Sagittarius' "lighten up and move along" winning ways, success is in the bag.

But whenever Sagittarius is involved, it's always possible that some overly permissive parent or grandparent served to spare the rod and spoil the child, and with an "I'm the boss" Capricorn ego and a high-and-mighty Sagittarius personality, arrogance can be a problem. If there's too much self-importance and presumptuousness in these people, they get pretty high-handed and pushy. They're quite adept at making people feel used and abused by smiling at them one minute and ignoring them the next. This kind of behavior needs to be avoided at all costs. Being less than kind never benefits Sagi-magi-ragi-ttarius.

Finally, promises are important here. Sagittarius knows the power of a promise better than any of the other signs, so these Capricorns are likely to use them to motivate, encourage, and inspire people. And as long as they deliver—fine! But promising more than they deliver is a recipe for disaster. An earthly, wise Capricorn knows this deep inside, and that practical wisdom needs to be heeded. A happy middle ground between Capricorn's thoroughness and Sagittarius' leaps-and-bounds optimism is a sure-fire path to the winner's circle.

CHAPTER 15

THE AQUARIUS SUN SIGN
AND ITS RISING SIGN PERSONALITIES

THE AQUARIUS SUN SIGN
January 20–February 18

Relax, don't be defensive, and keep an open mind. For Aquarians, it's all about attitude! There's a friendly, electric, magnetic side that glows like a beacon when Aquarians decide to put their best foot forward, and they've a "good fellow, well met" about them that gets their foot in the door to leave a powerful impression. But with a sour, uptight attitude, they're so disagreeable and contentious they end up with a chip on their shoulder, arguing with the wall. If they leave people laughing and saying, "Gee, I kinda like that guy," they earn the cooperation they need to get what they want out of life. My familiar refrain, "We've no problems that can't be resolved with more awareness," is never more applicable than here with Aquarius. If these people are aware of their unusual stress level and realize that they think in terms of right and wrong rather than being open to what is unfamiliar, all is well. When their purpose is to be helpful rather than right, they'll wait patiently until whomever needs assistance is ready to listen. Good parents know this! Instead of argument and opposition, their knowingness brings back gratitude and respect. And if they'll relax enough to let their humor show through, they put people at ease and make everyone feel like they're part of the team. There's more to life than declaring others wrong, but no other sun sign in the zodiac thinks what they want to think, regardless of the facts, like Aquarians do. Their attitude creates an opinion, and it's obvious as a neon sign: People can see their position before they open their mouths!

They sometimes wonder what it was they said that riled someone, when, in fact, it wasn't *what* they said, at all … it was *how* they said it. The attitude far outweighed the words, and attitude makes or breaks an Aquarian's image every time. These folks need to be forever mindful of what they're displaying to others in order to bring back the desired response.

Electric Light Bulb Aquarians are plugged in, both literally and figuratively. They've a knack for technology that makes them feel quite at home in this computerized Age of Aquarius. They know the information superhighway like the back of their hand, and their career path often follows a high-tech trajectory. But Aquarians are also perpetually "plugged-in" in the sense that they react quickly to things, with no need to warm up. They're tightly wound and ready for emergencies. They cover their bases ahead of time, leaving themselves well-prepped to handle anything and everything that comes their way. For them, the unexpected is rarely truly unexpected. Even first impressions, which for many people are illogical, highly biased, and generally untrustworthy, are more often than not "right on" for Aquarians.

This "plugged-in" networking quality makes Aquarians an indispensable part of the team, and no one understands teamwork like Aquarians. They're innately able to see their peers as teammates rather than rivals, and they believe completely in the system. They're regimented and always at attention, and if they keep a good attitude through thick and thin—avoiding the temptation to be overly argumentative, overly opinionated, and overly defensive—they can win friends and influence people in the most charismatic ways imaginable.

Aquarius Born Around Dawn:
Aquarius with Aquarius Rising

These are the best grinners and grippers in the zodiac! A friendly smile and a firm handshake puts them in good standing with the people they meet. But when it's double Aquarius, attitude is doubly important! Aquarius' friendly, electric, magnetic side has more potential with Aquarius rising than with any other rising sign—but it takes self-awareness. Aquarius' funny-boned, good-fellow-well-met needs to always shine through.

Sometimes that comes easy, and sometimes it doesn't. Aquarius' natural alertness is hyper-alert in this combination. These people are born to handle emergencies and are always perched to "ready, set, go!" on the edge of the seat, convinced that the crap is about to hit the fan. This constant vigilance is highly useful to Aquarians in the workplace, especially if their work is dangerous. Aquarians are often found in the armed forces or the fire station, the cockpit or the police cruiser. But it's important they remember there's a healthy reason why sailors are allowed shore leave and firefighters are given long breaks. Stiff joints and high blood pressure are common problems among Aquarians, and they really do need to relax, although learning to do so isn't easy for them—it might even be a lifelong struggle. It all depends on their Jesus Jupiter faith in life. If they stay flexible and limber in their minds, hearts, and bodies, and always keep a good attitude, they end up healthy, wealthy, and wise. Frequent diversions into things that interest them, whether it's reading for pleasure or a few sets on the tennis court, are a very good idea. And anyone who can make them laugh, and keep them laughing, becomes a true friend and teammate for life.

Double Aquarians have a wonderful ability to find common ground and express oodles of community spirit. They're totally committed to the systems in which they work, and at home they view their neighbors as comrades in arms. They know inherently that "what I do to you, I do to me." At their best, they're entirely "all for one and one for all" and they're strict adherents to the Golden Rule, "Do unto others as you'd have them do unto you." They're also apt to be interested in technology and might work with computers; these folks are rarely strangers to the World Wide Web. A great many Electric Light Bulb Aquarians can be found in radio and television. And with Aquarius' affinity for powered flight, careers with airlines or in the Air Force aren't uncommon. But wherever they work and live, their keys to fulfillment are their level of serenity and their attitude. With a good, positive faith in life and a willingness to take a break now and then, success is always in the cards.

Aquarius Born Shortly After Dawn:
Aquarius with Pisces Rising

These gentle-hearted Aquarians are whimsically serene—and sometimes exotic!—on the outside, but they might be nervous wrecks deep down. Still, with the most silently shrewd and gentle personality of all teamed up with the electric funny-bone, they sometimes earn wealth and fame. There's an alluring magnetism here and possibly a photogenic quality that adds to the appeal and popularity of these somewhat delicate and more peaceful Aquarians. A Peaceful Pisces rising sign cancels out some of the stressed-out tendencies that accompany Aquarius. Regular meditation might suit them wonderfully. And remember: Pisces rising always makes for people who think better with their shoes off. They literally let go of stress through their feet.

Pisces' universal love principle coupled with their Florence Nightingale "let me help" motives often leads Aquarians born shortly after dawn into careers in people-helping institutions, be they hospitals, sanitariums, or schools. But with an eye for beauty and a keen sense of what's popular or trendy, these Aquarians are sometimes adept advertising executives or marketers of fineries. They might be friendly, magnetic salespeople with a knack for creating return customers. And Pisces is almost always drawn to photography, especially here with Aquarius' technological savvy. Even if cameras are only a hobby, these people don't need anyone to explain to them what an f-stop or a zoom lens is. They might even have their own dark room.

The delicate quality of Pisces is usually quite obvious in these people and sometimes dominates the impression they leave, but with an Aquarius ego there are also sudden and surprising spurts of assertiveness. There can even be some of the stiff-spined argumentativeness, though it's more common in other Aquarians. A Pisces personality makes them better listeners. They blend their watery Pisces emotions with their suddenly intuitive Aquarius awareness to come up with the most original and enlightened solutions. And they understand innately that the peaceful way is the most productive and easiest. But they do have their opinions and they will stand their ground; they know what they think and usually can't be accused of being wishy-washy. The key to whether their Big Attitude Aquarius causes problems or difficulties is self-awareness. If they'll focus on the way they're being received the way photographers zero in on their subjects, they'll be able to keep the negative traits in check and enjoy their popularity!

Aquarius Born Mid-Morning:
Aquarius with Aries Rising

These friendly, electric Aquarians rarely need a jump-start! They're plugged in and ready to go, showing up early, bright-eyed and bushy-tailed, zipping through the workday, and expecting everyone else to keep up. When they're in positions of authority, they don't tolerate laggers and slackers. They keep the system rolling, the machine humming, and the workers hopping. But they're not slave-drivers. They completely understand and are devoted to the team, and they pitch in just as much—and usually more—than anybody else. They might lack a "rest easy, all is well" serenity, but they're not usually pushy or insensitive. They've the inherent Aries ability to earn trust with honesty and the Aquarian ability to make people feel like they're part of the team. They love teamwork!

There's a "best foot forward" here that's usually quite charming because it's not only sincere and honest—it's friendly and magnetic with a becoming physical appearance. And they keep people listening with humor: They have a unique ability to use humor to open a window on reality, easing people into the cold, hard facts with a joke that's hilarious but right on-target. And at their best, they do this with enough tact to preserve team spirit and boost morale. Their priority is the "all for one and one for all" success of the team. So everyone gets respect.

Long-term hopes and aspirations are paramount to Aquarians born mid-morning. They live in their tomorrows, always going through today with tomorrow in mind. As kids, they talk about what they're going to be when they grow up, and as adults they remain extremely driven toward a distant destination sometimes decades down the road. Feeling that tomorrow's more important than today, they're often over-achievers and are great at inspiring others to look toward the future with anticipation and hope. But they need to remember that while it's wise to plan ahead—who can forget the grasshopper and the ants?—it's not always productive to completely sacrifice today's rewards for a tomorrow that may never come. Implementing an agenda for the future makes sense, but it's no sin to enjoy the present. And with the high energy of Action Aries rising and a funny-bone Aquarius good attitude, the present might be the most important time after all.

Aquarius Born Around Noontime:
Aquarius with Taurus Rising

A good attitude is always important with a serious Taurus, the Banker, personality. These people have staying power second to none, but they're awfully intense. They just take themselves and life too seriously. But they're affectionate, with a warm touch, and they usually show personal concern for others. They like to make people comfortable and are sometimes lavishly generous toward the people who are closest to them and whom they depend on. But they can also be fiercely intimidating with a bullish posture, totally convinced that their way is the only way.

These take-charge Aquarians elevate themselves to positions of authority the old-fashioned way: They earn it. But their plugged-in Aquarius ego enables them to do it with technological savvy. They might be overly serious, making them unpleasant to work for, given their "my way or the highway" Taurus personalities, but they run a tight ship that glides into port successfully and on schedule, making it all look so easy.

Once these people learn their lessons, they're invaluable to the team because their steady-as-she-goes Beast of Burden kicks in. They understand the system and remember the routine. But if Taurus' bull-headedness is too overpowering and Aquarius' disagreeable side is too often triggered, learning their lessons doesn't always come easy. Aquarians with Taurus rising need to lighten up and keep their eyes, ears, and minds open to better ideas; they need to be willing to listen to others and realize that something can be unfamiliar and complicated but true. They too often stop listening when things get difficult to understand and dismiss good ideas and worthwhile concepts as worthless, untrue, or just plain wrong. "Don't bother me with the facts" is never a productive strategy here. Aquarius and Taurus are both fixed signs, so a little flexibility always sweetens the pot. With flexibility and a good attitude, Taurus' financial sensibility enables Aquarians to be enormously successful as Wall Street professionals or marketers of products of extremely high quality. They tend to excel in jobs that everyone else considers too demanding or too high pressure. And their generosity and community spirit might also equip them to be great fundraisers, almost uncanny in the way they drum up dollars for worthwhile programs. Yes, they'll always need a lot of independence, and remembering to keep an open mind might be a lifelong challenge, but that's an effort that pays off a hundredfold and allows Aquarius' magnetic, electric, funny-bone to shine through and work its magic.

Aquarius Born Early Afternoon:
Aquarius with Gemini Rising

If these quick-minded, chatty-faced Aquarians emphasize the "best foot forward," funny-bone side of their Aquarius ego, they'll entertain and fascinate people with cordial conversation and be adored and appreciated. "Gee, I kinda like that guy" never worked out better than it does with congenial, interesting Gemini rising. The stiffness of Aquarius benefits tremendously from a flexible Jitterbug Gemini personality. Remember: Gemini's the "icing on the cake" of the zodiac. Not only are these folks typical Aquarius team-players, but they're highly effective multi-taskers to boot, juggling three or four duties without ever dropping the ball. Their versatility enables them to do almost anything, but they often find special success and satisfaction in teaching posts or a dispatcher's seat, where they can inform and direct people with their glib silver tongues. Navigating familiar city streets, delivering newspapers, packages, or the daily mail might also be dream jobs. They love to share information!

There are busy and curious minds at work here; the intellectual engines are always humming, so Aquarians born early afternoon usually love to challenge themselves with crossword puzzles, anagrams, or other sorts of problem-solving diversions that keep their minds whirring and help them stay sharp.

And as usual with Gemini, there's a tendency to talk, talk, talk. These Aquarians hatch new ideas by the hour and are compelled to share them. So with a sense of humor and a good attitude, they make their point and prove their case with amazing congeniality. But if that stiff-spined, contentious Aquarius side shows itself, they ramble on endlessly about whatever opinion is on their mind or argue insatiably over trivial matters. A tendency to argue simply for argument's sake is a taxing trait when it's wielded by someone who never shuts up. And if a bad attitude doesn't manifest itself through specific words, it still shows up in things like body language, facial expressions, and the tone of voice. If these Aquarians find themselves constantly on the defensive, hearing themselves say "I didn't say anything!" they need to realize that when their attitude is on display like a neon sign they don't need to say anything to be offensive. That's why a good attitude is always their ticket to a bevy of friends and an interesting life full of conversational enjoyment.

Aquarius Born Mid-Afternoon:
Aquarius with Cancer Rising

Here's a cautious personality with a strong Aquarian ego. The emotional sensitivity of Cancer is likely to obscure a lot of the classic Aquarius qualities, so these might be people who don't obviously resemble their Aquarius sun sign. There's less contention and egotism here, and Cautious Cancer often leads these Aquarians away from the typically high-stress, flashing-lights-and-sirens, where's-the-fire? vocations that might otherwise appeal to them. But they're still big-time worker bees, even if they do exercise their nonstop diligence closer to home and hearth rather than at accident scenes or on aircraft carriers. Aquarians with Cancer rising are often very involved homemakers, but can just as often be found staffing real estate or insurance offices or running an establishment that requires a lot of face-to-face contact with customers. The friendly Aquarian ego works well with Cancer's accommodating qualities. Lending institutions might also be a good fit. Just because Cancer is more apparent than Aquarius, it doesn't mean we're dealing with people who don't leave the house.

Still, if there *is* too much shyness here, these Aquarians will benefit enormously from turning loose some of that friendly, magnetic, funny-bone Aquarius ego that's always inside them. And, of course, their cagey Cancer sensibilities let them know just how and when to do that most effectively. If it's their thin-skinned Cancer fear of rejection that stifles them, they need to remember how charming their closest friends and loved ones find them. Other people will feel the same way if they can catch a glimpse of their always-present magnetism. Aquarians born mid-afternoon are often very enlightened people, and they do the community a big favor when they speak up and spread a little illumination. This might not come easy sometimes, but it will bring them the popularity that Aquarius thrives on and a wonderful sense of fulfillment.

Finally, there's some sentimentality and nostalgia whenever Cancer rises, and a mid-afternoon birth brings the ability to benefit from other people's resources, so friends made long ago and kindnesses shown in years past might come back to haunt them—in the most favorable ways! These Aquarians shouldn't look a gift horse in the mouth, as they say. Their diligence has earned them all the rewards that come their way.

Aquarius Born Around Sundown:
Aquarius with Leo Rising

With a robust demeanor and a striking appearance, an attention-getting Leo personality leaves a big impression all by itself, so Aquarians with Leo rising need to put their "best foot forward" to rally support and inspire confidence. Friendly and magnetic triumphs over sour and disagreeable every time, but look-at-me Leo ups the ante tremendously. These people are usually so full of stage presence that they love drama and might well be involved in theater, stand-up comedy, or other performing arts. A fondness for jewelry or other ornamentation is also common. But attitude is everything! They need to avoid being defensive and taking themselves and life too seriously. They're energetic and confident, but they still feel challenged from the moment they wake up in the morning. When they face the world with a brusque and snarly attitude because they expect a battle before breakfast, they'll almost always get one. It's a self-fulfilling prophecy. If they want some enjoyable companionship, as sundown births usually do, they need to stop opposing everyone who rings the doorbell.

Better that they emphasize their more charming traits that keep people coming back for more. With objectivity and self-awareness, these Aquarians are highly effective at putting themselves in the other person's shoes, and their generous concern is heartfelt. From the moment they allow themselves to relax they become more and more sensitive, until their sunny Leo personality and their wonderfully romantic qualities bring them all the love and respect they crave. This is why these Aquarians are often so good with children: Around kids, they feel more in charge and don't need to be defensive.

Finally, Lordly Leo the lion brings a fearlessness to these emergency-prone Aquarians that makes them bold and confident in the face of danger. Their behavior can be downright heroic. But they need to avoid succumbing to a "daredevil syndrome" that puts them in dangerous situations unnecessarily. A long life surrounded by family and friends is more likely with a dose of common sense—and, of course, a good attitude!

Aquarius Born Early Evening:
Aquarius with Virgo Rising

An intelligent, friendly person with an unassuming and helpful personality—what a joy! These people are always willing to consider the other person's position, and they usually come back with the most original and enlightened ideas for their consideration. Aquarians with Virgo rising busy themselves with whatever's begging for improvement, be it a misunderstanding, a squeaky door, a crooked shelf, or an inefficient filing system. They'd prefer to improve the situation rather than react intolerantly to error. With Virgo's love for what's most productive, they're just not as disdainful of unknowingness as other Aquarian types.

These intelligent tinkerers are never bored as long as they've problems to fix and puzzles to solve. When they're academically inclined—and they often are—they ace the test. There's a whole lot of brain power here, and sometimes it completely overshadows their emotions. Aquarians born early evening aren't usually inclined to discuss emotional hang-ups at the kitchen table or get weepy over melodramatic TV movies. Their attitude is to cure emotional ills with a positive thought rather than dwell on them with an emotional willowiness. And that almost works for them, because they sort through their thoughts for all their understanding anyway. Loving logic as they do, they don't always consider their feelings while making judgments. This can be altered by other astrological influences, but neither Aquarius nor Virgo are known for their emotional awareness.

One of their most positive traits is their Virgo modesty. They're more interested in function than impressions: They derive more satisfaction from solving a problem than from the accolades they get. They're disarming and nonthreatening even when they're the most stylish and popular people on the block, and they're almost never resentful. However, with a tightly-wound Aquarius ego, and a less confident Virgo, the Worry Wart personality, these folks can be paranoid wrecks if they don't acknowledge and manage their anxieties. They need to relax, bolster their confidence, and apply to themselves and their circumstances that reasonable, objective, analytical eye that serves them so well when they're solving equations or troubleshooting the computer. "Worry" is reasonable only when experience indicates that a probability really exists. When there's lightning and thunder, it's intelligent to feel nervous about swinging a metal golf club on an open golf course—so we're wise to refrain until the storm blows over. But worrying about being struck by lightning on a clear day is a prescription for paralysis. These people need to remind themselves that no one ever drowns in the desert. If they'll put away unreasonable fears and superfluous worry, and keep a good, positive attitude—always an issue with Aquarius!—they'll excel in whatever career they choose, whether they're accountants, department store managers, computer salespeople, or doctors or nurses. Their modesty, intelligence, and cooperative team-player spirit all work together to guarantee their success.

Aquarius Born Mid-Evening:
Aquarius with Libra Rising

A likable, obliging Libra personality is a true complement to a magnetic Aquarius ego. If we give Aquarius' good-attitude, "Gee, I kinda like that guy," friendly side some polite Likable Libra social skills, we get the most congenial, easy-to-work-with diplomats on the planet. They love interaction, and they're a joy to be around. And they're much more open-minded and willing to consider what they don't agree with or understand easily than most other Aquarians. If Aquarians with Libra rising avoid the argumentative, disagreeable side of their tightly-wound Aquarian ego—and that shouldn't be too difficult here—their popularity grows by leaps and bounds. They're always in good favor with friends and co-workers—and even children like them! These people are sometimes so magical with kids that the neighborhood children think of them as their favorite adults. They're amiable and upbeat and innately able to put kids at ease. There's usually a warmth here that's not always present with Aquarius. Also, in professional or financial situations, Libra's willingness to "wait and see" gives them diplomacy and more time to consider their options before committing themselves to one direction or the other.

But always trying to please everyone as Libra often does can get them trapped into becoming the neighborhood taxi service or the granddaughter's full-time babysitter, too. It's important for these Aquarians to slow down and stay centered when other people's demands become unreasonable. Aquarians with Libra rising are always doing for others, and neighbors, co-workers, and family members sometimes take them for granted. They often have trouble saying "no," and if they're not careful they'll run themselves ragged doing nice, obliging things for everyone but themselves. They owe it to themselves to let other people handle their own problems once in awhile. Going overboard with obligation isn't the worst fault in the world, but it can sometimes create an overly concerned meddler.

Still, with all their magnetism and social charms these folks are legitimately interested in the well-being of the people around them, and that fact earns them good favor and preferred consideration from the important people in their lives, time and time again.

Aquarius Born Around Midnight:
Aquarius with Scorpio Rising

With an intense, Mysterious Scorpio personality and an on-guard alertness, these people are always vigilant, on their toes, and ready for anything. They show up full of purpose and generally have a "come hell or high water" attitude. They're not very tolerant, but when Aquarians born around midnight channel their energy in positive directions, they're able to move mountains. There's a lot of motivation here and a "grab the handle" eight-cylinder gusto to match. No one ever accused these people of being lazy! And they keep their cool in emergencies because they're always convinced the crap is going to hit the fan. Scorpio's handiness coupled with Aquarius' technological prowess usually produces some high-tech wizardry, and with Scorpio's eye in the back of the head and Aquarius' intuition, they come up with some remarkable insights. It's hard to hide from these people! They usually have jobs that facilitate the use of these skills. Whether they're computer programmers, back-room researchers, Inspector Gadget types, or whiz kid engineers, they consider every possibility and investigate every angle, leaving no stone unturned. And they probably have a computer in the spare bedroom that they use to surf the Internet for their own amusement. Aquarians with Scorpio rising who haven't discovered the information superhighway should give it a shot; there's an aptitude for it that may be untapped.

Because these people have a deep aversion to feeling vulnerable, they too often hide their agenda and draw suspicion from others with unnecessary secrecy. When they work against themselves with their refusal to bring people into the loop, they deny themselves the cooperation they need. It becomes hard for them to endear themselves to others and gain the popularity that Aquarians crave if they always leave folks to wonder what they're up to. They might never be entirely comfortable in huge crowds, but they benefit from cultivating at least a few close friendships, creating an inner circle they love and trust. Too much hush-hush breeds isolation.

Also, any uptight Aquarius needs to avoid being overly suspicious, and a Scorpio personality is usually just that. Cautious vigilance in potentially dangerous situations is one thing, but suspicion around-the-clock is nothing more than paranoia. These Aquarians need to trust their plugged-in, emergency-prepared Aquarius intuition and their always investigative Scorpio insight. There's no reason for these people to be constantly glancing over their shoulders—if there's trouble brewing, they'll spot it a mile off. If they'll think positive, be objective, and charge full-steam-ahead, they'll be more successful than they ever dreamed.

Aquarius Born in the Wee Hours:
Aquarius with Sagittarius Rising

Friendly, electric, "Gee, I kinda like that guy" Aquarius coupled with the winner of the zodiac? There's so much positive energy here it's almost unfair! Magnetic Aquarians never looked better than they do with a winning smile and an encouraging word. These people set a great example for those less fortunate or those with less faith in life. There's a wonderful compassion here, and usually a forgiving attitude and forward-looking vision that benefits everyone. And they're naturally better at "Do unto others as you'd have them do unto you" than any other sun sign/rising sign combination. Sure, with Big Attitude Aquarius there's always the danger of argumentativeness and unreasonable opinions, but with a Happy-Go-Lucky Sagittarius personality the likelihood of negative attitudes is practically nil. There's so much delightful enthusiasm, and such a love of the outdoors and the community, that they might show up as the neighborhood Good Humor man. Sagittarius loves sweet things, and ice cream will do just fine.

These Aquarians are usually well-connected, well-read, in-the-know, and very popular. Persuasive and inspiring, they make superb salespeople, and as politicians they're known for their genuine concern for their community and constituents. They come up with brilliantly original ideas and are adept at selling them on the basis of how they'll brighten everyone's future. There's nothing selfish in their motives: Their Aquarian team player always looks for the common good. They're very capable schoolteachers, and might also be involved in the fine arts, possibly performing on stage or raising money for the local symphony orchestra or ballet troupe. But whatever their vocations or hobbies, they've a volunteer spirit that's appreciated throughout the neighborhood and a keen awareness that their God-given purpose on this planet is to care for living things.

When Aquarians born in the wee hours think and live positively, they almost glow with enthusiasm and their influence is immeasurable. Yes, with a bad attitude, these people might be high and mighty and look and talk like Attila the Hun, but there's so much electric optimism here that—on this tree, at least—it's hard to find a bad apple.

Aquarius Born Pre-Dawn:
Aquarius with Capricorn Rising

These people play by the rules. If it's not in the book, we're not doing it that way! They're bureaucrats who believe in the system. And as is usually the case with sober, responsible Capricorn, they do what's expected, plus. There's no need to go looking for these folks—they're right where they always are: at work! They're the same "show up early and stay late" keepers of the keys that we usually see with Capricorn. These Aquarians tend to be comfortable with late shifts, long hours, and work that takes them away from home for long periods of time. Without a purpose they're lost; so they usually feel a duty to something or someone that totally motivates them, and, most likely, that motivation is career-related. Their self-esteem is completely connected to how well they fulfill their commitments and they always know exactly what they're aiming for. With a good attitude—and attitude is cornerstone when Aquarius is involved—they achieve the boss's office and stay there. Often they've designed and implemented some aspect of the system or the machinery themselves and are rewarded for their incomparable contributions. And if they're *not* appreciated or respected—watch out! They won't be there long.

However, even though it's words to the wind with these overly serious types, Aquarians born pre-dawn really do need to lighten up, sweeten it up, and stop taking it all so seriously. They need to let their electric Aquarius magnetism shine through their sour, dour Wise Old Goat exterior. There's a tendency to be stone-faced and bossy and not a lot of inclination to talk about the day's events over the dinner table in any emotionally sensitive way. These Aquarians will probably never feel really comfortable being mushy and gushy, and they shouldn't feel that they need to be; but wearing a smile and generating a little warmth can go a long way. At work, they respond best to cold, hard facts rather than emotional persuasion. They aren't easily swayed, but it's not because they're close-minded: They're concerned for the best interests of the team, and they won't compromise those interests for someone's fuzzy hunch. They hold fast to what's been proven, and if, down the road, they're proven wrong—with facts, of course!—they'll almost always make the proper adjustments. But this calm, cool, and collected, highly-reasoned, "lockstep with the data" demeanor doesn't always play as well at home with the loved ones as it does at work with the technicians and bureaucrats—so they need to show a little tenderness. With some visibly friendly Aquarius in the mix, everybody's happy, and life gets a whole lot easier.

CHAPTER 16

THE PISCES SUN SIGN
AND ITS RISING SIGN PERSONALITIES

THE PISCES SUN SIGN
February 19—March 20

These people are the psychic sponges of the zodiac. Kind, whimsical, idealistic Pisceans are some of the most cooperative and unassuming people on the planet. They've a delicate receptiveness that puts them in tune with the vibrations around them, and they filter their perceptions through their emotions automatically. With their mouths shut and their ears open, they learn by absorbing information rather than rigorously processing, analyzing, and sorting it. They listen before they speak; in fact, getting the most innocuous information out of them can be a lifetime chore. But they're blessed with oodles of talent and amazingly vivid imaginations that usually benefit their artistry. Inspired to pursue the things they love, Pisceans sometimes become the stereotypical starving artist, quitting their day job in the naïve belief that a masterpiece painting, a blockbuster novel, or a starring role is magically just around the corner. They're wizards at living on thin air for as long as it takes to realize their dreams.

There's a delicate and fragile quality in Pisceans that sometimes manifests itself even in their physical appearance. At times their cosmic consciousness gets weighed down by the sobering requirements of life on this cold-as-stone planet. They're truly the gentle cosmic travelers, longing to soar above the material and the mundane, and they absolutely wither in the face of intensity. So, POOF! They disappear. No one vanishes into the night quicker than these scaredy-cats. But the nighttime energizes them. Nocturnal by nature, they sidestep crowds by shopping in the evening and often prefer the late shift at work and in their leisure, too. They find serenity in solitude, and they avoid disagreement simply by clamming up and refusing to take a position. Deploring confrontation and insisting on keeping things peaceful and flowing, they shrewdly circumvent intense situations. Sometimes there's an unceasing anxiety that others will totally disapprove of them no matter what they do. So they find it easier to withdraw and keep silent, as if muteness absolves them of any responsibility. This might be a fairly effective way of avoiding confrontation, but at the same time it isolates them from the people who care the most about them. Their friends and loved ones are left to wonder, "What's on her mind? Where is she? How's she feeling?" While Pisceans are off hiding from the harshness of the world, others are made to feel left out.

Pisceans are gentle, kindhearted people with a bit of Florence Nightingale in their demeanor; their simple purpose is to care for living things. They need to realize that heavenly kindness comes with earthly protection. Taking courage and stepping out into the light brings them more opportunities; having enough courage to speak their mind allows people to know them better and to appreciate their gentle hearts and vivid imaginations. Of course, Peaceful Pisceans always do better when they feel less threatened; they're the masters of illusion, always adept at pulling off a slick disappearing act. But there's tenderness and talent here that shouldn't be boxed or bottled up, and courageously swimming to the surface and into the open—for all to see—will guarantee success and unparalleled achievement.

Pisces Born Around Dawn:
Pisces with Pisces Rising

Pisceans with Peaceful Pisces rising are extra soft-hearted, whimsical, and kind, and they're sometimes fascinating and glamorous. They've an obviously delicate quality about them, and they draw people to them with their empathy. They mean to be helpful, but when faced with people who are just too emotionally needy, they feel the pain so keenly that they transfer it to themselves. Sometimes, however, if they're more in tune with their spiritual side, they can magically let the pain pass through them, relieving both the other person and themselves. There's a genuine Florence Nightingale spirit here, and a wonderful ability to patiently listen, but they're so very delicate. They might be very white-skinned, with long, slender fingers and toes, and they sometimes have very full lips. And they think better with their shoes off. So if they've big issues to consider, it might be a good idea to kick off the old Nikes.

In the workplace, if Pisceans born at dawn are left alone to perform their duties without being subjected to undue intensity or pressure, they complete things with precision, always finely polished and on time. They won't require fanfare, challenge the boss, or make waves with colleagues. But once voices are raised and confrontation is at hand, they'll either disappear—POOF!—or break down under the intensity. And when they're extremely talented and accomplished—and they often are—there's a potential for arrogance, in which case they won't take kindly to even the most constructive criticism. Sadly, there's sometimes a prima donna lurking just beneath the surface. They're often drawn to medical careers, movie sets, or the fine arts. And they deal with the strains of those conditions by making themselves scarce. They're master allocators when they need to be, conveniently disappearing behind a closed door or the velvet curtain to allow others to carry out their duties and put on the show—but always with the same freedom they request for themselves.

However, they do need to avoid becoming *too* incommunicado. A little solitude is one thing, but a full-blown vanishing act is another. They need to remember that even when they're silent or unseen, they're still responsible for the impression they leave. And if they'll courageously and confidently reveal themselves, the impression they leave will always be deeply appreciated and respected—because their compassion and concern for others is genuinely a beautiful thing.

Pisces Born Shortly After Dawn:
Pisces with Aries Rising

Now here's a delicate person with a childlike charm. Attractive and absolutely fascinating, these Pisceans just can't go unnoticed, although they might prefer to. Drawing attention and attracting a crowd is rarely Pisces' ultimate objective. And if there's too much heat and intensity, these people are apt to disappear like a beautiful tropical fish, darting away or blending into the coral. These are the less obtrusive but still provocative movie stars for whom the flashing cameras and the endless line of paparazzi are a bit too demanding. Aries' childlike honesty, bubbly enthusiasm, and boundless energy make these people less withdrawn and secretive than other Pisceans, so it's easier for them to build trust with people. They're less likely to isolate themselves. But they're still Pisceans, so they'll take cover if there's too much scrutiny and pressure. And that's not always bad! They do need their time alone to regenerate themselves.

With Pisces' interest in medicine and Aries' quick, hard-body efficiency, these folks make marvelous doctors. In any vocation, they surprise their peers with their effectiveness. But a Pisces sun sign takes the edge off of Aries' brash impatience, so they're less likely to show up inconveniently early. Pisceans never want to be an inconvenience. Rushing, bothering, and annoying people is certainly going to invite confrontation—and Pisceans abhor confrontation! But the energy level here is still amazing. With Pisces' penchant for the nighttime and Aries' early morning vitality, Pisceans with Action Aries rising can work two shifts a day and still enjoy dinner at the nightclub or take in a late show with friends. Bright-eyed and bushy tailed Aries is alive and well in this combination, and four or five hours of sleep a night and a catnap here and there is sometimes all these people need.

As long as these Pisceans allow themselves their solitude when they feel they need it, they'll be able to face each day with eagerness and confidence. But, sometimes, when the telephone is ringing off the hook, they'll do well to back off and let the answering machine handle a few calls.

Pisces Born Mid-Morning:
Pisces with Taurus Rising

Sturdy Taurus' steady-as-you-go practicality and good taste are a fine complement to delicate Pisces' idealism. Taurus, the Banker, brings quality, focus, and determination to Pisceans' wondrous ways. Plus, their mid-morning birth gives these folks a vision for tomorrow, so with Pisces' vivid imagination and Taurus' focus there's an ability to set goals and accomplish them.

Pisceans with Taurus rising might still be soft-spoken, but a Taurus personality equips them to speak up if they've a contribution to make. Bullish Taurus doesn't do much "shrinking violet." And Taurus' materialism gives these people a greater appetite for earthly comforts. There's a tastefulness here, and a love for the material, that looks for—and revels in—goods and merchandise of higher quality. These people usually have a rather dignified demeanor. But they're genuinely kind and generous. They willingly share with others, and when they meet with financial success—as they often do—their Pisces Florence Nightingale fuels a philanthropic spirit that makes them much beloved benefactors. And their methods of attaining success might look amazingly easy to the casual onlooker. Taurus' powerful ability to attract people, things, and opportunity is alive and well here, coupled with Pisces' fascinating concepts. Remember, Pisceans are masters of illusion. They might seem to be way out in front, pushing for their agenda, when in fact it's their "keep it simple" shrewdness in the back room that cements the deal.

The key for Pisceans born mid-morning is to curb the intensity of their Taurus personalities. Bullheaded intolerance is always possible when the Beast of

Burden enters the picture, but if anyone is ill-served by heavy-handed intensity it's Peaceful Pisces. We always get what we want in life by enhancing the positive traits of our sun sign. Especially for these peaceful people, inviting unnecessary confrontation is a prescription for disaster. Self-awareness is cornerstone to avoiding rough waters and ensuring the smooth sailing that Pisces loves.

Pisces Born Around Noontime:
Pisces with Gemini Rising

A peaceful, "don't rock the boat" Pisces with a chatty, "icing on the cake" personality and a willingness to take charge and give direction—now that's a special set of characteristics! Most take-charge types are more intimidating than these folks, but here there's a craving for open dialogue with everyone, whether it's their underlings or the boss. Youthful, spry, and almost always inoffensive, Pisceans with Gemini rising are the most conversant Pisceans of all. They're the friendly folks you want to ride in the elevator with, always offering a nicety for the day: "Hi, how are ya? Where ya from? I've been there. See ya later." Their cordiality is sincere and even entertaining. There are quick minds at work here, powered by a fanciful imagination; their curiosity is insatiable. They usually love to read, and fiction is often their literary cup of tea. And if they've read an interesting book or heard an interesting tidbit of information, they'll readily share it at the water cooler.

But these Pisceans need to double-check their information to avoid gossip and innuendo. Pisces is a believer and Gemini is a busy mind, so misinformation is their nemesis. The tongue is a double-edged sword, isn't it? With a heartfelt "howdy-do" and a profusion of winsome words, these people have a wonderful knack for making others feel accepted and at ease; but if the talk turns to half-baked ideas or—heaven forbid!—hurtful gossip, negative impressions are left, reputations are injured, and friendships are compromised. Yes, Pisceans with Jitterbug Gemini rising are quick-minded, but they don't always concentrate well and get to the bottom of things; they might come to erroneous conclusions by collecting small pieces of information here and there and believing they've put together a complete picture, when actually all they have are unrelated fragments. Without discipline, they can find themselves spreading stories that are partly true and partly dreamed up, but always misleading. To avoid coming off as superficial nitwits or the kings and queens of useless information, it's important they slow down, get an overall view of the issue, and be certain they've verified their facts.

But they're well-intended, nice people and gifted managers—their noontime birth usually puts them in charge. They hire good people, they facilitate cooperation and teamwork, and they leave their team alone to do their jobs their own way. They value their own space so much that they usually give others the same consideration. Some of their downtime might even be spent in meditation: It helps them center and calm their restless minds and peaceful egos. Even a little quiet concentration now and then might be just the ticket to ensure that they've organized their thoughts enough to communicate clearly, truthfully, and effectively the next time they exercise their silver tongues.

Pisces Born Early Afternoon:
Pisces with Cancer Rising

So much depends on how wisely objective these people are about themselves and their circumstances. There's a lot of totally subjective watery emotion here that can quickly turn in on itself, so if they're unable to stand off and see themselves in context they're apt to be too influenced by the opinions of others. Pisceans with Cancer rising are some of the most unassuming, gentle-hearted people on the planet. They're very involved in the lives of their loved ones; family is all-important to them, and nurturing loved ones is usually their Number One priority. And they're extremely industrious. When Cancer's willing-worker kicks in, everyone within shouting distance is well fed and bedded down comfortably. These Pisceans are buzz saws on the job, and after hours and on weekends they apply the same energy and industriousness to sniffing out bargains and wheedling good deals. Cancer's thrifty nickel is in full bloom here. They use the shrewdness of Pisces and the cageyness of Cautious Cancer to come at things sideways, getting what they want in the cleverest of ways. They're superb at letting people think they're up to one thing when they're really up to something else—reading their motives can be a challenge. But their light touch is so inoffensive! They're not Scorpion dangerous, but a crab will still pinch you. Nonetheless, they're beloved in the neighborhood because they have the greatest garage sales and their soup bowl is big enough to feed everyone. They're sometimes painfully aware of the necessities of life, so they save everything; their attics are bulging with things they're fully convinced will be of use in the future. And if not, they'll give the stuff to some poor family—or sell it at the garage sale!

But it's Pisces' fear of disapproval and Cancer's fear of rejection that sometimes gets the best of them. They have a hard time being straightforward with their opinions, and might cave in immediately after finally mustering the courage to speak their minds. In these cases, they do put their cards on the table, but when the other party asks, "Is that so?" they back off with "Well, maybe I overstated things." These Pisceans need to avoid being wimpy and stand their ground. They too easily let others lean on them unhealthily and often take people under their wing who don't make a contribution of their own. When this happens, they end up as enablers rather than the helping hand. They need to realize that if these people continue to perpetuate the same bad behavior, all they're doing with their help is throwing good energy after bad. Sooner or later resentment sets in and they break the cycle—but the better strategy is to avoid these situations in the first place by being more discriminating in their judgment and more objective in their relationships.

Pisceans born early afternoon deserve recognition and gratitude for their wonderfully gentle efforts, their endless contributions, and their common decency. They really need to be appreciated for their delicate, nurturing nature, and they deserve the same emotional support they so willingly give to others. The key here is objectivity and a willingness to stand their ground. Because these kind-hearted, industrious worker bees reap their rewards the old fashioned way: They earn them!

Pisces Born Mid-Afternoon:
Pisces with Leo Rising

Now here's a wild imagination teamed up with an ability to leave big impressions. And when an artistic Pisces ego teams with theatrical Leo the actor rising—you get people who love drama! They're masterful at creating an image and presenting it in the most impressive ways. And they're adept at selling themselves and their concepts. Now that's a switch for reclusive Pisces! The natural shyness of Pisces is all but lost with Leo rising, and with their up-on-the-stage demeanor and their craving for attention, these folks might not be easily recognizable as whimsical Pisceans. There's usually a penchant for jewelry here, too. But Pisces is fascinating and Leo says "Look at me!" so a little outlandishness might be exactly what's intended. There's no Piscean "shrinking violet" hide-and-go-seek routine here! These people present themselves as sturdy and capable, with a heaping helping of out-front, lion-hearted courage. They inspire confidence with an "I can handle it" attitude. But they're still Pisceans, so their motive may be totally obscured. They're not apt to shy from center stage, but it's anybody's guess as to what they're really up to. Just remember that Pisces is a master of illusion, so buckle up for a surprise ending. And don't step on their pride!

Pisceans born mid-afternoon are usually quite robust and may not need a great deal of sleep. They tend to be night owls, staying up working—or playing—into the early hours but still greeting the morning with enthusiasm. Sometimes, their physical constitution just doesn't require much downtime.

They're exceptionally affectionate and romantic, and they adore children. They're often the kinds of people who can entertain the nieces and nephews for hours with magic tricks, riddles, and playacting. They give of themselves so freely! There's nary a complaint and, given time, their generosities often come back full circle. With these Pisceans, it isn't uncommon for old kindnesses to be repaid tenfold, some years down the road.

But the key here is using that Lordly Leo personality to get attention, spark interest, and open doors. With their heavenly kindness, artistic talent, and vivid imagination, Pisceans have a lot to offer the world—they're just sometimes so doggoned hard to find. They hide themselves as if they've something to be ashamed of. A dose of "Look at me!" Leo is just what the doctor ordered.

Pisces Born Around Sundown:
Pisces with Virgo Rising

For a helping hand or a shoulder to cry on, these gentle hearts are the people to call. But there's a firm lesson in life for these kindly Pisceans born around sundown. They're so prone to the universal love principle of Pisces that they often sell themselves down the river, ending up with less than their fair share of consideration. They too often give without good judgment. They need to consider whether or not their helpfulness is constructive for the recipient and will be answered with gratitude and respect. Though it's certainly righteous to give selflessly, it's of primary importance that these people learn to treat themselves fairly while giving to the people they care about the most. Helpful and obliging Pisceans with Virgo rising are simply too modest, unassuming, and no-maintenance. They can always be counted on to do their fair share, and with Virgo there's a bit of the "neat freak," so they're quite willing to follow after their loved ones, picking up the mess. There's just too much subservience here! If they'll implement their Virgo cleverness and Pisces imagination, they can create very viable exchanges wherein everyone is well-served and happy—including themselves. The effect in their lives of learning this fairness-to-themselves principle is stupendous: Their contribution is sizably increased because they don't waste their time in unproductive situations. That's a great bargain for these sweet, often stylish, people who are so adept at putting themselves in the other person's shoes.

There's a needle-sharp intelligence here. These Pisceans are superb bean-counters, never losing track of a single penny. They excel at anything that requires precision. And with Virgo's analytical skills and Pisces' fervent desire to help and heal, they might be expert medical researchers or very capable doctors or nurses. Also, Virgo's keen attention to detail and Pisces' talent for listening makes these people highly sensitive to variations in pitch and tone, so they're often very proficient musicians.

With so much going for them, it's important that these Pisceans don't undermine their vast potential by investing themselves in incompatible relationships. In tandem with Pisces' fear of confrontation, Virgo, the Worry Wart, can create the consummate "cave-in" artist. They need to avoid going from helpmate to human doormat. Sometimes, there's a fine line between the two, and without good judgment and a strong backbone these Pisceans can cross that line without ever noticing it. But if they learn to be as fair to themselves as they are to others, the sky's the limit.

Pisces Born Early Evening:
Pisces with Libra Rising

Well, let's create some harmony and some win-win situations for everyone! These exceptionally kind, considerate people strive to be productive, care for living things, and help others realize equitable solutions. They're superb at striking a happy medium and keeping everyone satisfied. After all, Pisces is the best listener in the zodiac, and Likable Libra wants to be fair. With their wonderful social skills and an innate ability to "share and share alike," These Pisceans constantly earn favor with their polite words and kind deeds. They're more outgoing than many other Pisceans and much less fearful of disclosure. And Pisceans born early evening aren't as wary of confrontation because they know how to nip contention in the bud with their agreeable diplomacy. There's a keen understanding here that "one hand washes the other," so these folks almost always know just what to bring to the table to be well-received and still complete their purpose. And if worse comes to worst and no agreement is possible, their Libra sense of "wait and see" enables them to go with the flow until the fog dissipates and the options improve. But don't pressure them for decisions! They're waiting for an inspiring option to appear.

And the word does get out about them. People remember how pleasant these Pisceans were to work with and how imaginative, insightful, and—above all—useful their input was. So, as usual, Likable Libra benefits tremendously from word-of-mouth. True, Pisceans don't usually prefer the limelight—but these people are sought out for their good company because they're fascinating! They're apt to blush when praised because their subjective and somewhat inhibiting modesty takes over. They just need to realize that the compliments are genuine and cornerstone to their success in life. And, if they'll take it at face value, all the feedback they get from people can be very useful.

But there's still a lack of objectivity here that's too often inherent in us all. So these people need to be particularly wise about their involvements, both business and personal. It could be said that their relationships will either make or break them. Many prospective partners and colleagues may come knocking, but these Pisceans need to be selective and remember that truly compatible relationships are supposed to be easy, not difficult. This is especially true with close friendships and romance. Compatibility is essential here. If their relationships are flawed, they'll be pulled off-center and lose their way. There's too much "I don't wanna be alone" with sharing Libra. Their obliging nature and their "keep it peaceful at all costs" Pisces caves in far too easily, and ultimately they cheat themselves out of their just rewards. They just need to be fair to themselves to ensure success and happiness.

Pisces Born Mid-Evening:
Pisces with Scorpio Rising

It's anybody's guess where these people are coming from. All you can do is look for warmth in their eyes and watch their behavior—and there's apt to be lots of behavior to watch! Scorpio's "full of gusto" is alive and well here, so these Pisceans are tremendously active and big contributors to boot. Scorpio's intensity creates a lot of desire, and they tackle their chores with carnivorous purpose. They're simply "do it now and think about it later." They know exactly what they came for, and they fully intend to go home with it. But getting them to actually state their case might be impossible. Putting their cards on the table just doesn't come naturally to them.

Both Pisces and Scorpio have a deep aversion to feeling vulnerable, so they hide themselves: Pisces hides to avoid confrontation, and Scorpio hides to control and manipulate. So Pisceans with Scorpio rising are apt to be very difficult to find sometimes. As adults they usually outgrow the shyness that characterizes their childhood, but they still need their peaceful solitude. Still, there's a lot of sexy Scorpio at hand, and alluring Pisces is always fascinating. So although they rarely welcome it, they're never short on attention from others.

The handiness of Scorpio and the vivid imagination of Pisces gives these people a lot of artistry, however they choose to express it. But whatever their occupation, they prefer to be left alone to fulfill their duties at their own vigorous pace, focused and undistracted. They don't like to be interrupted by micromanaging bosses or by colleagues who want to take a break and chat about their plans for the weekend. With good character, they work hard for their money and invest their resources wisely. But with poor character, there might be some shifty behavior because they soon discover that they're masterful at covering their tracks, and they believe—usually with solid evidence—that they'll get away with it. This is a dangerous path for anyone to travel, not just Pisceans, because not only is it just plain wrong, it's earthly foolish. It never shows a profit over the long haul. Eventually, it will be time to pay the piper. So Pisceans with Mysterious Scorpio rising are well-advised to be a little more outgoing, a little more visible, and on the up-and-up. There's always a healthy dose of Florence Nightingale in the Pisces ego, so helping people and caring for living things brings them a peace and a fulfillment that's fully satisfying. They're most beloved when they're gentle and willing and courageous enough to keep from—POOF!—disappearing when people have come to trust and depend on them. Emphasizing their positive traits is their ticket to happiness.

Pisces Born around Midnight:
Pisces with Sagittarius Rising

If any sun sign/rising sign combination was born with a ticket to ride it's Pisces with Sagittarius rising. An exuberant, Happy-Go-Lucky Sagittarius personality brings Pisces out into the open and fuels the confidence of these wonderfully sharing and caring, Florence Nightingale types. These people are kind-hearted good listeners with winning ways; they've an "it's okay, we'll do better next time" attitude, and—usually—a bright-eyed, toothy smile. They're encouraging, forgiving, and generally tolerant of error. Continually earning trust with their obvious compassion, they're the masters of encouragement, whether they're giving a pat on the back to the Little Leaguer or having a brief but uplifting visit with a friend laid up in the hospital. These Pisceans are just downright inspiring. And they're very often in the right place at the right time. They've the gift of good timing!

Seeing as Sagittarius is the sign of celebration, these people love a party like no other Pisceans. Some Pisceans hyperventilate at the thought of mixing and mingling, but Sagittarius rising might show up looking spectacular and expecting to be noticed. They'll even plunk out a few tunes on the piano. And if it's nighttime—Katie, bar the door! They love the nighttime.

Pisceans born around midnight feel their "God within" from moment to moment, and it shows. With Sagittarius' winning ways and Pisces' whimsical nature they're seldom offensive or unsuccessful. It's their kindness that gives them their good fortune, and if they know not to be arrogant and inconsiderate, they're truly the salt of the earth. But if anything can get them off track, it's the "poison candy" syndrome: Being inspired about something that's obviously not good for them. If they've learned to keep it real and look at things objectively, all is well. But viewing the world through rose-colored glasses can create problems. Sure, their good fortune usually protects them from the most dire consequences, but still they run the risk of letting more rewarding opportunities pass them by. This is especially true in their personal relationships. They allow people to perpetuate bad behavior by accepting "I'm sorry" for an apology rather than demanding improvement. They need to know that "I'm sorry" is not an apology; it usually means "I'm gonna do it again." A genuine apology promises improvement! These Pisceans are better served by slowing down and being objective than almost anyone else in the zodiac. If they'll be honest with themselves about their hopes and aspirations, and objectively ponder both sides of the issue, they'll always wind up in the winner's circle.

Pisces Born in the Wee Hours:
Pisces with Capricorn Rising

Here comes the "keeper of the keys." These people are always in favor with the boss because they do what's expected plus, with an "I hope I can do everything right and keep everything peaceful" Pisces attitude. They're among the most dependable and silently helpful folks on the planet. With a calm, cool, collected Capricorn personality, these "walk softly" Pisceans carry a big authoritarian stick. They bide their time and go with the flow, scrupulously avoiding confrontation and intensity as all Pisceans do, but less from Piscean fear and more from respect for others. They're wonderful at giving people their space. And even if there's error, they'll respectfully give you all the rope you need to hang yourself. The Wise Old Goat gives these Pisceans a more earthly-wise understanding of the bad-joke planet Earth; they're realistic and sensible and not as given to unrealistic anxieties because they understand the ways of the world. They build and depend on the approval they've earned since kindergarten— they've always pleased their teachers, parents, and every other superior they've encountered, so they know they're in good stead with the people in charge and rest easy in that knowledge.

When there's a need for self-motivated individuals, these are the folks to call. As employees, they put in an honest day's work; as bosses, they allocate responsibly and give their underlings the space they need; as neighbors, they're unceasingly helpful, rendering assistance wherever they see an opportunity to lend a hand. They treat their material possessions with respect, conscientiously maintaining their cars and polishing their furniture, and getting 150 percent usage out of everything. Pisceans born in the wee hours are by-the-book managers and inspiring but demanding teachers—if they're teaching music or other Piscean fine arts, they masterfully instill discipline, respect, and organization, enabling their students to "be all they can be." And they might be running immense operations such as the local hospital, where their Florence

Nightingale Pisces can work hand-in-hand with their business-is-business Capricorn. There's a lot of imagination here, too, and maybe a proclivity for reading fiction or writing fanciful and fascinating stories.

But as always with Capricorn, there's not a lot of obvious warmth, so these Pisceans do need to avoid appearing cold, un-giving, and even calculating. When shrewd Pisces blends with "play the angles" Capricorn, there's an ability to manipulate people, and that can be productive if they're fair in their manipulation. They just need to make it clear from the beginning that they have everyone's best interests at heart and that the best manipulator of all is in the front office, and always called "the boss." Getting what they want while making sure that others benefit equally is the boss's job. As long as all parties understand that everyone's going to have their cake and eat it, too, these Pisceans will never make an enemy—and for Peaceful Pisces with respectful Capricorn rising, that should always be the ultimate goal.

Pisces Born Pre-Dawn:
Pisces with Aquarius Rising

Imagination teams up with ingenuity! What a deal! With Aquarius' original approach to everything and the Piscean eye for illusion, these people can conceive of the most wondrous things, from a glamorous painting on the wall to the most beautiful crescendo you've ever heard. Cosmic Pisces and galactic Aquarius aren't so encumbered by earth and its ways—in this life they've come to earth with talent and wizardry. And if they've learned to apply it, the sky's the limit. It might even be their destination—the sky, that is.

This is an incredibly fascinating sun sign/rising sign combination. They're often found producing radio and television shows where they can be involved with glamour, fame, and fortune without being in the spotlight. And they're masterful advertising executives, talent agents, and scriptwriters. Pisceans with Electric Aquarius rising are so plugged-in they can conceive, produce, and slickly market any goods or services imaginable. They know what's popular—or what's going to be. They've a superb eye for what will sell. And with a good blend of peaceful Pisces and Aquarius funny-bone they're not pompous, bristly, or sour. But don't mess with that stiff-spined Aquarius attitude! Pisces is slick and sneaky and can get away with things. They'll find a way to get the last word in any argument—and if they zap you, you'll never know what hit you!

These Pisceans are always sitting close to the people in charge. Their talents don't usually go unnoticed when there's a powerful purpose at hand, and they love being part of the team. They're often the gatekeepers of power because they're innately wary of people, but they need to avoid going overboard with that. If they develop an overweening "everybody's trying to rip me off" distrust that follows them into their personal lives, it will obscure the more gentle and kind qualities of Pisces. Sure, there's a time and a place for requiring explanations and checking credentials, but it's not while hanging out with friends or sitting at the dinner table with loved ones. Lowering their guard a little when it's time to relax and enjoy good company is highly recommended here. These folks have enough Pisces Florence Nightingale within them to bandage people's wounds and warm their hearts, so if they'll share their tender mercies wherever they're needed they'll be known to all as awesome power brokers and genuinely nice people.

ABOUT THE AUTHORS

William Lamb is "The Horoscope Man," a witty, no-nonsense astrologer who appears regularly on radio stations from Orlando to Los Angeles, Baltimore to Houston. He has made appearances on Orlando's CBS and Fox affiliates, as well as the nationwide "Fox and Friends." He lives in Orlando, Florida. **www.williamlamb.com**.

Webb Harris, Jr. teaches English at Seminole Community College in Florida. His essays and short fiction appear regularly in academic quarterlies and literary magazines.

Also from Fair Winds Press

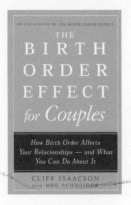

THE BIRTH ORDER EFFECT FOR COUPLES
by Cliff Isaacson with Meg Schneider
ISBN: 159233-023-1
$14.95 (£9.99)
Paperback; 192 pages
Available wherever books are sold

Birth Order—Your Secret to Success in Love!

• Are you struggling to communicate with your Fourth Born lover?
• Does your Second Born spouse reduce you to tears with constant criticism?
• Are you an Only Child looking for love in all the wrong places?
• Are First Borns and Third Borns a hopeless match?
• And what does your mother have to do with it?

In this entertaining and enlightening book, Cliff Isaacson applies his groundbreaking *Birth Order Effect* to relationships—showing you how birth order shapes you, your partner, and your happiness together in surprising and meaningful ways. This understanding will allow you to improve your relationship across the board—emotionally, physically, spiritually, and sexually.

With *The Birth Order Effect for Couples*, you'll learn:

• Which birth order personality you are (not necessarily chronologically!);
• Which matches are best for you;
• Which birth order personality your significant other is;
• What your compatibilities as a couple are;
• What your potential clashes may be, and
• How to resolve those clashes, regardless of birth order.

The Birth Order Effect for Couples will transform your relationship, whether you're already married or are still looking for that special someone. With this book in hand, you have everything you need to create, nurture, and maintain a love that lasts a lifetime!

ABOUT THE AUTHORS
Cliff Isaacson is a the author of four books about birth order, and founder of the Upper Des Moines Counseling Center, where he continues his counseling practice.

Meg Schneider is an award-winning writer and journalist with more than a decade of experience in television, radio, and print media.